BETWEEN TWO WORLDS

BETWEEN TWO WORLDS

My Life and Captivity in Iran

ROXANA SABERI

HARPER ● PERENNIAL

NEW YORK ● LONDON ● TORONTO ● SYDNEY ● NEW DELHI ● AUCKLAND

HARPER ● PERENNIAL

A hardcover edition of this book was published in 2010 by Harper, an imprint of HarperCollins Publishers.

HarperCollins books may be purchased for educational, business, or sales promotional use. For information please write: Special Markets Department, HarperCollins Publishers, 10 East 53rd Street, New York, NY 10022.

FIRST HARPER PERENNIAL EDITION PUBLISHED 2011.

Designed by William Ruoto

The Library of Congress has catalogued the hardcover edition as follows:

Saberi, Roxana.
    Between two worlds : my life and captivity in Iran / by Roxana Saberi. — 1st ed.
        p. cm.
    Summary: "A chronicle of the Iranian-American journalist's imprisonment, as well as a look at Iran and its political tensions"—Provided by publisher.
    ISBN 978-0-06-196528-9 (hardback)
    1. Saberi, Roxana—Imprisonment. 2. Women journalists—United States—Biography. 3. Women journalists—Iran—Biography. 4. Women political prisoners—Iran—Biography. 5. Journalists—Crimes against—Iran. 6. Iran—Politics and government—1997– 7. Iranian American women—Biography. I. Title.
    PN4874.S23A3 2010
    070.92—dc22
    [B]
                                                                    2009051764

ISBN 978-0-06-196529-6 (pbk.)

11 12 13 14 15   OV/RRD   10 9 8 7 6 5 4 3 2 1

For my cellmates and all other brave souls
standing up for human rights, freedom, and dignity

When a bird realizes that it is other than the cage,
it is already free.

—Saeb Tabrizi,
SEVENTEENTH-CENTURY PERSIAN POET

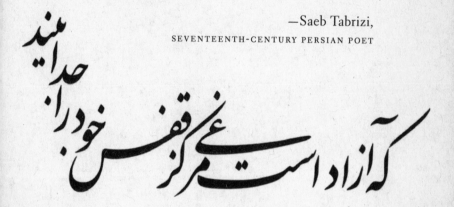

AUTHOR'S NOTE

This book aims to convey what I experienced in Iran, particularly during my one hundred days in Evin Prison in 2009, when I saw the dark and bright sides of human nature, including my own. I hope the lessons I learned in prison can inspire readers to overcome adversity in their own lives. I also hope this account can help shed light on events unfolding in Iran, where many people have gone through similar or much more difficult ordeals, but few have been free to speak of them.

Although I tried to write as openly as possible, I omitted details that I believed could put others in danger or invade their privacy. In place of some names, I used either pseudonyms, which are marked with asterisks, or initials. I also altered the identities of certain cellmates, while attempting to keep them and their stories as true-to-life as possible. I received permission to use the actual names of a handful of my cellmates.

When referring to some intelligence agents and prison guards, I created nicknames because they never told me their real names. And after I was freed, I learned that the names of certain officials dealing with my case were likely pseudonyms.

In prison, I was prohibited from having a pen and paper, but I had plenty of time to review conversations and events over and over in my mind, and after my release, I spent much of the next several weeks writing down my recollections. Of course, memory has its shortcomings, and not all of the dialogue from my imprisonment is repeated verbatim here. Even so, I have reconstructed it, as well as the scenes in this book, as accurately as I could.

Before my arrest, I was writing a different book about Iran, where I had gone to work as a journalist when I was twenty-five. I had planned to stay for one or two years. But I became so captivated by the country that after nearly six years, I found myself still enjoying my life in Tehran—unaware that I would soon be jolted out of my comfortable routine in ways I had never imagined.

CONTENTS

PART I
TRAPPED   1

PART II
ANGELS IN EVIN   115

PART III
ON TRIAL   225

EPILOGUE   295

ACKNOWLEDGMENTS   307

GLOSSARY   313

NOTES ON SOURCES   315

SELECTED BIBLIOGRAPHY AND SUGGESTIONS
FOR FURTHER READING   319

PART I

TRAPPED

CHAPTER ONE

T an pantyhose were selling for 1,000 tomans, assorted head-scarves for 2,000.

"Red with white flowers, black with turquoise stripes!" a plump woman hawker cried out as she pushed her way through the packed train car.

Like my fellow female passengers on Tehran's metro, I craned my neck to catch a glimpse of these $1 to $2 items, but all I could see from where I stood jammed in the corner were the backs of heads covered in mandatory hejab.

The metro screeched to a halt. Some women got off; others snatched up the vacated seats in our subway car, one of two set aside for female passengers who chose to sit separately from the men. I remained where I was, tired but content that with my trip to the holy city of Qom behind me, I had come one step closer to finishing the interviews for the book I was writing.

I hadn't intended to write a book when I moved from America to Iran nearly six years earlier, in February 2003. Instead, I wanted to get to know my father's native land and its rich culture and history, learn the Farsi language, and realize my dream of becoming a foreign correspondent. Everything was going more or less according to plan when, in 2006, the Iranian authorities unexpectedly revoked my official press credentials.

I could have left Iran then, but I chose to stay. The loss of my press pass, I realized, might actually be an opportunity. I had gained more time to explore Iran, a country that remained exciting and mysterious to me and a place many outsiders seemed to misunderstand. And so I had decided to work on a book about life in Iran as seen through the eyes of a wide range of Iranians.

I believed if I didn't do this before leaving Iran, I would be too caught up in the next stages of my life to have another chance. Besides, I wasn't in a big hurry to go. I had fallen in love with Iran, had made many good friends, and for now, would have rather been here than anywhere else.

S everal taxis crawled by when I got off the metro at a bustling central Tehran square. They were all full. Since fuel rationing had begun in 2007 in this oil-rich, gas-guzzling nation, cabs seemed to have become harder to find on the streets.

My boyfriend, Bahman, had urged me to always use a taxi agency instead of privately owned taxis and shared cabs, in which total strangers often sat next to one another. I usually heeded his advice, but this evening, I just wanted to go home, take off my hejab, and unwind.

"*Darbast!*" (literally, "exclusive") I shouted at an approaching four-door Peykan, Iran's most popular car before it was discontinued a few years earlier because it was a heavy polluter.

"Get in," said the driver, a young man with gelled hair and a tight T-shirt.

As we entered the highway, he cranked up the Iranian rap music on his stereo and began to hum along. It was one of those songs available only on the black market but largely tolerated by the authorities if played in private. I turned to look out my window. A gray cloud of smog hung in the air, obscuring the Alborz Mountains to the north of Tehran. If I hadn't known they were there, I would have thought they didn't exist.

"So where are you from?" the driver yelled over the music.

"Iran!" I yelled back. Although I had been an American citizen since birth, I was in Iran on my Iranian passport.

He turned down his music and glanced back at me. "You look Japanese," he remarked.

"Yeah," I said. "My mother is Japanese."

"Really? The Japanese are very hard workers."

My cell phone rang, saving me from going into any more detail about myself. Bahman was on the line. Even though he was visiting his sister in Los Angeles, he still called regularly to check on me. I gave him a rundown of my previous twenty-four hours, then we hung up the way we always did, with the words *Dust-et dâram*, a term of affection meaning "I like you" or "I love you."

Gradually, the car wove its way north up Sadr Highway, which Iran's authorities had named, like many streets and freeways, after a "martyr," this one, a grand ayatollah who had been executed by former Iraqi President Saddam Hussein's regime. Since Iran's 1979 Islamic Revolution, the Islamic Republic had tried to equate the idea of martyrdom, a concept highly revered in Shiite Islam, with self-sacrifice for the state. Many Iranians were lured to the front lines of the Iran-Iraq War in the 1980s with the promise that if they died, they would become martyrs and go to heaven.

I got out at my neighborhood grocery store, where I picked up the ingredients for my dinner—some eggs, fresh bread, and a bag of imitation nacho Doritos. The grocer smiled warmly at me as he handed me my goods.

My apartment complex sat at the end of an alley a block away, past a pastry shop, three fast-food restaurants, and several high-rises. When I walked through the front door, I found the elevator broken as it often was. On my hike up five flights of stairs, I bumped into the building caretaker, Gholam.

"Miss Saberi," he said, "is your heater working well? The weather's going to get colder soon."

My heater had been pumping out more cold air than warm, I informed him. He told me he would call the handyman.

As I unlocked my door and entered my apartment, giggling children burst out of one neighbor's unit and chased each other down the stairs, while Voice of America Persian boomed from another neighbor's illegal satellite TV.

I took off my long, black chador, which I had worn on my trip to Qom to blend in with the conservatively dressed local women, but instead of hanging the cloth on a hook as was customary, I returned it to its role of keeping the dust off my piano.

I began to whistle "Silent Night" as I prepared my dinner. My home was my refuge. I felt a sense of calm here, even though I suspected that my life within these walls wasn't completely private. As an Iranian-American journalist, I assumed that my telephone and e-mail might be at least occasionally monitored—a fact of life for many journalists, foreigners, and certain others in the Islamic Republic.

It was Christmas, which few people celebrated in this largely Muslim nation. Other than e-mailing holiday greetings to some friends abroad, I would spend my evening like most other nights: logging interviews, doing research for my book, and typing on my laptop. For a break, I might play the piano, call a friend, or visit my elderly widowed neighbor, who always welcomed me with gossip and honey-filled pastries. Then I would e-mail or video Skype my parents in North Dakota to tell them all was well, scrub the pollution from my clogged pores, and go to sleep, usually long after midnight.

I expected to more or less repeat this routine for the next three months, until late March. By then, my book would be finished, and perhaps with Bahman, I would leave the country to move on to the next chapter of my life.

CHAPTER TWO

I sank my head into my flannel-covered pillow and pulled my down comforter over my cold ears. It was the last day of January, and more than five weeks had passed since Gholam had promised to send the handyman, but still my heater was broken.

Most mornings, I was awakened by the sounds of hammering, drilling, and sawing, as construction workers erected one new apartment complex after another in my upper-middle-class neighborhood. But on this Saturday, the first day of the Iranian workweek, the only sound that reached my ears was the ticking of my clock.

My eyes turned toward it: 9:00.

D*ing-dong.*
I flinched. So it was the doorbell that had woken me up. I rolled over and closed my heavy eyelids. I wasn't expecting any visitors. Someone was probably mistaking my doorbell for a neighbor's on the console downstairs as usual.

Ding-dong.

If I got up to answer it, I wouldn't be able to fall back asleep. *Brain won't function if don't get eight hours of sleep.*

Ding-dong.

Whoever it was obviously wasn't giving up.

I stumbled out of bed and across my living room. The monitor on my video door phone was lit up, displaying a black-and-white image of an unfamiliar middle-aged man.

"Yes?" I asked in Farsi.

"Miss Saberi?" the man inquired with a friendly smile.

"You are?"

"You have a letter."

It was a mailman, I realized.

"Could you bring it up, please?" I was too groggy to go downstairs. "I'm on the fifth floor."

"Certainly."

I buzzed open the door to the building, then dragged myself back to my bedroom, put on a white headscarf, and slipped a knee-length black *roopoosh* over my pajamas.

A light rap sounded at the door. I opened it just a few inches. The mailman was standing there with an indecipherable smile on his face and a piece of white paper in his fist. Saying nothing, he handed the paper to me through the crack.

My eyes scanned the page, skipping over most of the words, trying to figure out what this was all about. My modest Farsi-reading skills, combined with a growing sense of unease, were hindering my comprehension of what appeared to me as:

> *Qeruzjiojitenajkfasdf*
> *azntxcjviorgtneafn*
> *24 hours serjiojasfkjzfnty*
> *znernagyrhgbfg Evin Prison ewatngnmdfv.*

Evin Prison?

I ran my eyes over the last line again.

"Evin Prison."

My heart began to pound. This Tehran jail was notorious for having held Iran's most famous political prisoners, including students, academics, and activists. Torture was common, and hangings and a mass execution had taken place there.[*] In 2003, Iranian-Canadian

---

[*] Statistics vary, but Amnesty International says 4,500 to 10,000 political prisoners were executed in Iran's prisons between August 1988 and February 1989. The regime has never acknowledged the mass executions.

journalist Zahra Kazemi was detained in Evin and shortly afterward, died suspiciously. No one had ever been held accountable for her death.

"Excuse me," I said to the man at my door, attempting to conceal my mounting fear. "I don't read Farsi very well. Could you give me a moment to look at this more carefully?"

I tried to shut the door but couldn't. He had propped it open with his right foot and was now sneering at me.

"No," he grunted, forcing the door open just as three other men filed out of the elevator behind him.

I shuffled a few steps back in horror as they pushed their way into my apartment and quietly shut the door.

Two of them had the same look as the "Mailman": middle-aged, with scruffy beards and untucked shirts hanging over dark trousers. The third was well groomed and younger, perhaps in his early thirties.

No doubt about it—these were Iranian intelligence agents.

What could they want from me?

"Did you just wake up?" one of them asked in Farsi, as he glanced at my pajama pants sticking out of my *roopoosh*.

Before I could answer, another remarked, "Yes, she goes to sleep late and gets up late."

I turned to look at the agent who had just spoken, shaken that he knew my sleeping patterns. He was the youngest member of the group, a clean-shaven man who didn't fit the typical intelligence-agent profile. Wearing blue jeans, a black leather jacket, and hard-soled shoes that clicked as he strolled across my tiled living room floor, he could have fit right in with the youth—or *javân*—of northern Tehran who often had a Westernized look. "Javan" (who as an agent would never disclose his real name) surveyed my living room with indifference, except for a faint look of disgust when he spotted my chador draped over the piano.

"Do you know why we're here?" the tallest man said, fiddling with a set of *tasbih*, or prayer beads, in his right hand.

I opened my mouth to respond to "Tasbihi," but no words came out.

"We have the right to interrogate you," he said evenly, without waiting for a response. "And if we are not satisfied, we can take you to Evin Prison tonight."

This had to be a very, very bad dream, worse than any nightmare I could remember.

"Don't worry," Tasbihi continued, flashing an unsettling grin. "If you cooperate, you'll be back home this evening. Just do as we say, and don't leave our sight."

I wanted to make a dash for either my phone or the door, but all I could do was nod. I recalled what I had heard about Zahra Kazemi. As the story went, she had been arrested after taking photos of some prisoners' families outside Evin and then responded defiantly to her interrogators. Hard-line authorities initially tried to cover up the cause of her death and later said she died from head injuries resulting from an "accident." But according to a doctor who said he examined Kazemi's corpse and escaped Iran to disclose his findings, the journalist had been raped, her nose broken, and her skull fractured. She might have made it out all right, an Iranian official had once told me privately, if she hadn't resisted.

The four men started sifting through my belongings in the living room. The Mailman was packing up my laptop and flash drive. Another was tossing some of my notepads into an empty garbage bag he had taken from my kitchen.

"You'll get all these back later," Tasbihi told me, as I looked on, frozen in place in the middle of the room. "We just need to do a little research first."

Javan began scanning the titles on my bookshelf. A few books were in Farsi, including two or three written by the leader of Iran's Islamic Revolution, Grand Ayatollah Ruhollah Khomeini. The agent skipped over these, as well as my favorite classics in English, such as *Plutarch's Lives*, and turned to other texts I had brought from America. Many had to do with Iran, the Middle East, and Islam.

"I'm impressed, Miss Saberi," he said with obvious sarcasm. "You are quite a scholar! What do you do with all these books?"

"I've collected them over the past six years I've been living here," I heard myself say, "and now I'm using some of them to research a book I'm writing about Iran."

As if he didn't know already. I had always assumed the authorities knew about my book, even though it didn't require government permission to research and write. It was an independent project I had openly described to the dozens of Iranians I had interviewed to ensure the regime would realize I had nothing to hide.

Javan didn't say anything and continued to peruse my small library. He paused with interest when he came to two English-language books covered with portraits of Iran's hard-line president, Mahmoud Ahmadinejad.

"What are these about?" he asked.

They were ordinary books about Ahmadinejad and his policies, I replied.

He threw the books into the trash bag, which was by now half filled with the spoils his colleagues had collected. Then he spotted my cell phone on the kitchen counter and stuck it in his pocket.

The four men made me move on with them to another room, where they dug through my desk and file cabinet. They confiscated several music CDs, old videotapes, and bank statements.

When the Mailman came upon my American and Iranian passports, he smiled triumphantly. I felt my knees weaken and had to lean against the desk to steady myself. Without these documents, I wouldn't be able to leave the country. And with no U.S. Embassy in Iran, there were no American officials here to help me.

"Don't worry," Tasbihi said, echoing his earlier words. "Cooperate with us, and you'll get these back later."

But I was more than worried. I was frightened, bewildered, and furious: frightened at the prospect of landing in Evin Prison, bewildered by the presence of four strange men seizing my belongings, and furious at this violation of my privacy.

My eyes followed the agents as they combed through some note-books from my college days that I referred to for journalism tips and background on international relations. One of the men began pulling dusty papers and folders out of the closet. He sneezed. I had meant to throw out that useless stuff, but I had procrastinated.

Meanwhile, Javan was peeling two photos, one of Bahman and the other of my family, off the wall. He dropped them into a fresh garbage bag. Then the men made their way to my bedroom where, speechlessly, I watched them rummage through my closet and dresser.

"Change into your regular attire," Javan ordered me, after the agents declared their search complete. "We're taking you elsewhere for interrogation."

"Why?" I asked. "What do you want from me?"

"Just cooperate," he said curtly.

Cooperate. I had no idea what kind of cooperation these people were talking about.

The men left me alone in my bedroom with the door open a few inches. I looked out my window. I wished I lived on the ground floor. From this height, I couldn't expect to survive if I jumped, and I had neither enough guts nor enough bed sheets to swing my way down to safety.

My impractical plots unraveled with a knock on my door. It was one of the men, telling me to hurry. I changed into jeans and a T-shirt and put on my wristwatch before throwing on my hejab again.

The four agents escorted me out of my apartment, lugging their loot with them. The hallway was eerily quiet, just as it had been when they had entered two hours earlier. Usually my neighbors or their kids were coming or going or socializing there. Maybe they had seen the agents and were nervously peering through their peepholes from the safety of their apartments. I thought of screaming for help, but I knew that no one would dare interfere with these men, who were undoubtedly armed.

I was instructed to sit in the back of the first of two white Peykans, with the Mailman beside me and Javan next to the driver. As we got onto the highway and headed toward central Tehran, I stared numbly out the window. The scenes were so familiar, yet they seemed otherworldly, as if I had fallen into a horrible fantasy. If only I had known a few hours earlier what was in store for me today.

I hadn't realized until I had climbed into bed at four that morning how exhausted I was.

My weariness stemmed from having sat at my computer for hours that night and from a growing uncertainty about my future. During the previous few weeks, as the date of my departure from Iran had rapidly approached, I had lost much of my usual sense of optimism as I came face-to-face with questions I had been trying to ignore.

What will come of my book? I had wondered. I hadn't even found a publisher yet. *And what will happen to me once my book is finished?*

As a journalist in Iran, I felt I had discovered some purpose in my life through my work by providing news coverage from a country where few foreign journalists could live and operate.

That was why, when Iran's Culture Ministry pulled my government-issued credentials in 2006, I felt a sudden emptiness. I had lost not only my press pass but also a large part of my identity.

A few other dual-national journalists before me had been forced to give up their credentials, and many foreign journalists had seen their visas either revoked or not renewed. The situation had worsened after Ahmadinejad was elected president in 2005, replacing a reformist administration with hard-liners. Iranian officials gave me no clear reason for their decision to pull my press pass, although they hinted it was part of a larger effort to restrict the Western media from reporting in the country.

I believed, however, that outsiders had a greater need than ever for independent news from Iran, and I felt an obligation to help provide it. So I decided to keep reporting but in a limited way that didn't require a press pass according to Iranian law, as a few other journalists in similar situations had done.

The Iranian authorities were aware of my continued news reporting and had never told me to stop. I figured they didn't mind that I was sharing news briefs and a few features about Iran with the outside world.

A little later, I started working on my book on Iran. My hope was to portray the lives of everyday Iranians more thoroughly than I could in short news stories.

More than two years had passed since then. Now that my book was almost finished, I had no idea what I would do next—which country I would move to, whether Bahman and I would continue our relationship abroad, or what I was going to do with my life.

But did any of this really matter? I asked myself as I lay in bed. *No. In fact, nothing really mattered.*

I had been grumbling to God a lot lately, as I often did in times of self-doubt and uncertainty. Having been raised by my parents to explore various faiths, I had created a general vision of an infinite and gracious God, a Higher Power to which all major religions pointed in one way or another.

But lately I had been feeling that God didn't really care what I was doing.

I had started to think that despite my efforts, my life didn't have much meaning, and I was tired of trying to give it meaning. In the end, we would all die anyway. It didn't even matter if I continued to live beyond my thirty-one years. I couldn't recall why I had ever been so resolved to try to make a difference in the world.

Yet I had plenty to be thankful for, I reminded myself as my eyes grew heavy—a loving family, good friends, my health . . .

I drifted asleep as the call to morning prayers arose from the local mosque.

Where are we going?" I ventured to ask.

"We're bringing you somewhere to ask you a few questions," Javan said, without looking back at me. "As my colleague told you earlier, if you cooperate by this evening, we will take you home. If you don't, we will escort you to Evin."

A cell phone rang. The tone was muffled but familiar, arising from the agent's pocket.

"Who's 'Mr. Z'?" he asked, reading the name off my phone's caller ID.

Mr. Z was a man I had interviewed for my book a few months earlier on a trip to Zahedan, I explained, referring to the capital of the southeastern Iranian province of Sistan-Baluchestan. His nongovernmental organization was working to alleviate poverty and disease there.

"Put it on speaker phone and answer it," the agent ordered as he gave the phone to me. "Act naturally. Tell him you are in a meeting and will call him later."

As he spoke, I recalled an incident a few years back, when two plainclothesmen stopped me after a human-rights news conference in Tehran and confiscated my videotape from the event. I had objected, but my close friend Hassan,* who was with me at the time, told me to hand it over. He later advised me that arguing with intelligence agents was both pointless and dangerous, and I should do as they directed.

"Hello?" I said into the phone.

"Miss Saberi?" asked the man on the other end.

"Sorry, I'm in a meeting, can I call you back later?" I said in one breath.

"Sure. I apologize for disturbing you."

I placed my phone in Javan's outstretched hand, and he shoved it back into his pocket.

Our two cars soon pulled up to a building by a park in central Tehran. I had driven past the park before but never noticed this building. It was unmarked, as were many structures maintained by Iran's intelligence and security forces. The agents took me inside, past a guard, and up a set of stairs into a windowless room. Three of the four men left. Only Tasbihi remained. He sat on a shabby couch, and I sat on another, with a coffee table between us.

As he toyed with his prayer beads, Tasbihi began to question me.

Where was I born and raised? What did my parents do? Where did my father's relatives live in Iran?

I was born in New Jersey and raised in Fargo, North Dakota, I replied. My mother, Akiko, was a pathologist. My father, Reza, was an author of books on philosophy and a translator of Persian poetry into English. Most of his relatives still lived in northwestern Iran, in his birthplace of Tabriz, but I seldom saw them.

"Can you write your answers in Farsi?" Tasbihi asked.

"I can try," I said. He handed me a pen, but after watching me struggle with my spelling, he took it back and told me to dictate my replies while he wrote them.

Why had I come to Iran, he wanted to know, how often did I go back to America, and for what?

I answered these questions, and he asked more. This wasn't so bad, I thought, as the minutes turned into two hours.

Then Javan entered the room. He was carrying a stack of brown file folders crammed with papers of various colors and sizes. He glanced at the pen in his colleague's hand.

"Why are you writing for her?" the young agent growled. "She can write Farsi by herself!"

With that, he slammed his folders on the coffee table, making both Tasbihi and me jump, and thrust the pen into my hand. Staying on his feet, he began to read the responses Tasbihi had collected from me so far, shaking his head silently from time to time.

As Javan examined the papers, I was able to get my first good look at him. He was fairly slim and of medium height. His nose was a little hooked, and his receding hairline accentuated the slight upward angle of his eyes. His eyebrows appeared permanently raised, as if he were in a constant state of skepticism. When he set aside the papers and turned his dark, opaque eyes toward me, I shuddered.

Finally, Javan said in a calm but menacing tone, "We have not been making enough progress with you."

He waved Tasbihi aside to make room for himself on the sofa. Evidently the younger man was going to take over. "Miss Saberi," he said, as he opened one of the brown folders, "we know you have been doing a lot of research and conducting many interviews over the past several months."

"Yes," I said. "As I mentioned earlier, I am writing a book on Iran."

"Why were you interviewing so many people?"

"I have been studying different sectors of Iranian society, and I want the book to reflect a diversity of views," I explained. "I don't want to talk to only a few people and say they represent the entire country. That would create an unbalanced picture of Iran for English-language readers abroad."

"We know whom you were interviewing," Javan said smugly. "Fortunately, one of them, Mr. M, called us to report that you were asking him suspicious questions."

Mr. M? He was a wealthy merchant I had interviewed about the Tehran bazaar for the economics chapter of my book. I explained to the interrogator that I had asked Mr. M about the bazaar's role in Iran's economy, politics, and society.

Javan leafed through a few pages in his folder, then looked up and asked: "And why did you interview reformists? You know that some of them are very critical of the regime."

Iran's reformists had enjoyed the height of their formal political power under the previous president, Mohammad Khatami, and were now working to make a comeback, focusing on the June 2009 presidential election. Many reformists had criticized Ahmadinejad's social restrictions, economic policies, and confrontational stance on Iran's disputed nuclear program. They also advocated better relations with the West and greater democracy within the framework of the Islamic

Republic.

"I interviewed politicians from across the political spectrum," I replied. "I also interviewed conservative members of parliament."

"We know you did," Javan said sharply, "including a few on the National Security and Foreign Policy Commission."

"What's wrong with that?" I asked. "They wanted to share their perspectives with foreigners through my book, and how am I supposed to accurately describe conservatives' opinions without talking to them?"

The interrogator deflected my question with another question.

"What business do you have interviewing all these people anyway?" Javan demanded. "Who told you to interview them?"

"No one," I answered, taken aback. "It was my own decision to interview them for my book."

"Does anyone have any copies of what you've written so far?"

"Yes," I said. "My mother does."

"Why her?"

Every few days, I would e-mail my mother a copy of my latest writings. I was aware that Iranian plainclothesmen had raided the homes of some journalists and intellectuals, and even though I didn't think this would ever really happen to me, I felt more secure knowing that my mother had a backup copy on the other side of the world. Besides, she was giving me helpful feedback on my writing.

"She reads my chapters and gives me her advice," I explained.

"Nobody else has a copy?"

"Nobody else," I replied, uncertain why he was raising this question.

Javan nodded slowly, then began paging through another folder. "Let's go back to 2003. You prepared some TV reports for Fox News. You realize Fox is an arm of the Pentagon?"

I knew this was a view held by some Iranian officials, but I didn't want to get into a discussion about it with the agent. So I simply explained that the Culture Ministry had given me permission to send those reports to Fox. *Anyway,* I thought, *if those stories had been such a problem, why was this man bringing them up six years later?*

"You did a report for them on the Shahab 3," Javan said pointedly. The Shahab 3 was an Iranian missile that could reportedly reach Israel and some U.S. bases in the region, although Tehran said it was meant for defense. I searched my memory, trying to recollect what I had stated in my story.

"I think it showed footage of the missile from Iranian state-run TV," I said. "And I believe I included a statement from Iran's Foreign Ministry spokesman about a successful test launch."

"And you did another report for Fox on al-Zarqawi," he continued.

I couldn't remember exactly who al-Zarqawi was, except that at one time he was said to be a leader of al-Qaeda in Iraq. I explained to the interrogator that as far as I could recall, my report had referred to Tehran's denial of allegations that al-Zarqawi had fled to Iran.

"You provided analysis in these reports," he said with increasing animosity.

"I reported what observers and Iranian officials were saying."

"But it was analysis."

"If it was analysis, it wasn't *my* analysis," I argued. "It was *other people's* analysis."

"Analysis is exactly what the *Si-â* wants from Iran," Javan declared, pronouncing "CIA" with a Farsi accent.

You can't be serious, I wanted to say. Unfortunately, he probably was. Iranian hard-liners liked to maintain that foreign intelligence agencies, particularly the CIA and Britain's MI6, were relentlessly seeking ways to supplement their spotty information about the Islamic Republic. By bringing up the CIA, Javan was taking me into perilous terrain and signaling that I could be in much deeper danger than he and Tasbihi had earlier indicated.

"I highly doubt the CIA relied on any of my news reports for analysis," I told Javan.

Without responding, he handed me a piece of paper marked with some unintelligible handwriting in red ink.

"Sorry, I can't read this," I said. "I can read Farsi only if it's printed neatly—as if it's typed."

The interrogator took the sheet back and read out with a tinge of irritation, "It says, 'What types of reports did you do for Fox News, and how did this help the CIA?'"

He returned the paper to me. "Now write that you did analysis for Fox News about the Shahab 3 missile and al-Zarqawi, and this benefited the CIA," he commanded.

I wrote down the first part of his answer but changed "and this benefited the CIA" to "and perhaps someone at the CIA watched those reports."

Javan read my answer impassively, then gave me another sheet. Again, I couldn't read his handwriting.

"It says, 'Why did you see Mr. A when he came to Iran?'" he said, articulating each word as if I were a preschooler.

I saw my American friend Mr. A when he was visiting Iran to set up a student-exchange program with his Ivy League university, I explained.

"As you know, Miss Saberi," the agent said, "Washington uses such exchange programs to gather intelligence about us through the young Iranians it brings to America and through the American students it sends to Iran."

He ordered me to write that I had met Mr. A in Iran and helped him with his exchange program, which was aimed at spying on the Islamic Republic.

I wrote that I had met my friend in Iran and had not helped him with his exchange program, which as far as I knew, was merely an exchange program.

Javan read my answer, again without reacting. Then he handed me another piece of paper with red scribbles on it. "It says, 'Who's paying you to write your book?'"

"No one," I answered. "It's a personal project. I don't even have a publisher yet."

"We know you are also preparing news reports," Javan said. "You have continued to send them after your press pass was revoked in 2006."

I pointed out that I was aware the Iranian authorities had known this and that the limited reporting I had been doing did not require a press pass. Besides, I added, if they had a problem with it, they could simply tell me, and I would stop.

"How much do you earn for each news report you send from here?" Javan asked.

I gave him an approximate figure. The amount was insignificant but helped pay my bills.

"You haven't been doing many reports," he said, "so how can you afford to work on a book?"

"I have some savings from the years I worked as a full-time journalist," I explained, "my parents lent me some money, and I don't have major expenses." I didn't have to pay rent because my father had bought my apartment for me to live in, I added.

"So who's paying you to write your book?" the agent asked again. "Who told you to write it?"

"No one," I repeated. "It was my own idea."

He sighed, lowered his eyes, and leaned back. Then he pointed to the folders on the table. "Miss Saberi, we have several dossiers on you. This is just a small sample of what we have built up over the years."

I shrank into the couch. I had never suspected I was monitored to this extent.

"When you lie to us," he continued, "we know, and we think you are not cooperating. That will not be good for you, and we'll have to take you to Evin."

"But I'm not lying," I said, my voice now sounding strained.

Would they really take me to Evin?

In recent years, Iran's Intelligence Ministry had begun detaining prominent dual-national activists and academics, mostly Iranian Americans, though they had been primarily dealing with politically charged ideas or exchanges of intellectuals, writers, and civil-society activists. I had always thought if the authorities had questions about my work, at most they would interrogate me. I knew some journalists who had been routinely questioned for a few hours, then released. I longed for the same thing to happen to me and hoped this man's threats would turn out to be empty.

Javan stood up and said he would give me some time over lunch to think about whether I wanted to start cooperating. Then he left the room. Tasbihi, who had been listening quietly, tagged after him.

Another man entered and handed me a Styrofoam container, along with a bottle of *doogh*, an Iranian yogurt drink.

"Make sure you eat," Javan said, poking his head in from the hallway. "You'll need your energy."

I opened the container, releasing a burst of thick steam. With one look at the rice and chicken kebab, I shut the lid. I had no appetite.

I wished that my cell phone, which was still buried in the agent's pocket, would ring again and that it would be Bahman. He normally called by this time of the afternoon. He was probably busy editing his latest film. If only he would call, I could somehow hint to him that I was in trouble.

Javan returned momentarily. This time, he was alone. He sat down and opened another brown folder.

"Why did you meet with Mr. J, and what did he want from you?" he demanded.

Mr. J was a Japanese professor I had met when he was visiting Iran. He had asked my opinions about Iranian society, I explained.

"You know very well that he works for Japanese intelligence," the interrogator stated with apparent conviction.

So the *Japanese* were suspect, too. I didn't know what to say, except, "If he really was an intelligence agent, how would I know?"

Javan moved on to the next topic, the Aspen Institute. Aspen was an American NGO that had recently chosen me for a regional youth-leadership program, something the interrogator had likely gathered from monitoring my e-mail. Didn't I know, he said, that this organization was pursuing the "soft overthrow" of Iran's Islamic regime?

This line of thinking sounded uncomfortably familiar to me.

In recent years, Iranian hard-liners had argued that whether or not Washington was attempting to remove the Islamic regime through military means, it was striving to unseat it through a soft or velvet revolution, similar to what had occurred in Czechoslovakia in 1989 and later in countries such as Georgia and Ukraine. In those nations, mass movements had ousted Soviet-style governments through nonviolent revolutions.

Iranian hard-liners claimed that such movements were not homegrown but masterminded by the United States. They said one way Washington was trying to achieve similar upheaval in Iran was by using American think tanks and foundations to invite Iranian intellectuals, students, and opinion makers to take part in conferences, workshops, and fellowships. The goal, the hard-liners asserted, was for these elites to then use the media and civil society groups to spread antiregime ideas throughout Iran's population, which would eventually rise up against the ruling establishment. In arguing their theory, these officials liked to point to the Bush administration's "Iran Democracy Fund," which they alleged was aimed at changing Iran's regime—a charge Washington had denied.

I told Javan that the Aspen program that had selected me was focused on community service, wasn't paying its fellows anything, and as far as I knew, hadn't received any funding from the U.S. government. Anyway, I added, the fellowship hadn't even begun.

The agent looked at me blankly. I couldn't tell whether he believed me or even cared what I said. I would be faced with this seeming indifference many more times over the next few hours, as Javan would read out a question, and I would reply. He would then order me to write my answer before he followed with another question.

We had produced a small pile of completed sheets by the time the servant entered the room and offered us tea. I declined. Javan stuck a sugar cube between his teeth and raised his cup to his lips.

"So tell me more about these interviews you've been doing," he said, slurping his tea and leisurely crossing his legs.

"As I said, they were for my book," I told him. "I interviewed a wide variety of people: artists, women taxi drivers, veterans of the Iran-Iraq War—"

"It's not possible you could be conducting so many interviews only for a book," the agent interrupted, taking another sip and setting down his cup.

"But I am," I objected. I proceeded to give him the outline of the book and its various chapters.

He cut me off again. "We *know* your interviews weren't only for a book."

I couldn't understand what he was getting at.

"*Someone* told you to gather this information," he went on.

"What do you mean?"

"The U.S. government told you."

"The U.S. government?" I exclaimed. "Really, the interviews were meant only for my book."

"More specifically than the U.S. government," he said, "a certain *part* of the U.S. government: the intelligence apparatus, the *CIA*."

My pulse quickened, and my stomach twisted.

This man was now accusing me not only of informing the CIA through my news coverage but also of *spying* for it.

The idea was ludicrous, but I should have known my interrogation would lead to this. Iranian hard-liners seemed to believe that foreign spies were lurking behind every corner. As proof of their claims, they often pointed to news reports of covert activities against the Islamic Republic and the role played by U.S. and British intelligence agencies in the overthrow of Iran's democratically elected prime minister in 1953. But while the Iranian regime had legitimate security concerns, hard-liners frequently exploited these concerns by blaming domestic problems on foreign "hidden hands" and by using their cries of "espionage" to justify tightening their grip on power. Some Iranians, including journalists, had also been accused of spying, especially if they had foreign contacts and were openly critical of the regime. Much of Iranian society had learned to see such charges as bogus and politically motivated.

"*I am not a spy*," I told Javan firmly. "I have absolutely nothing to do with either the CIA or any intelligence service of any country."

"You were using your book as a *cover*," he said in a cold voice. "You were using it as a cover to gather intelligence for the CIA."

"A *cover*?" I said. "You have confiscated my flash drive and my laptop computer. You can see for yourself the chapters I've written using quotes from the various people I've interviewed."

"We know that you were using the book as a cover," he repeated slowly and deliberately. "The CIA and foreign governments do this all the time. They know that journalists and writers have good access to high-ranking people in other countries and use them to gather intelligence."

Was this man really so paranoid? Did he really believe that everyone I had met or interviewed was linked to an effort to gather intelligence on the Islamic Republic? I recalled with some irony the words of a foreign journalist once based in Iran: *The Iranian authorities think we are all spies because they themselves use their journalists as spies.*

Just then, my cell phone rang. Javan fished it out of his jacket. "It says 'Bahman,'" he said, as the phone rang again. "Who's he?"

Finally, Bahman was calling me.

I replied that he was my friend, though I was almost positive Javan already knew about our relationship.

"Put it on speaker phone," he directed me. "If you want to go home soon, speak as you normally do. Tell him you're in a meeting, and you'll call him back later. Remember, if you cooperate, you'll be freed by this evening."

I didn't know what to say. I wished Bahman and I had some sort of code. If I told him outright that I was in trouble, my captors wouldn't free me. They might crack my skull or pull out my fingernails as I heard was done to Zahra Kazemi. But if I cooperated, maybe these men really would let me go.

"Bahman," I said, my voice slightly quivering, "I'm in a meeting."

"OK," he said, "call me when you can."

"All right. But . . ." *How could I signal to him that I was in danger? We were supposed to have dinner that evening for his birthday, and he knew I wouldn't miss his birthday for anything.*

" . . . sorry, Bahman, I might not be able to make it tonight."

"OK," he repeated, sounding a bit distracted and apparently oblivious to my hint. "Call me when you can a little later. *Dust-et dâram.*"

And just like that, he hung up. Devastated, I returned the phone to Javan.

His eyes, steady and penetrating, were pinned on me. "As I was saying, Miss Saberi, we know you are cooperating with the CIA."

"I am not."

"You are cooperating with elements that are either in the CIA or linked to the CIA."

"I don't know how else to tell you, but I have nothing to do with the CIA," I insisted. "If you don't believe me, give me a lie detector test."

"We don't trust those," he countered. "People get training to pass them."

"But I didn't get any training."

Javan looked at me scornfully and went on to his next question. As the hours passed, he kept claiming that my book was a cover for espionage activities, and I kept denying it. I knew that asking to see proof of his allegations would be of no use. In this country, people like him needed no more than their own words to send someone to jail for years.

Finally, he shut the latest folder he had been studying and announced, "We are not making progress." It was 7:30 P.M., and he wanted to finish up for the day.

"We didn't want to take you to Evin," Javan said nonchalantly, "but we gave you a chance, and you didn't cooperate. Now we have no other choice." He began to gather his numerous dossiers.

I felt the blood suddenly drain from my face. "But I have been telling you the truth. Please, believe me!" I begged.

"You haven't been cooperating," he said calmly.

"What do you *mean* by 'cooperating'?"

"You have to *confess*."

"Confess to *what*?"

"To using your book as a cover to spy on Iran for the CIA."

"I swear to God I have nothing to do with the CIA!" I exclaimed, throwing my arms in the air. "*I—am—not—a—spy.*"

"Suit yourself," he said, as he rose to his feet.

As Javan headed for the door, images I had once seen on Iran's state-run TV flashed before me. In 2007, one program highlighted what its producers claimed were the confessions of three detained dual-national scholars—Haleh Esfandiari, Kian Tajbakhsh, and Ramin Jahanbegloo. I couldn't recall the details of the video, except that it made them appear to admit their work was aimed at undermining the Iranian regime through a soft revolution and that their statements seemed forced. A few months before that, Iran had broadcast video clips of captured British sailors and marines "confessing" to illegally entering Iranian waters—a charge London disputed.

These videos were soon followed by the captives' release, as if confessing on tape had been a prerequisite for their freedom. Critics in and out of Iran had ridiculed the videos as mere propaganda, and a few of the captives had recanted their confessions once they were released.

Yet forced public confessions, in which prisoners often expressed regret for their actions, denounced colleagues, and asked for forgiveness, were an institutionalized feature of Iran's intelligence apparatus. The practice was largely designed to suppress dissidents, intimidate like-minded people, and bolster the regime's claims of subversive plots.

The thought that I might have to make such a confession filled me with rage and contempt. "So now you're going to torture me until I confess on video to a crime I didn't commit," I snarled at Javan.

The agent turned around with a smirk on his face. He seemed amused by my sudden burst of boldness.

"No, no, it's not like that at all," he said quietly, showing me the door.

I staggered out of the room and down the stairs, where his three colleagues were waiting for us. The street was crowded with cars and passersby going about their daily activities. I thought again of yelling for help, but I doubted anyone would come to my rescue, and creating a scene would infuriate my captors. Besides, maybe they had only wanted to scare me so I would stop writing my book, and now they planned to take me home.

I resigned myself to the unknown and got in the car. We started driving back toward northern Tehran. When we passed the turnoff to my apartment, my heart sank. The driver kept going, straight to Evin Prison.

CHAPTER THREE

I had been to, or rather, *outside* Evin, once before.

An Iranian friend had insisted on driving me past the prison, which was located on a hill in an upper-class neighborhood of northern Tehran, close to the Alborz Mountains. I had asked him not to linger: Just seeing its tall walls and barbed wire made me tense, and I suspected that cameras were recording video of anyone in the vicinity.

Now, as our car pulled up to the prison gate, I could no longer deny the reality of what was happening to me. For the first time that day, I felt truly terrified. *Some people come here and never leave.*

"I don't understand why you are bringing me here," I said to the Mailman, who was sitting beside me in the backseat of the car.

"Don't worry," he said with a sly smile. "If you prove your innocence, you'll be set free."

"Why should I prove my innocence?" I asserted. "A person is supposed to be presumed innocent until proven guilty. If I am guilty, *you* are the ones who have to prove it."

The man shrugged and turned his head away.

A guard waved us through the blue metal gate. We drove up a winding road and parked in front of a brick building, where I was told to get out of the car. Tasbihi gave me a dirty, white blindfold and ordered me to cover my eyes. He told me to pull the cloth just high enough so I could see his black shoes in front of me. I followed him into the building, groping the walls as I stumbled down a hallway and up a flight of stairs. I trembled, thinking of how many thousands of prisoners had been detained, tortured, and executed in this prison since it was built by Mohammad Reza Shah in the 1970s and expanded after the Islamic Revolution.

At the top of the stairs, Tasbihi told me to face a wall. I heard him ring a buzzer. Then came the sound of a heavy door opening. A frosty hand seized my wrist and pulled me inside a corridor. The door banged shut behind me.

"Remove your blindfold," a woman whispered to me.

I did as I was told. Standing before me was a solemn-faced, heavy-set woman wearing round glasses and a black chador. She must have been a guard. She guided me down a quiet, brightly-lit corridor past five or six steel doors on the left. We stopped in front of the last one, which stood open. "Go in," she murmured.

I entered a small cell with lime green walls and a thin, worn-out brown carpet. The room was lit by one dim, yellow lightbulb.

"Remove all your clothes," the woman directed me.

I took off my headscarf and *roopoosh*, then stopped and looked at her. I wondered whether she was going to turn around or keep staring at me.

"Go ahead," she said, remaining glued to her spot with her eyes wide open.

I stripped down to my underwear.

"Take that off, too," she said.

When I was completely naked, the guard told me to face the wall and open my ponytail. She ran her fingers through my long hair, evidently to see if I had hidden anything in it. Then she handed me a large pair of underwear, some synthetic, beige-colored sweatpants, and a matching sweatshirt to wear in place of my own clothes. The only personal item she allowed me to keep was my socks. No bra. No watch. No shoes. Instead, I was given men's oversize, white plastic slippers—the cheap kind many Iranians wore to the bathroom in their homes. The guard took my tote bag, made a list of the belongings it contained, and had me sign a form and fingerprint it.

Like a robot, I did as she instructed.

She then had me put on a *maqna'e* to cover my hair and neck, a *roopoosh* that hung loosely on my small frame, and a dark blue chador that smelled like unwashed socks. When I was dressed, she grabbed my arm and led me back down the corridor and, once I was blindfolded again, out the door. From there, I walked clumsily beside her a few steps down another hallway and into a room on our left, where she told me to unfasten my blindfold.

I found myself in a small, one-room dispensary. A young male doctor was sitting behind a desk. He stood up and checked my weight, blood pressure, and pulse, silently noting the results until he announced, "You're very healthy."

How unfortunate, I moaned to myself. *If I were gravely ill, maybe these people would release me. Or maybe they wouldn't. Maybe they'd be glad if I were dead.*

"Are you an athlete?" the doctor asked.

"Yes," I replied.

"What sports do you play?"

"Soccer."

The doctor ran down a list of illnesses. Regrettably, I didn't have any.

"Have you ever been depressed?" he asked.

My captors wouldn't want to keep a suicidal woman here for long, would they? I thought. *There was that time years ago when a counselor told me I had a mild case of depression . . .*

"Well, I get depressed once in a while," I replied.

"Everyone gets depressed once in a while," the doctor said.

"And athletes shouldn't get depressed," interjected the guard, who was standing next to me. I glared at her.

"Are you on any medications?" the doctor asked.

I told him I had been using a special acne ointment, which was in the bag I had brought to prison.

"Your skin looks fine," he said. "You don't need it." With that, he turned to the guard and told her to take me back to my cell.

The steel door clanged shut behind me, automatically locking. I had never been any more cut off from the outside world. I had never been any more alone.

A disposable plastic bowl of cold baked beans was sitting on the ratty carpet. I slid the dish aside with my foot and began to survey my new surroundings.

The guard had left four frayed military blankets in one corner for me. She had told me to roll one up as my pillow and to sleep on two others. She had also given me a towel, a miniature bar of soap, a toothbrush, and a travel-size tube of toothpaste.

The cell, which measured about seven by nine feet, was clearly made to hold only one person. By raising my arms to the sides, I could almost touch both walls. A few feet above the door, beyond my reach near the ceiling, was a closed, barred window covered with a sheet of tightly woven metal mesh. There was a small window in the door, too, but its shutter was latched from the outside.

Nailed to one wall was a sign with some instructions in Farsi, which I ignored. Against another wall stood a rusty iron sink. The guard had warned me not to drink the water. She had also told me the old toilet beside the sink no longer worked. If I needed to use the bathroom down the hall, I was to push a black button near my door. This would activate a green light outside my cell, signaling that I needed to be let out.

Attached to the opposite wall was a heater with a white metal cover. It was engraved with various comments left by previous detainees. I knelt to examine them.

"National solidarity for the freedom of Iran," stated one in Farsi.

"18 Tir 1386," read another. This date on the Iranian calendar marked the eighth anniversary of the 1999 peaceful student protests that had rocked various Iranian cities before the authorities violently suppressed them. Every year since then, students had commemorated the anniversary of the protests with fresh demonstrations, which were consistently put down by force.

Ahmad Batebi was one of the students who took part in the original protests. After his photo appeared on the cover of *The Economist* magazine, holding up a shirt splattered with the blood of a fellow protestor, he was given a death sentence, which was later reduced to several years' imprisonment in Evin. I had read how Batebi's captors had tried to get him to say what they wanted by beating his testicles and legs and by holding his head in excrement until he inhaled it. In 2008, when he was briefly allowed out of prison for medical treatment, he escaped to neighboring Iraq and was later granted political asylum in America.

Toward the top of the heater, someone had drawn several parallel lines, apparently indicating the number of days she had been jailed. "One, two, three . . ." I counted. "Eighteen!" I could not handle even one night here.

I puzzled over how my predecessors had made these engravings without any sharp objects at their disposal. I tried using the bottom edge of my tube of toothpaste. It was solid enough to carve into the paint.

"GOD . . . SAVE . . ." I etched into the heater, "IRAN." I had to keep myself from adding, "from these awful people." The guard might later inspect what I had written. Who knew, maybe she could read English.

As I was finishing my artwork, I heard a whimpering sound coming from the other side of the wall through the perforations in my heater.

Then I heard a neighboring cell door open.

"You must eat something," I heard the guard say.

The whimpering paused.

"I can't," a woman said in a voice barely louder than a whisper.

"OK, it's up to you," the guard replied. "You're only hurting yourself, not us."

The door closed.

"Is she still refusing to eat?" asked someone, who must have been another guard.

"Yes," came the reply.

Poor woman. I wondered why she was here and what ghastly things had been done to her.

I lay down on my blankets and shut my eyes. The air was thick with dust, and my cell smelled like a junkyard of metal and cement, devoid of life and activity. The heater wasn't working, and the room was chilly. With two blankets under me and only one left as a cover, I was shivering. So I placed two blankets on top of myself and kept only one beneath. I was a little warmer, but now my bones were grinding against the frigid cement floor.

Without a watch or clock, I had no clue what time it was. It must have been near midnight, but I wasn't sleepy.

Anger roused me. Anger at the people who had put me here. Anger at U.S. policies that gave my captors a pretext to accuse people like me of plotting against the Islamic regime. Anger at God.

"Why are you punishing me?" I whispered. *Is it because I complained to you last night about my life? I'm sorry. I didn't mean it. Please help me. Where are you? Why have you abandoned me?*

I was also angry at myself. I had been such an idiot to think that my research wasn't that risky, that I would at most be interrogated and not land in prison, that Iranian intelligence agents would be rational enough to see the harmless nature of my work, and that they would believe me if I told the truth.

A few tears of self-pity trickled down my cheeks as I lay awake for what seemed like hours. I wished I could turn back time. I would have never begun writing a book about Iran. I would have left the country in 2006.

"Aaa-eee!" came a man's anguished howl from somewhere in the distance.

What a terrible, terrible place!

CHAPTER FOUR

Acall to morning prayers reverberated through the air, startling me awake.

"*Allaho akbar, Allaho akbar!*" a muezzin's voice bellowed through the prison loudspeakers, "God is great, God is great!"

Tall walls appeared all around me as I opened my eyes and felt the cold seeping through my body, reminding me that the previous day had been all too real.

The guard from the night before opened my door to hand me a plastic cup of tea, along with some white bread and a sliver of cheese. I felt queasy. I didn't touch the food and sat against the wall, speculating about what new horrors this day might bring.

After what seemed like an hour, a loud buzzer sliced through the silence. This was followed by the sound of footsteps scuttling past my cell, pausing, and scuttling back, until they stopped outside my door. This time when the door opened, I saw a slim woman guard in her midtwenties. She told me to put on my *roopoosh*, chador, and blindfold. I was going to see my *bâzju*, or interrogator, she said.

I was led out of the women's ward, down the hallway, and through an open door padded with leather, where I entered a room and was told to sit down. When I tipped back my head, I spotted a plastic school desk with a writing arm, facing a foam-covered wall. I blindly inched forward, trying not to trip over the ends of my chador, and maneuvered myself into the desk.

"Hello, Miss Saberi. How are you?"

It was the cold, measured voice of Javan, the young interrogator the guard must have been referring to as my *bâzju*. A tremor passed through me.

"OK," I said.

"We're giving you one more chance to cooperate with us today," he said. "But if you don't, we will have to take you to court, where *tafhim-e ettehâm mishi*."

I had never heard this phrase before. "What does that mean?" I asked.

"It means you will be told the charge against you."

I heard the screech of a chair behind me, followed by the clicking of heels approaching and what sounded like a heap of papers being thrown on my desk. Then the shoes clicked back to where they had originated.

"Raise your blindfold slightly so that you can write," Javan commanded.

I obeyed and saw a pen and a pile of blank forms before me.

"Write your name and nationality on the top of the first page," he directed. "As I'm sure you know, Iran does not recognize dual nationality."

I did know that. Based on this practice, Iranian authorities claimed that their treatment of dual nationals like me was an internal matter.

"So even if you were born and raised in America," my *bâzju* continued, "you are an Iranian according to our law. You enter and leave our country as an Iranian. You must write down that you are an Iranian. Anyway, America cannot help you here. In fact, no one can help you here."

I figured it would be futile to object. I did as he ordered, and the interrogation began anew. Similar to the day before, my interrogator would pose a question, I would verbally answer it, and then I would write down my reply, all in Farsi. Once in a while, another interrogator would jump in with a comment or question. By listening to the different voices bombarding me from behind, I concluded that at least four men were in the room.

I wrapped my chador tightly around me. Accounts of sexual assault in Iran's prisons were not uncommon, and I didn't know if these men would touch me, or worse.

Their questions flew at me in no apparent order.

Why had I traveled to Qom? To interview various clerics for my book.

Why had I gone to the French Embassy in Tehran? To sign up for classes to brush up on my French.

"Why did you interview a Hezbollah official in Beirut?" Javan asked, adding, "You questioned him about ties between Iran and Hezbollah."

Iran had helped create the Shiite Muslim militia in the early 1980s to counter Israel. Washington accused Tehran of supporting the Lebanese group with military training and equipment, but Tehran said it offered only "spiritual" support.

I explained to my *bâzju* that I had interviewed the Hezbollah official about various issues. The relationship between Iran and Hezbollah was only one of them.

"You should have known we would learn of these things from our friends in Hezbollah," he snorted. "They tell us *everything*."

I was at a loss to understand why Javan considered the interview a crime. "If you're saying it was illegal to ask these questions," I reasoned, "then should the U.S. government also detain me for having interviewed Iraqi Kurdish officials about their ties to Washington?"

"We *know* you went to Iraqi Kurdistan," another interrogator cut in. He was referring to the region in northern Iraq where ethnic Kurds lived. Millions of Kurds also lived in Iran, Syria, and Turkey. They were considered the world's largest ethnic group without its own state, although the Kurdistan Regional Government in northern Iraq had recently won formal autonomy.

I bit my lip. I had unwittingly provided my interrogators with a transition to the next item on their list.

"You interviewed several Kurdish officials in Iraq about their government's relations with Tehran."

"Yes, I did," I said. "Their comments are online in the news report I wrote."

"Who helped you set up those interviews?"

I hesitated. Bahman had helped me.

As an Iranian-Kurdish film director, Bahman had made movies in Iraq and was closely acquainted with a few top Kurdish officials there. I didn't want to bring up his name again. He already had enough problems with Iran's Culture Ministry, which he often referred to as the Intelligence Ministry's little brother.

"We know it was Bahman Ghobadi," Javan said haughtily, "just as we know all these other things about you. When you don't volunteer this information, we know you're not cooperating."

I released a sigh tight with tension. I must have carelessly discussed this trip with Bahman on the phone at some point.

"So Mister Bahman helped you with those interviews," Javan said.

"But he wasn't doing anything wrong," I insisted.

"You also interviewed Kurds in *Iran*," the agent continued, sounding mildly annoyed. "Why did you focus so much on Kurds, anyway?"

My captors were obviously sensitive about the issue of ethnic minorities. Although a unifying Iranian identity pulled many of the country's people together, Iran was home to a variety of ethnic groups with distinct identities. Persians constituted around half the population, while Azeris, Kurds, Baluchis, Arabs, and others made up the rest. The Kurds, many of whom were Sunni Muslims, were of particular concern to the Shiite Islamic regime. Some Kurds had called for more autonomy, or even separation from Iran in order to form a "Greater Kurdistan" state with their counterparts in nearby Syria, Turkey, and Iraq. Many others, however, preferred to focus on gaining more rights within Iran.

"I interviewed several Kurds for my book," I answered frankly, "and I have many Kurdish friends in Iraq and Iran."

Javan then asked me, as he had the day before, if anyone had a copy of my book, and I replied again that my mother did.

I heard papers rustling behind me. The men must have been leafing through those horrid dossiers.

My *bâzju* brought up a trip I had made to Israel. I explained I went there years earlier on my American passport to do some freelance reporting.*

"We also know you went to Afghanistan to see your brother," he said.

Javan was clearly aware that my brother, Jasper, was in the U.S. Army, a piece of information I had not volunteered but knew was available on the Internet.

"I couldn't have met him in Afghanistan because I went there to report in 2004, and he didn't go until 2005," I explained, adding that what little I knew about Jasper's work then had to do with fighting the Taliban, which Tehran claimed was its adversary, too.

My *bâzju* asked me a few more questions, then paused.

"Miss Saberi," he said in his controlled, self-assured way, "we have been monitoring you since the day you first set foot in Iran in 2003. We have shot hours and hours of video of you, and we even took some trips with you, flew on flights with you."

"I hope you enjoyed Paris," I quipped under my breath, even though a sinking feeling was rapidly overcoming me.

Suddenly I remembered how a friend had told me a few months earlier that he had spotted a man and a woman filming us in a park. After my friend waved at them and smiled at the camera, they had abruptly departed. We had both thought the filming might have to do with our mutual acquaintance who was jailed at the time.

I wondered if any part of my life over the past six years had been private, whether in Iran or abroad, or if every moment had been recorded on tape and in those dreadful brown files. From what Javan was telling me, he and his colleagues had invested a lot of time,

---

* The Islamic regime does not recognize Israel and says holders of Iranian passports are not entitled to travel there. Some Jews living in Iran have traveled to Israel through a third country.

money, and manpower in following me. I had never fathomed I was this important to Iran's intelligence apparatus.

"We also know you wanted to publish your book abroad," Javan said, "and that you wanted to leave Iran in a couple of months."

I had mentioned this in a few phone conversations. "Yes," I replied.

"Why did you want to publish your book outside Iran?"

"Because it's in English, and I wanted to find a publisher who could promote it in the West."

"No," he spat. "It's because you knew that publishing a book in Iran requires government permission, and you thought you wouldn't get it."

I didn't answer. I was trying to figure out the logic of these seemingly haphazard questions. Was my crime visiting foreign embassies in Tehran, conducting interviews the authorities didn't like, or writing a book they could not censor?

Another interrogator told me to stand up. I had a phone call, he informed me, from the interrogators' boss at the Intelligence Ministry, a man he referred to as Haj Agha, a term often used to show respect to men. With my blindfold back in place, I tottered after the interrogator down the hallway. Every few feet, I bumped into a desk or chair or barely dodged the shoes of a few seated men I assumed to be prison employees.

When we finally reached the end of the hallway, the interrogator handed me a telephone receiver.

"Miss Saberi," came a voice, gruff despite its singsong accent particular to central Iran, "if you cooperate today, by tomorrow evening, you will be continuing this conversation with my colleagues in the comfort of the Esteghlal Hotel, not in Evin Prison."

The Esteghlal Hotel was just down the hill from the prison. Other journalists had told me that big hotels such as the Esteghlal were popular venues for Iran's intelligence agents and that it was common for them to hide recording devices in the hotels' restaurants, lobbies, and rooms. Still, I would have preferred the Esteghlal to Evin any day.

"OK," was all I could muster.

"But if you don't cooperate," Haj Agha continued, "you could end up staying in prison for a long, long time. That would be a pity."

"OK," I repeated in a choked voice.

"No one can help you here but us. Cooperate, and we will help you. This is the only way. Do you understand?"

"But Haj Agha," I squeaked, "I *am* cooperating. I am telling the truth."

He hung up, and I was taken back to the interrogation room, where my captors continued to question me.

Why did an American acquaintance of mine want to sell vitamins in Iran, why had I gone out for coffee with an American journalist in Tehran, and why had I tried to help my jailed Iranian acquaintance a few months earlier?

I answered openly, clinging to what had become a tiny shred of hope that I could convince my interrogators their suspicions about me were unfounded. Yet every time I responded to their questions, they twisted my replies to sound as though I were guilty of undercover intelligence work. They ordered me to write down their responses, which I stubbornly tried to twist back into mine.

As the hours passed, my frustration and fatigue grew, and I had to struggle to stay completely focused. Sometimes the men shot out one question after another so quickly, I hardly had time to reflect on my answers. Other times they jumped from topic to topic, disorienting me. They also repeated certain questions many times but in different ways, as if to see whether my answers would remain the same. This was most conspicuously the case with my book, which appeared to be their main object of interest.

"The interviews you've been doing," an interrogator said, "why don't you just tell us whom and what they're *really* for?"

I summoned the energy to sit up erect in my chair. "The interviews inside Iran that you've asked me about were *really* for my book," I maintained, "and those I did outside Iran were *really* for either news reports or my book."

"It's *not possible* you could be doing so many interviews just for a *book*."

"I have a habit of doing a lot of research to comprehend a subject well," I explained. I was now cursing myself for this.

Someone exhaled slowly and heavily behind me.

"Miss Saberi, we are still waiting," came Javan's voice from the same direction. "We are waiting for you to tell us who told you to use your book as a cover to spy for America. What information did you gather, and how did you give it to them? What else did they want you to do? In return for what?"

"I don't know what you're talking about!" I was desperate now and almost shouting. "Just read the chapters of my book on my flash drive, and you'll see I'm not a spy."

"Miss Saberi," Javan said again, continuing in his quiet, restrained way, "I have an *allergy* to the word *book*. If you want to get out of here, don't use it anymore."

"But when that's the truth, what else am I supposed to say?" I felt my fists clenching.

"Well," the agent said, as I heard him stand up behind me, "we gave you another chance, but once again, you didn't cooperate. Unfortunately, now we'll have to take you to court to see the prosecuting magistrate."

This time when I was loaded into a car, a male guard handcuffed me. Never in my life had my hands been bound. As I watched him turn the key in the lock, I felt as if he were shackling someone else's wrists.

I recognized neither the driver nor the guard who sat beside him, holding on his lap a bulky, black pouch—just large enough to carry a handgun.

As we drove toward central Tehran, I feverishly scanned the streets, longing for Bahman to somehow walk or drive past our car and spot me—wishful thinking, in a city of more than 8 million people. He knew it wasn't like me to disappear for twenty-four hours, and he must have been trying to contact me since I had failed to call him back the day before. My parents were also probably confused as to why I hadn't e-mailed them as usual. They might start to suspect I was in trouble, but not trouble like this. If news of my arrest were to reach my father, I dreaded to think what effect it might have on him. He was already suffering from high blood pressure, and he had undergone quadruple bypass heart surgery a few years earlier. I had to get out of Evin as soon as possible.

We reached a middle-class neighborhood I recognized as Mo'alem. I had been to this area several times before, but never to the building we were now approaching.

"What is this place?" I asked the driver.

"The Revolutionary Court of Tehran," he replied.

I gasped. Iran's revolutionary court system ran parallel to the country's other courts. It tried cases such as crimes against national security and slandering the supreme leader or Islam. Women's rights activists, students, unionists, journalists, bloggers, academics, politicians, and many others had been summoned here on political charges, although the regime liked to refer to them as "security" prisoners, not "political" ones.

The state's security-oriented approach toward society, which had somewhat relaxed under Khatami, had become more prevalent under President Ahmadinejad, who had installed hard-liners as the heads of various ministries, including the Intelligence Ministry and the Ministry of Culture and Islamic Guidance. These ministers and their associates seemed to believe that tightening restrictions on society was necessary to counter what they claimed were foreign (mainly, U.S.) efforts to undermine the Islamic regime. The authorities had rolled back social freedoms, increased suppression of the student movement, and hindered political, ethnic, and social activism. Books, music, and films came under tougher restrictions and more censorship. Local journalists and bloggers continued to be interrogated or given prison sentences.

The guard removed my handcuffs and led me to the second floor of the building. We walked down a drab hallway lined with chairs, passed a few women in chadors, and entered a small antechamber connected to three rooms. The guard took me to the one on the far left.

A dark-bearded man who appeared to be in his midfifties was sitting behind a large desk. I assumed he was the magistrate. He motioned at me to take a chair in one of several rows facing him as he talked to another man, who I assumed was his assistant.

"Start him off with one week in solitary confinement and one phone call," the magistrate said. His assistant nodded and sat down at a desk on the other side of the room.

"Where are you from?" the magistrate asked me casually, as if simply making small talk.

"I was born and raised in America," I said. "I've been living in Iran for the past six years."

"You are being charged with acting against national security," he said in the same easygoing manner.

My lips parted to speak, but I couldn't find my voice. I knew that this was a common charge, one so vague it allowed Iranian authorities to punish people for a variety of peaceful activities.

"Have you colluded with the CIA?"

"No," I said weakly.

He tilted his head to the side and looked at me, his eyes narrowing slightly, as if trying to size me up.

"Want a cookie?" he asked.

For the first time since my arrest, I could feel my stomach growling.

"Yes, please," I whispered.

"What did you say?"

"Yes, please," I repeated, a little more loudly.

He held out a box of sugar cookies with his right hand. Large gemstone rings adorned his ring finger and little finger.

I took a cookie, ate one bite, and set it down.

Then the magistrate gave me a pen and a piece of paper and said, "Write down your defense."

With a tremulous hand, I wrote something like: *I protest my detention and object to the charge against me. I am not a spy, and if I have ever had any contact with anyone in any foreign intelligence service, I was not aware of it. I was simply writing a book to provide a comprehensive view of Iranian society to English-language readers abroad.*

The magistrate picked up the sheet, reminded me I would be treated as an Iranian citizen despite my American nationality, and told the guard who had brought me to take me away.

That was all? He hadn't even informed me of my legal rights. I wished I had studied some Iranian law, although I had a feeling that no matter what the law was, my captors could interpret it as they wished or even act above it.

"Excuse me," I said. "May I get a lawyer?"

"When your interrogation is complete," the magistrate replied.

As if that would do me any good. I needed a lawyer now.

"How long will my interrogation take?" I ventured.

He shrugged. "Maybe one week, maybe one month, maybe longer. It depends when your interrogators are satisfied with your answers."

One month or longer?

"How long do I have to stay in solitary confinement?" I asked, wondering whether the magistrate's ruling for the other detainee would be the same for me.

"Maybe one week, maybe one month, maybe longer," he repeated. "It depends on your interrogators."

My guard was gesturing at me to get up.

"But could I at least make a phone call?" I pleaded.

"Yes," the magistrate answered. Then, looking at the guard, he said, "She can make one phone call today from prison."

As we were leaving, I glanced over my shoulder to read the sign outside the antechamber where we had just been.

SECURITY DIVISION OF THE PUBLIC PROSECUTOR'S OFFICE OF TEHRAN, it read. I repeated this phrase many times, mouthing it silently. I would tell it to Bahman as soon as I could make my call.

The guard loaded me into the car again, and the handcuffs came back on.

As we headed toward Evin, I gazed damp-eyed through the window. Colored lights decorated the streets in observance of the Ten Days of Dawn, commemorating the period between Khomeini's return from exile to Iran on February 1, 1979, and the victory of the Islamic Revolution nine days later. I yearned to walk freely in those crowded streets, like the college students carrying backpacks, like the housewives haggling over fruit prices, like I was two days ago.

But this trip to the magistrate had wiped out what little hope I still had that I might be freed soon. I pictured myself jumping out of the car, leaving behind the two pot-bellied men in the front seat, and sprinting down a busy Tehran sidewalk. I would throw aside my chador, rip a headscarf off a random woman, and tie it around my own hair to blend in with the crowds. Then I would leap into a Dumpster, like a fugitive in the movies, mixing with the rats while the two agents ran by me unaware.

Who was I kidding? I couldn't even open the car door. The driver had turned on the safety lock.

It must have been late afternoon when I was returned to the interrogation room, my eyes wrapped once again, and I informed my captors that the magistrate had said I was allowed to make a phone call.

"Whom do you want to call?" Javan asked.

"Bahman."

"Why do you want to call him? As I told you, no one can help you here—not Bahman, not your parents, no one."

"I want to call him anyway."

"Wait until later," he said.

I heard someone saunter toward me and order me to lift my blind-fold a little. I obeyed and saw that Javan was waving a pamphlet below my eyes.

"We found this in your home," he said. It was a research article that his colleague must have dug out of my closet the day before. I hadn't seen it in ages.

"Is there something wrong with it?" I asked.

"We found several of these in your apartment," he replied. "Where did you get them?"

I explained that I had received many such articles at the Center for Strategic Research, where I had attended conferences and, at the request of a friend, corrected the English grammar of a few articles. I had hoped this might help increase understanding about Iran outside the country.

Javan must have already known about my association with the center, a governmental think tank in northern Tehran that published books, journals, and articles about local and international issues. Many moderate analysts, professors, and ex-diplomats worked there. Some were close to former President Khatami and his predecessor, Akbar Hashemi Rafsanjani, a leading centrist and top rival of President Ahmadinejad.

I told the agent that employees at the center knew I was interested in a wide range of topics and often gave me articles to read. I had also bought a few, which were available to the public, I said.

"And how many did you have?"

"I don't remember exactly," I said. "Maybe ten, fifteen."

Then Javan held up the pamphlet again and said adamantly, "This is a *secret* document."

He had to be lying. "No, it's not," I said with certainty. "It's public information."

"It's secret."

"If it's really secret, where's the stamp on it?" I had heard that se-cret documents in Iran were marked with a stamp.

No answer came. Instead, my interrogators' questions—and my defense—resumed.

"Why did you borrow a book in Tehran using your friend's library card?"

"Mine had expired, and I had to wait a few more weeks for the library to renew it."

"Why did you translate some interviews for an Iranian journalist, who later published them in his moderate newspaper?"

"Because he didn't know English."

"How much did he pay you?"

"Nothing. I did it for free."

"We don't believe you."

"It's true. He was my friend, and I just wanted to help him."

"Who were Mr. B, Mrs. C, Mr. D . . ." Javan asked, leaping to the next subject, after I wrote down what he must have considered yet another unsatisfactory answer, "and what did they want from you?"

These were various American friends, acquaintances, or interviewees I had been in touch with in one way or another over the previous six years. None of them wanted anything from me, I told my interrogators. One was a journalist friend who had e-mailed me a few weeks earlier from America.

"We know he works for the *Seattle Post-Intelligencer*," one of the agents said.

"Yes," I said. "He's a photographer there."

"That paper is an arm of the CIA," he continued.

"What do you mean?"

"It has the word *intelligence* in its name."

I almost scoffed in disbelief. "As far as I know, the newspaper is not connected to the CIA in any way," I said. "I truly do not know *anyone* in the CIA."

"What did all these people want from you?" Javan asked again.

"Nothing."

"Nonsense!" he barked. "We know that one of these Americans

wanted you to use your interviews and research for your book as a cover to gather intelligence for the U.S. government. Tell us who. How much money did you get for it? What information did you provide?"

"I wasn't gathering intelligence for anyone," I said, raising my voice. "As I told you, the book I have been writing is a personal project and not for any institution or government."

"And as I told *you*, I am *allergic* to the word *book*," Javan retorted.

"But it's the truth," I insisted.

"You are lying, you are lying," he said, drawing out the words as if tasting them before they left his mouth.

"I'm not lying!" I erupted. I could not sit quietly while these men insulted my integrity. "Just give me a polygraph test," I pleaded, as I had the day before, "and you will see that I am telling the truth!"

"Fix your hejab!" another interrogator thundered at me. "Do you think you're in America?"

Amid my outburst, my chador had slipped back on my head, exposing a few strands of hair.

"Sorry," I whimpered. I tugged the cloth forward and cowered in my desk.

A chair scraped against the cement floor. One of the men behind me stood up and started pacing slowly back and forth. My head turned from side to side, trying to follow his movements.

Back and forth.

Back and forth.

"Miss Saberi," came my *bâzju*'s voice, dark and intense, "if you don't cooperate, we will have you sentenced to ten years in prison. That could be extended for another ten years."

He paused to let the words sink in. They flooded my ears and were beginning to drown me. *Ten years? Twenty years behind bars?*

"Picture what you'll look like after twenty years in prison. By the time you are released, you will be an old lady."

Much as I wanted to ignore this cruel forecast, my mind flashed forward to a gray-haired, fifty-one-year-old woman, broken, emaciated, dim-witted, useless. Javan seemed completely serious about this threat. I shriveled farther into my seat, as if my school desk could shield me from the agent's piercing words.

"You certainly won't look like you do now," my *bâzju* continued. "You can't stay young forever."

The pacing stopped.

"Did you ever think you'd end up in prison?" he asked.

"No," I said, my voice hoarse, "never. I still don't know why I'm here."

"Yes, you do."

"No, I really don't," I said. "I thought if you had questions, you might interrogate but not imprison me."

"Well," he said, with a snide chuckle, "we wanted to wait and see if you changed your ways on your own. When we saw that you didn't, we had to detain you."

His words confused me. I couldn't comprehend why he cared whether I was going to "change my ways" when he knew I was planning to leave the country soon. If I really was such a threat to national security, it didn't make sense that my captors would wait to detain me until just before my departure. They could have easily arrested me months or years earlier at the Tehran airport when I was making one of my frequent trips, as they sometimes did to academics and activists entering or leaving the country.

The men behind me had begun whispering to one another. I strained to hear but couldn't make out what they were saying. The room had grown warm and the air, heavy. I leaned my head on my right palm and used my chador to dab perspiration from my upper lip. Having eaten practically nothing for two days, I felt that my body and mind were withering away.

Then Javan spoke, his voice lower now: "Miss Saberi, your crime is very serious. Espionage can also result in the death penalty."

My heart thudded in my gut, and my mouth became dry. Iran

ranked second in the world, after China, in number of executions. Human-rights groups claimed that many executions took place after a kangaroo trial or no trial at all. Group hangings often made headlines, with many victims accused of drug trafficking and armed robbery, although human-rights activists believed some were political prisoners. Juveniles were sometimes executed, as were some prisoners found guilty of security-related crimes, including an Iranian telecommunications salesman convicted of espionage who was hanged in 2008.

The hangings, some of which had taken place in Evin, were often conducted secretly. If I were executed, maybe no one would ever find out. The local papers might refer to me simply as "R.S.," who, along with a bunch of other initials, "was hanged at five A.M. on Friday."

"Could I please call Bahman now?" I asked timidly.

"What do you want to tell him?"

"I want to tell him where I am," I replied, inwardly hoping that Bahman could raise a fuss over my arrest in the media and among his many fans and Kurdish contacts.

"I want you to realize something," the young interrogator said gravely. "If you cooperate, you will be freed by tomorrow or at the latest, the day after. But if you tell him where you are, this won't be possible anymore."

"But," I said in a thin voice, "I don't understand. What exactly do you want from me?"

Javan remained quiet for a moment, then said, "Maybe we can reach some kind of deal."

A *deal*?

"First, confess to gathering intelligence for the CIA," he said.

"But I wasn't—"

"Secondly," he continued, "we could use the help of people like you."

I didn't like the sound of this. "What are you getting at?"

"You know, *help* us," he replied. "Gather some useful information for us."

"About what?"

"About *whom*."

"About whom?"

"Foreign diplomats, other journalists—"

"You mean . . ." I stammered, "you want me to *spy* for you?"

"We don't have to call it *spying*," he said. "Call it collaboration."

CHAPTER FIVE

We have many people working for us," Javan said. "They come from all walks of life: students, athletes, artists, journalists like you . . ."

Ever since I had moved to Iran, several of my Iranian friends had warned me to be careful about what I said, where, and to whom. You never knew when the friend or stranger with whom you were conversing might be an informant for the regime, they would tell me. As a result, over the years I had found myself sharing details about my life with only my closest companions.

Now, based on what Javan was telling me, it appeared that my suspicions had been justified. Although much of my captors' information about me was incorrect or incomplete, they knew about certain aspects of my life that I had never communicated in e-mails or by phone—information that only a few acquaintances or friends knew. Maybe some of them worked for Iran's Intelligence Ministry. If so, I wondered who. Hassan, the friend who had advised me to never argue with intelligence agents, came to mind. Only he had known about some of the points my interrogators had mentioned. And on a few occasions, he had behaved suspiciously.

"We don't ask much of our collaborators," my *bâzju* continued. "They just help us gather a little information about who is doing what, saying what, going where, with whom. . . . Other detainees have agreed to work with us, too, in exchange for their freedom."

I felt so helpless, so powerless. I just wanted to talk to Bahman. But if I didn't at least pretend to consider this deal, I might miss my only opportunity to make a phone call.

"Maybe I could do that," I said, "but could I please call Bahman now?" I abhorred the sniveling, imploring tone of my voice but could not conceal it.

Javan heaved a deep sigh. "OK, but remember, if you tell him where you are, you won't be freed any time soon. If you are going to work with us, no one should know that you have been here, or your cover will be blown." He paused. "So tell him you are in Zahedan."

Zahedan? He must have thought this up because Mr. Z had called from Zahedan the day before.

"But Bahman knows I don't go out of town without informing him first," I said, trying to convince Javan this was a bad idea. "He won't believe me." In reality, I didn't want to say anything that would make it harder for Bahman to locate me.

"Just explain to him you made a last-minute trip to do some research on your book, you forgot your cell-phone charger, and you're in the countryside, where there are no telephones," he said, the lies rolling off his tongue. "If you do, we promise you will be back with Mr. Ghobadi tomorrow or at the latest, the following morning. If you don't, we will make sure you'll remain here. So tell him you'll be back from Zahedan by the day after tomorrow."

"Um . . ." I knew if I didn't agree, Javan wouldn't let me call, "OK."

Tasbihi's black shoes reemerged beside me to lead me down the hallway, where my cell phone could get a signal.

"Remember what your *bâzju* advised," he said. Then he told me to lift my blindfold, which I had been ordered to lower when I got up to leave the interrogation room, and handed me my cell phone. It was turned off.

As soon as I unlocked the SIM card, the phone rang. It was Bahman! My heart raced. He must have been calling nonstop since the night before.

"Hello?" I said.

"Where on earth have you been?" he cried. "I've been worried sick about you!"

"Talk very normally," Tasbihi whispered in my ear.

"*Azizam*, my dear," I began, attempting to sound calm, "please, don't worry."

"Of course I'm worried," Bahman said, clearly agitated. "Why has your phone been off?"

Somehow, I had to indicate to him that I was in a bind, without angering my interrogators. The only scheme I could think of was to tell him I was sorry I didn't make it to his birthday party the previous night and that I hoped his other guests weren't upset. This might alert him that I was in danger because Bahman knew we had been planning a private dinner, just the two of us.

"Where are you?" he asked. "You haven't been answering your home phone, either."

Tasbihi had leaned his head toward me to hear our conversation, so closely that I could sense his warm, oniony breath on my cheek.

"*Azizam*," I repeated, still trying to control my voice, "I'm sorry, I had to make a last-minute trip to Zahedan, but I'll be back the day after tomorrow. I'm sorry I didn't make it to your birth—"

"What? Zahedan?" he exclaimed. "Why didn't you tell me before you left? You have no right to call me ever again!"

Click.

"Bahman? Bahman?" I called into the phone, but all I could hear was the blood pulsing in my ears. We had argued in the past about my going off alone because he felt responsible for my safety, and he probably thought I had traveled to Zahedan without telling anyone. Bahman's own problems with the Intelligence Ministry, which had occasionally interrogated him and recently suggested he move abroad "for his own good," had only made him more insistent to know my plans ahead of time. I wasn't surprised his concern for me had now turned to anger, but his timing couldn't have been worse.

"What happened?" Tasbihi asked.

"It got cut off," I sputtered. "There's no reception here. I need to tell him not to worry if my phone will be off for a couple of days."

"OK," the agent said. He guided me farther down the hallway, up a few steps, and into an outdoor, walled-in area. "The reception should be better here."

I hit the redial button, but Bahman wasn't picking up. I dialed his number again. Now his cell phone was turned off. I dialed his home number. No answer. I dialed it again. Now the line was disconnected. I dialed it again. And again. No use. Trying to hide my panic, I quickly wrote a text message to him, using my chador to screen the note from the agent:

> Sorry I couldn't make it to your party last night. Please apologize to your guests.

I pressed the send button, but the message wouldn't go through. I hit send again and again. It was no use. Bahman's cell phone was still turned off.

"Give me the phone," Tasbihi demanded, reaching for it.

I swiftly deleted the unsent text message and returned the phone to him.

My hands were shaking badly. I had lost my only chance to inform someone in the outside world of my capture. Now if something happened to me here, who would know? If I died like Zahra Kazemi, would anyone ever find out?

And of all the cities Javan had to choose from, Zahedan was among the worst. It was in what was said to be the most lawless and unsafe province of Iran, where Sunni Muslim militants and armed bandits had reportedly kidnapped and assassinated civilians and officials. Once Bahman learned of my disappearance, he would suspect rebels or bandits, not the regime, which would likely pretend it knew nothing of my whereabouts, even if my captors killed me and threw my body in a ditch.

Tasbihi led me blindfolded past the open door of another room, from which came the sound of a man weeping and beseeching someone to believe in his innocence. Only a victim of torture could sound like that. I feared I might soon be reduced to the same state.

Back in my interrogation room, I crumpled into my chair, my eyes covered and my ears alert, as I waited for the unknown.

"Did she do as I instructed?" Javan asked his colleague.

"Yes," Tasbihi replied.

"Very good."

My *bâzju* then claimed again that I had possessed several secret documents, and I again denied this accusation, although I couldn't understand why he kept repeating this lie, and with such confidence.

"Miss Saberi," he continued, ignoring my response, "with all this evidence against you, you'll never get out of here without our help. Admit you've been spying for the United States. Tell us which one of the Americans we discussed wanted you to use your book as a cover. We won't tell anyone about any of this because we want you to collaborate with us, and that would compromise your cover. And we will make sure the magistrate you saw today at court sets you free."

I couldn't speak.

"Repent of your mistakes, and we will forgive you," he said. Then he added icily, "If not, as we said, you could be here for quite some time . . . or much, much worse."

I was beginning to feel faint. The smell of fresh paint from somewhere nearby mingled with male body odor, filling my nostrils and clouding my already foggy mind. Sweat was dripping down my armpits, and I felt the walls of the small, stuffy room caving in on me.

"You should also know," another interrogator began, "we have agents all over the world, even in America. We can easily find your family."

My body stiffened. *My family?* Would these people really send someone after my parents and brother? I had heard that physical threats against prisoners' family members was one torture technique used in the Islamic Republic. The Iranian state must have had more pressing priorities than chasing down a couple in their sixties in North Dakota—but my captors didn't seem to care whether I lived or died, so why would they be any more sympathetic to the rest of the Saberi family?

The interrogators continued to warn of what would happen to my family and me if I didn't "repent of my crime," earn their trust, and consent to spy for them.

As the day wore on, my mind began to reel, desperately, frantically, searching for a way out.

If I pretended to agree to spy for these people, then they would free me, and I would somehow escape from this country.

But to be released, I would also have to "confess"—just like the confessions I had seen on TV. Hadn't those confessions seemed coerced and unconvincing?

And if all those other people had to confess to win their freedom, who was I to resist the warped way things worked here? In the Islamic Republic, I was an Iranian citizen who could be locked up in solitary confinement, cut off from the world, wrongly convicted, and then executed.

My interrogators were threatening to lead me toward this very outcome. In this prison, these hard-line fanatics held all the power, and according to their worldview, I couldn't possibly be innocent.

I struggled to come up with what I was supposed to confess. How could I admit to something I knew nothing about and make up a story my captors would believe enough to set me free? Then I understood that these men had already provided me with a story line. I just had to fill in their blanks.

I wanted to bury my face in my hands. I couldn't believe what I was contemplating—I, who had felt guilty on the rare occasions I had told friends a white lie just to make them feel better.

It was then that I came to a terrible realization: The truth meant

nothing here. Only lies could save my family and me. My only way
out was to admit to a crime I did not commit and to ask for forgiveness.
I would have to select a scapegoat, but that person would be far from
here, out of harm's way. I could always, like many before me, recant
my lies once I was freed.

"Fine!" I cried out. "Just tell me what you want me to say!"

All at once, the room fell silent. No more shuffling of papers, tap-
ping of pens, shifting in seats. It took what seemed like a minute
or two until I heard two chairs sliding toward me.

"You may take off your blindfold now," I heard Javan say. His voice
sounded almost conciliatory.

I pulled the cloth down below my chin and saw him sitting to my
right, his knees almost touching mine. I drew my legs in under me,
trying to make the movement seem natural.

The agent was wearing the same black leather jacket and jeans as
the day before. His eyebrows were still arched in suspicion, but his
eyes had softened a little. Sitting next to him was a middle-aged man
I didn't recognize.

"Tell us which one of the Americans we asked you about wanted
you to spy for them," Javan said softly.

My insides churned. I wished I could simply invent an imaginary
person to accuse, but I knew my interrogators would never buy that.

"It's OK," he cooed. "Take your time."

Several seconds passed. I had no idea what lie to make up.

"Just tell us," he began again, "which one of them told you to use
your book as a cover to gather information on Iran for the U.S. government?"

I stared dumbly at my hands, which were lying lifelessly in my
lap.

"We already discussed the Americans you know," the other man
said.

Javan ran through their names, while my eyes remained glued to my hands. "Don't worry," he added. "Whatever you say will remain just between us."

I closed my eyes and stayed silent, frozen with fear. I knew I shouldn't trust these people, but I felt I had no other choice. My life belonged to them.

The faces of the individuals Javan had listed appeared before me, blankly staring straight ahead, unaware that I was being forced to arbitrarily pick one of them: Mr. A, Mr. B, Mrs. C, Mr. D . . .

Mr. D was an acquaintance I hadn't seen in years. He had no family in Iran, and I highly doubted he would ever come here. He had also been kind and helpful to me in the past. Surely he would want me to do what was necessary to stay alive.

I'm sorry, Mr. D! I have to pick you as my scapegoat. Please forgive me. You are safe in America, while I am in danger in Iran. Please understand that I have to fabricate a story about you to save my life. . . .

"It was . . ." I said, my voice cracking, "Mr. D."

"Who?" my *bâzju* asked.

"Mr. D," I repeated, as I raised my eyes tentatively.

A sly grin stretched across his face. "So Mr. D wanted you to use your book as a cover to gather information about Iran," he stated. "And he wanted you to interview various people to get this information."

"Uh . . ." my life now depended on playing along, "yes."

"So he told you to give him copies of interviews that you were doing for your book."

A chill ran through me. To lie and affirm this might demand further falsehoods, perhaps involving other innocent people. I wanted to stand firm for what I knew was right. But fear overpowered my principles. "Ye-yes," I said, "he wanted . . . transcripts of some of them."

"Did he give you a secret code to e-mail him if you would ever be in trouble, if your cover would be blown, like now?"

I guessed that spies were supposed to have secret codes. "Yes."

"What was it?"

I didn't know what to say. "Um, sorry," I began. "Actually . . . there was no code."

"Why did you just say there was?" Javan asked, a frown creasing his brow.

"I . . . I was nervous," I stuttered. "You all . . . scare me."

He tried to reassure me with a faint smile. "Don't be scared," he purred. "It's been a long day, and you must be tired. Why don't you go back to your room for the night, and we can continue tomorrow?"

"Yes, please," I said shakily.

"Just think about these questions: How much money did Mr. D give you for your work? What information did he request? What types of people did he want you to interview? What information did you give him—when, where, and how?"

My head spun as I began to realize how many hideous lies I would now be forced to tell. But I had to concentrate. I had to memorize these questions because I would have to think up a story based on them the next day—if I didn't want to be tortured, locked up for years, or killed.

I was taken back to my cell by a woman guard.

"Do they execute people here?" I whispered to her.

"Not usually," she murmured. "Trust in God," she added, as she raised her eyes toward the ceiling and slammed the heavy cell door shut behind her.

I collapsed on my blankets. I supposed it was near midnight, but now was no time to sleep. I had only a few hours to concoct a story unlike any I had ever imagined.

Strange, I thought. *Two nights ago I claimed I no longer needed to live, and now I am prepared to take almost any measure to avoid death.*

I tried to recall sayings that had inspired me when I was free. The Greek historian Plutarch had written something like, "Courage is the first step to victory." And what was it that Gandhi had said about fear? "I do believe I am seeking only God's Truth and have lost all fear of man."

But neither of these applies here, I groaned to myself. *It is impossible to be Gandhi in Evin Prison.*

God, I asked you for help, but you did not rescue me. And if you don't save me, who will? I have no choice left but to lie for my life.

CHAPTER SIX

L et's pick up where we left off last night," Javan said to me the next morning. "And don't think you can get out of here without confessing everything."

Today, he had allowed me to turn my chair around, slip off my blindfold, and face him. He was sitting behind a large metal desk, his face calm and determined. We were the only people in the interrogation room.

The sight of him made me squirm. I loathed and feared this man but needed to win his trust and approval to be set free.

"You were saying that Mr. D asked you to spy for him," Javan said, "that he wanted you to collect information about Iran, using your book as a cover."

I took a deep breath. I now had to pretend to be someone I was not: a repentant spy. This would only be temporary, I assured myself. My family and friends would understand I had to do this in order to survive. Once released, I would try to set things right. I had rehearsed my lines the night before, based on the questions I had anticipated. Now all I had to do was play this revolting role.

"Right," I said unsteadily.

"And Mr. D requested that you interview certain types of people," Javan stated. "Top officials? Members of the Revolutionary Guards? People in decision-making institutions?"

The agent was pretty much writing the tale for me.

"Yes?" I said, hoping this was the answer he wanted.

"And he asked you for copies of some of your interview transcripts."

"Right," I replied, repeating my answer from the night before.

"In what format?" he asked. "On a CD or through e-mail?"

I surmised that real spies probably wouldn't send information through the Internet. "On a CD," I answered.

"And did Mr. D tell you that he was in the CIA or connected to it?" Javan asked, leaning forward.

I hesitated. I knew what my *bâzju* wanted me to say, but I didn't want to say it.

"Neither," I answered.

"It had to be one or the other," the interrogator insisted, his voice taking on a rough edge. "Tell me, Miss Saberi."

I swallowed hard. Every word coming from my mouth was tormenting me.

"Fine," I said, "the latter." Of the two options, it was the less damning.

Javan nodded approvingly, then went on, "How much money did Mr. D pay you up front?"

I would have to guess what might be a reasonable amount. "Five thousand dollars?"

"That's *all*?" the agent asked, sounding surprised.

Uh-oh. Apparently $5,000 wasn't much in this line of work.

"But he said he would give me more later," I added hastily, trying to recover from my error, "when I was to bring him the CD."

"And when did you do that?"

I told Javan I hadn't done so yet, but when he repeatedly refused to accept this answer, I yielded.

"So when did you give Mr. D the CD?" he asked again.

"Um, when I went to America . . . last autumn."

"And how much did he pay you when you gave it to him?"

I paused. "Ten thousand dollars."

"That's *all*?" Javan repeated.

Uh-oh again. Wasn't $15,000 a pretty good amount for allegedly giving someone copies of a few interviews?

"Yes," I ventured, "but . . . he guaranteed more if . . . I'd give him more transcripts the next time."

"How much more?"

I had no idea what my *bâzju* thought would be appropriate.

"He . . . didn't say, but, uh, he said it would be worth my while," I fumbled, wondering if my interrogator was buying my increasingly absurd story.

"How did he pay you?"

If I said by check or wire, the interrogator might demand to see a receipt or bank statement. "Cash," I replied.

"Is that money in a bank here?"

"No," I said. I had stopped using my Iranian bank account long ago. I disliked standing in long lines for hours, and mounting sanctions on Iran had made transferring money from abroad more and more difficult. To avoid these problems, I had begun bringing cash with me each time I returned from America, keeping it in my desk at home, and converting some into tomans whenever necessary.

"Where is it, and how much is left?" the agent asked.

I quickly tried to recall how many dollars I still had from the last time I had visited the United States. "I spent most of it. But I think I still have a few thousand in my apartment."

"You also gave secret documents to Mr. D."

I shivered. Javan wanted to make my lies much worse than they already were. "No, I did not," I replied.

"We know you did."

"I didn't."

"But you had secret documents," he said.

"I didn't have any," I objected.

He fixed me with a hard, unblinking stare. "Remember, if you want to be freed any time soon, you must cooperate. We know you had secret documents from the Center for Strategic Research like the one we showed you yesterday. We found them in your apartment."

"Nothing I had was secret," I maintained, perplexed that he kept grilling me about things I didn't have.

"Miss Saberi, do you want to rot in this prison?" he yelled. "Now confess that you had secret documents. We already know what they are, but you must confirm them to us!"

My eyes dropped from my interrogator's distorted face to my desk, but I could still feel him glaring at me. It was obvious he wouldn't let me go unless he was satisfied with my confession, so I would have to admit to this trumped-up allegation.

"I had that pamphlet you told me yesterday was secret," I said, as I reluctantly lifted my eyes toward him.

"What else?"

I had hoped one item would suffice.

"Tell me, Miss Saberi," he said, his expression growing even more ominous.

I scanned my memory to recall what other old papers his colleague might have pulled from my closet—one with a title that might quench Javan's thirst. "And another article . . . about the U.S. war in Iraq?"

"How did you get it?" he asked.

"I copied it."

"You *copied* it?"

"Yes."

The interrogator arched one eyebrow, lifting it higher than its normal state, and nodded slowly.

My stomach lurched. Employees at the center had often allowed me to copy articles. Could I have copied something that was indeed secret? But I was certain I had never seen anything marked as such.

Over the next few hours, my interrogator asked more leading questions, to which I supplied more falsehoods to meet his unflagging demands. Instead of telling me exactly what to say, he frequently gave me multiple-choice questions, some of which had only two possible answers, and whenever I didn't pick his preferred one, he would make his disapproval very clear. He kept reminding me that if I didn't cooperate, I would perish in prison.

I couldn't think straight. I had hardly slept or eaten for nearly three full days, and the only thing ruling my mind was fear.

As Javan's threats continued, I began to answer yes to practically everything he asked me.

Did Mr. D tell you to keep quiet about this? Yes, so no one else knew about it. Did he ask you to recruit other Iranians to collude with you? Yes, but I hadn't found anyone to enlist yet. Did he want you to work for him somewhere else after Iran? Yes, but I wasn't interested. If Javan had told me to say I was a kidnapper or a drug trafficker, I would have said yes, if that's what it took for him to think I was "cooperating" so he wouldn't hurt me and would set me free.

When Javan was satisfied, he leaned back in his seat and clasped his hands behind his neck, his eyes glittering with a vicious glee that sickened me. Even though he had essentially dictated my false confession, he appeared to completely believe it.

He was glad I had finally cooperated, he told me, and now it was time for me to recount the whole story to his boss, Haj Agha.

Haj Agha was a broad-shouldered, middle-aged man with a graying beard and white hair. When he strode into the room, Javan sprang up, bowed slightly, and pulled out an extra chair. Once seated, Haj Agha folded his hands on the desk and gazed at me a moment with deep-set, unfeeling eyes.

In the same rough voice I had heard on the phone the day before, he introduced himself as the intermediary between my interrogators and the magistrate. He said that whatever he would recommend about me, the magistrate would accept. Then he told me to relate my confession to him. Stumbling over the details, I forced myself to repeat the same terrible tale that Javan had just extorted from me. When I finished, Haj Agha smiled with delight.

"You know, Miss Saberi, what Mr. D wanted from you is *exactly* what the CIA lacks in Iran: *analysis*," Haj Agha said, echoing the claim Javan had made two days before. "They can easily get a lot of *information*, but they struggle to get *analysis*."

I nodded, pretending to concur.

"My colleague tells me you have agreed to work for us," he went on.

I nodded again.

"We will have you collaborate with us for six months in Iran," Haj Agha said. "During this time, you will gather information about foreign diplomats and journalists here. You will work as a journalist to keep your cover. You know, *we* were the ones who pulled your press credentials. But I will return them to you."

I couldn't have cared less about getting my credentials back at this point, but I had to appear intrigued. "Which news organization may I work for?" I asked politely.

"Whichever one you like," he said.

"*Che âli*," I replied, trying to sound serious, "how excellent."

Haj Agha stared at me stolidly. I couldn't tell whether he knew I was being insincere.

"After six months, we'll have you go abroad to continue your work with us," he said.

"Exactly what kind of work do you have in mind?" I asked.

"For example, gathering information about U.S. officials and activities abroad," Haj Agha explained. "You can carry on your own life overseas, but once in a while, we will arrange meetings with you in a third country. We do this with many of our other agents, too. The money we pay isn't as much as you might like, but we'll provide what we can. And don't worry, if we ever think your cover has been blown, placing your life in danger, we'll permit you to stop working for us."

That's so very *kind* of you, I wanted to retort. My indignation, I knew, stood in stark contrast to my helplessness, but I would have been foolish to express it.

"I will do my best to get you out of here in a day or two," Haj Agha said.

Then he leaned forward in his chair. His face darkened, and his eyes turned steely.

"However, when you leave this place," he said in a voice pitched low, "if you talk about what has happened here, we will track you down and find you, wherever you are in the world. You can be certain I will *personally* sign your *death warrant*."

Every muscle in my body went taut, and my heart started to gallop. In the past, individuals in the Intelligence Ministry had been implicated in assassinations both in Iran and abroad.

"I have no qualms about that," Haj Agha added.

I couldn't look at him anymore and had to lower my head. I heard him stand up and exit the room, leaving me alone with my interrogator.

Javan had me spend the rest of the day and long into the evening writing out my false confession. I wrote slowly because it was all in Farsi, and I had to ask him how to spell certain unfamiliar words. At the end, he instructed me to write: *I was under no physical or psychological pressure when making these statements.* Instead, I wrote: *I was under no physical pressure, although I am feeling a little stressed.*

In all, my confession turned out to be around twenty pages. Twenty pages of lies that I knew could haunt me the rest of my life. I could only hope they would gain me the freedom I needed to take them back, before my captors could use them to try to blackmail me to do their bidding.

The sign on my cell wall, the one I had ignored two nights before, quoted Ayatollah Khomeini: PRISONS MUST BE COLLEGES FOR HUMAN IMPROVEMENT.

"Yeah, right," I muttered.

A few other lines were written below Khomeini's quote. Some regulations about how writing on the walls was absolutely prohibited and how often detainees could take showers and use the toilet. I didn't feel like reading the rest of the sign, so I lay down. I wasn't planning to stay here long enough to need to learn the rules anyway.

Whimpering arose from the cell behind mine, just as I had heard on my first night in Evin. The sound started and stopped. Started and stopped. I wished it would stop for good. It was getting on my already frayed nerves.

I had always thought I would be stronger under pressure. I couldn't believe I had given in to threats and invented such awful falsehoods.

But they were "expedient lies," I rationalized to myself—as Iranians called them, *durughe maslehati.*

Like people all over the world, Iranians often felt compelled to tell lies to get out of danger. Some believed this practice stemmed from centuries of foreign invasions and various authoritarian regimes, which taught Iranians to mask their true thoughts and feelings, particularly from people in power. Others cynically claimed they had a right to spin tales because their country's rulers themselves were so adept at it.

The idea was validated in Shiite Islam in a concept called *taqiyya*, or dissimulation. It allowed and even encouraged Shiites to conceal their faith to protect their property or themselves.

There was also the principle of *ta'ârof*—a complex system of formalized courtesy—which could often make social interactions seem insincere, for example, when a shopkeeper refused payment although he actually expected it. But Iranians viewed *ta'ârof* as good manners, and many found it preferable to being straightforward or telling the complete truth.

Of course, I had met Iranians who believed that honesty was the best policy, but many others felt the "expedient lie" was justified in a country where what you did or thought in private was often considered illegal or unacceptable by the regime. For instance, a secular person who wanted to get a government job or enter university in Iran had to keep his personal beliefs to himself to pass the required ideological exam. Or a mother who didn't pray at home told her son to say she did if he was asked about it at school.

In fact, as a friend had once declared to me, lying was not only expedient but also often necessary for survival in the Islamic Republic.

And my lies today were necessary, weren't they? My captors had threatened my life and the lives of my family members. I hadn't had any other choice—or had I?

My body went limp. The harsh reality was that I had abandoned my belief in truth as a fundamental tenet of my work, my life, and all humanity.

And poor Mr. D! If what I said about him ever got out, his reputation could be ruined, unless I got to him first and informed him of the horrific falsehoods I had been coerced to say. I vowed to myself that I would find him as soon as I was freed.

The whimpering next door continued. I wanted to cry, too, but I felt I didn't deserve even my own pity.

CHAPTER SEVEN

M ay I say something?" I asked Javan, after I settled back into my desk in the interrogation room on Tuesday morning, blindfolded and facing the wall once again.

"Sure," I heard him say cordially. He must have been content with the statements he got out of me the day before.

"The sign in my cell quotes Imam Khomeini saying, 'Prisons must be colleges for—'"

"'—human improvement,'" he finished the sentence for me.

"Right," I said.

"And?"

"Um, I wanted to share with you that I know I have made some mistakes," I continued, referring in my mind to my lies from the day before, "and I hope God will forgive me."

A few tears started to glide down my cheeks. I didn't know why I was expressing my remorse to a man who had pressured me to tell those lies in the first place, but I desperately wanted to share my agony with another human being, and he was the only one available.

"Well, we are certainly glad if we can be a medium for God," he said.

I didn't mean *you*, you lowlife, I seethed, as I wiped my face with the sleeve of my prison *roopoosh*.

"Before we release you," came the voice of another man from behind me, "we need to ask you a few more questions."

I felt a knot forming in my chest, unsettled that I would have to answer *more* questions.

"We want you to tell us about a few people you know," the same voice declared.

The knot began to throb. "I don't feel right doing that."

"We already know a lot about these people, but we want you to confirm what we know," Javan said, his voice now rigid. "And remember, if you want to get out of here any time soon, you will cooperate."

"But you told me before that I would be freed by today at the latest," I protested.

"I said you *might* be freed by today."

Is that what he had said?

"So when do you think I'll be freed?" I asked.

"By the end of the week," he replied. "We just need to take care of a few odds and ends, and then you can go."

"People will start to wonder where I am."

"No one will notice you're gone," he countered.

He stopped for a few seconds, then said in a solemn tone: "But remember what Haj Agha told you yesterday. When you leave, if you talk about any of this, be sure that we will find you. I think you have understood how capable our agents are. For example, if you go on a reporting trip to Afghanistan, we can easily eliminate you and make it look like a car accident."

With that, Javan tossed a stack of papers onto my desk and told me to raise my blindfold just enough to be able to read them. Written on the top of each page was the name of someone I knew, some well, others hardly at all. Some lived in Iran, others abroad. My interrogators must have collected most of the names from my e-mails, phone calls, and the list of contacts in my cell phone.

It was common knowledge that Iran's intelligence apparatus was obsessed with gathering even the most trivial information on virtually anyone, in many cases for no apparent reason, and that this was a routine part of the interrogation process for many prisoners.

I dug my nails into my lap. I wished I knew of some way to get out of this, but I felt I had absolutely no bargaining power.

The interrogators demanded to know how I knew So-and-so, where we had met, and what that person's job was. They began to call out each person's name, and I was to provide an oral and then written description of him or her.

Seeing no alternative, I described each person as generally and superficially as I could, trying to avoid giving any private information or volunteering any details. For example, I wrote: *So-and-so was an acquaintance from my Farsi class. She lived here one summer before returning overseas. I know nothing of her family.*

But sometimes my interrogators, who again numbered up to four that day, would refer to an e-mail or a text message someone had sent me, and they would berate me for failing to mention I had once lent money to Miss P or written a recommendation letter for Mr. Q to apply to a college abroad. I wasn't sure how they had obtained some of the other details they brought up, such as my having gone to Miss R's birthday party, where turkey sandwiches were served. I also couldn't understand why any of this mattered.

"As I told you, we already know what your answers should be," Javan said. "We just want you to state them. When you don't offer information, we realize you are not cooperating. And remember what the costs can be for not cooperating."

Still, I kept my descriptions as banal as possible. I also wrote them at a sluggish pace, thinking that the longer I took, the fewer pages I would have to complete.

As I was writing, a woman's high-pitched wailing emerged from down the hall. My knuckles went white around my pen. The woman was trying to say something, but her heavy sobs were garbling her words. A man, presumably her interrogator, was screaming at her.

Someone in our room stood up and shut the door. Despite the leather padding, it wasn't very soundproof.

"She's just being theatrical," Javan said.

"What's wrong?" I dared to ask.

"She won't admit to her crime."

"Oh," I said. I wondered what her captors claimed she had done.

"She's here for the same thing you are," he added.

Another accused spy? If these people said she was a spy, she was most likely innocent. I hoped she would figure out that her path to freedom lay not in futile tears but in confessing to the charge against her, whether or not it was true.

I turned to a new page to see two words that I had been praying would be spared my pen: *Bahman Ghobadi.*

I wished I knew nothing about him.

"Do I have to write about Bahman?" I asked quietly.

"Yes, you have to write about him," Javan said. "Tell me how you two met."

Saying nothing, I closed my eyes.

I remembered that night vividly. It was late one evening in June 2007 when I received an unexpected phone call from a Japanese friend I had met in a Farsi class a few years earlier. She was back in Iran on a visit, and she wanted to introduce me to Bahman Ghobadi.

I had never heard of him, but by surfing the Web before leaving for his apartment, I learned he was a director who had made the world's first Kurdish-language feature-length movie in 2000, and although his films had won many top international awards, the Iranian authorities had rarely allowed them to be screened in the country's theaters.

That night at dinner, Bahman told my friend and me he was planning to begin filming his fourth movie in a few months. The only problem was that the government, which controlled much of Iran's cinema industry, had not yet given him permission to shoot it. Some hard-liners accused him of having promoted Kurdish separatism in his films. He denied this and said he simply wanted to share his Kurdish culture with his audiences.

Bahman said many independent filmmakers like him were treated by the regime as "outsiders," as opposed to "insiders" who worked with the authorities and often made movies in admiration of Islam, the revolution, and the Iran-Iraq War. While this outsider-insider distinction was far from clear-cut, I had witnessed it in many of the regime's dealings with society.

Bahman's passion for his work, his warmth, and the way dimples formed at the corners of his mouth when he smiled captivated me during that first meeting. Shortly afterward, we started dating. We were almost never apart: We ate together, exercised together, and took trips abroad together. He was generous and compassionate, doing all he could for his six younger siblings and their families, and he supported many poverty-stricken Kurdish children, including some who had starred in his movies.

As the months passed, Bahman decided to defy Ahmadinejad's Culture Ministry and shoot his latest film—one about Iran's underground music scene—secretly. I helped him behind the scenes, while continuing to write my book. Now, I would have given anything not to have to reveal even the most mundane information about him.

M iss Saberi," Javan said, jolting me out of my reflections, "I am still waiting for your response."

"Sorry," I said. "What was the question?"

"I said, 'Tell—me—how—you—two—met,'" he spat, each word like the jab of a dagger.

Through a mutual Japanese friend, I explained.

"And how has Mr. Ghobadi assisted you with your work?"

I explained that he had introduced me to some cultural figures and a few others to interview for my book. However, now that I had been pressured to confess to using my book as a cover for spying, I added, awkwardly, "But he—or anyone else for that matter—was not aware of my espionage activities." I hoped this would help protect them.

"What kind of relationship did you two have?"

By this point, I had no doubt my *bâzju* knew that Bahman and I had been dating. But like many couples in Iran, we had never taken the precaution of getting a *sigheh*, or temporary marriage, which would have made our relationship permissible in the Islamic Republic. If I admitted this to my interrogator, Bahman and I could be subjected to lashings.

"We were . . . contemplating marriage," I faltered.

"But you two recently had some *problems* in your relationship, didn't you?"

What's it to you? I wanted to growl. I couldn't believe he was getting this personal.

"Didn't you break up for a few months?" Javan taunted me, without waiting for my response.

"Yes," I said, "but later we got back together."

"He only wants to be with you for your American passport," the interrogator said curtly.

"He already has a green card," I pointed out. "His sister is a U.S. citizen and lives in Los Angeles."

"Still," Javan continued, undeterred, "do you think he really loves you? He loves his work more. Besides, we know him well, and an artist like him can never be content with only one woman."

I didn't respond. I knew Javan was trying to break me down even further, to make me feel even more vulnerable and alone. But I refused to believe him.

"Write down your answers," he ordered me. "Describe what kind of relationship you two had and how he helped you with your work."

I wrote a few lines, but my eyes began to well up as I asked myself when I might see Bahman again.

I pulled my chador over the sides of my face. *I will not let these vile men see me cry again.* A tear splattered my paper, smudging my pen's blue ink.

"What's taking so long, Miss Saberi?" Javan asked.

"Sorry," I sniffled.

"Are you *crying*?" he jeered.

"No." I dried the page with one edge of my chador and continued to write: . . . *and even though Bahman and I may have had our oc-*

casional difficulties, I am ready to die for him. My captors wouldn't appreciate this sentence, but I didn't care.

Another interrogator wanted to know which embassies I had visited in Tehran and which foreign diplomats I knew.

"I don't know many," I replied. "Most of the ones I knew have left."

"When you collaborate with us, you'll have to get to know more," he said.

"How about the foreign journalists in Iran?" Javan asked. "Which ones are spies?"

"I don't know of any spies," I said. I couldn't resist adding, "Anyway, there aren't many foreign journalists left in Iran. You guys kicked most of them out."

"Like who?"

I started naming the foreign and dual-national journalists I knew who, in recent years, either had their credentials revoked or were told to leave the country.

"Fine, fine," Javan cut me off midlist. "Of the ones remaining, who are spies?"

"I don't know of any spies," I repeated.

The agents moved on to a few of the foreigners I had been questioned about in previous interrogations.

They also asked about Iranians, some of whom I had spoken to for no more than ten minutes in my life. Javan and his colleagues seemed to focus on reformist and moderate figures, as if digging for statements with which to discredit them. The agents asked me some questions about interviews they knew I had done. I responded by giving a few ordinary statements the interviewees had made on the record.

As the hours passed, my mind grew muddled. What did my captors really know? Had they hidden recording devices in my apartment? Could they have monitored my conversations and interviews through my cell phone even when I had turned it off as a precaution? Maybe some of the people I knew had been under surveillance or had informed on me. I began to wish I had never spoken to or interviewed anyone over the previous six years.

The interrogators started to ask about men I had dated before Bahman, as well as others I scarcely knew.

"We know you had sex with Mr. X," one agent stated, referring to a reformist figure.

My cheeks burned. "No, we were only acquaintances," I said, barely able to hide my disgust toward my captors.

"We don't believe you," came the reply.

Did they do this to all detainees? Sex was a sensitive topic in the Islamic Republic, and I was incredulous that these men, who must have had religiously conservative backgrounds, were bringing up this subject with me.

"How about Mr. Y?" another interrogator asked, without sounding the least bit embarrassed. "We know you two were dating at one time. Did you have sex with him?"

"We dated, but we never had sex," I replied.

"It's not possible."

It is possible, you sick bastards! I wanted to yell. They seemed to take pleasure in forcing me to talk about aspects of my life I didn't normally discuss even with my closest friends.

"How could you date someone and never have sex with him?" Javan asked, mockingly. "So what did you two *do* together?"

I cringed.

My interrogators kept asking, and whenever I would hesitate, they would threaten me and tell me I would never be allowed to leave unless I said what they wanted. They kept pressing and pressing, insisting I say I had sex with practically every man I knew, whether single or married, young or old, friend or acquaintance. I wanted to weep with humiliation.

As questions about this person or that person continued, I tried to avoid them by filling pages without stating anything of substance. I wrote my answers in large print and repeated the same sentences in different ways. In an attempt to dodge giving more information, I kept maintaining that my memory was sketchy.

Sometimes my interrogators claimed I knew people I had never heard of, such as a woman named "Silva" and "a Canadian journalist who was planning to visit Tehran soon." After repeatedly stating I didn't know these people, the agents finally forgot about them. Late in the day, they brought up Hassan, almost as an afterthought. I explained that although we had once been close friends, we were no longer in touch.

My interrogators eventually announced that they were tired and wanted to go home for the night. I had no way of knowing how long I had been sitting there. Eight hours? Ten hours? My body had grown stiff and my hand, cramped.

On his way out, Javan handed me a half-sheet of paper with some lines of his illegible handwriting.

"Study these topics tonight, and think about how you will answer them tomorrow on camera," he ordered me.

I had a feeling this was coming. Getting videotaped was inevitable if I was to be freed, just as it had been for many of the political prisoners before me who had endured similar ordeals.

Javan stood over me and read out the list. It was long and daunting.

One of the agents led me back to the women's ward. I hung my head as I walked. While I had tried my best to state only innocuous information that day, in a few cases, I had succumbed to my captors' threats and told them what they wanted to hear. I was horrified to think of what they might do with my statements. I could have— should have—refused to speak even a single word—even if it led to my death.

A guard left me in my cell with a heavy plastic bag. I looked inside it to see bananas, oranges, and small cartons of juice.

I threw the gift bag in the garbage and myself on the floor.

Guilt and shame consumed me as tears started to stream down my face. I had always wanted to do good in my life. Why did I have to do so much bad?

I was so ashamed of what I had done in this prison. My fear had made me forsake my ethics and morals. I had been so weak.

Please forgive me, God. Please don't let anyone get hurt because of me. Please protect my loved ones. Please, God, please. Please, God, please. Please, God, please. Just let me live long enough to make my horrible deeds known to others before they can do any damage.

I glanced at the list of what I was supposed to present on camera the next day, but I felt so broken, I couldn't concentrate. Exhausted, I curled myself into a ball and fell asleep.

CHAPTER EIGHT

In preparation for my on-camera appearance the next morning, Javan instructed me to take a few notes. As I reviewed them, he decided to share with me some news from that day's paper. As far as I could tell facing the wall, he was the only person in the interrogation room with me.

"The Obama administration is threatening new sanctions against Iran," Javan read out from behind me.

I heard him set the newspaper down. "When will the Americans learn we don't care about their 'carrots and sticks'?" he asked.

He was referring to the approach of offering incentives to Iran to halt its most sensitive nuclear activities, coupled with the threat of new sanctions or other punishments if it refused. Iran was already under various U.S. and UN sanctions over its disputed nuclear program, which Tehran claimed was purely peaceful.

"Sanctions have only made us stronger and more self-sufficient," Javan declared, as he turned a page.

He was echoing Tehran's official line, which some Iranians agreed with. But many others, including some of those who considered nuclear energy their nation's right, did not. They complained that sanctions were hurting their pocketbooks and helping to isolate Iran. I decided it would be unwise to bring up any of these issues. "I see what you mean," was all I said.

The pages of the newspaper fluttered.

"*This* story is the perfect example of how sanctions have done nothing to hinder Iran's technological development," Javan continued.

Tehran had announced the day before that it had successfully launched its first domestically made satellite, called *Omid* [Hope], he read aloud. Iran said it was intended for research and telecommunications. I guessed Washington was concerned about how the satellite might be linked to Iran's missile program, but Javan didn't mention anything about this.

"You see," he said, "Iran has reached this level of technology without anyone else's assistance."

He folded the paper and set it aside. But he kept talking, as if he fancied discussing politics with me.

"And now Obama has become president and promised 'change,'" he said. "But he won't bring any change in U.S. policies toward Iran."

Barack Obama, who had taken office on January 20, just eleven days before my arrest, had pledged to step up U.S. diplomatic efforts with Iran, although he had also said Washington should not take any options, including military action, off the table.

"In fact," my interrogator was now telling me, "America's Democrats are more dangerous than Republicans." He asserted that while Republicans openly admitted they aimed to change Iran's regime, Democrats pretended to favor diplomacy while quietly pursuing the same goal. Even if the threat of a U.S. military attack on Iran appeared to have subsided under President Obama, Javan said, Washington would intensify its "soft warfare" to undermine the Islamic Republic and its Islamic ideology.

Javan's words reflected the belief of many hard-line Iranian leaders that Washington was not genuinely interested in engaging Tehran in serious negotiations because ultimately it sought to overthrow the Islamic regime. Many other Iranian elites, however, were less certain of Washington's intentions and were more willing to give engagement a chance, especially after Obama's inauguration.

"And the Americans say we don't have democracy here," my *bâzju* continued, "but our supreme leader's powers are restricted by the As-

sembly of Experts." He was referring to a council of eighty-six clerics that elected the supreme leader and in theory could remove him,
though Javan neglected to mention that its members had to be vetted
by jurists who were either directly or indirectly chosen by the supreme
leader himself. "Also, our president can't take office without the supreme leader's approval."

Having lived in Iran for six years, I had become aware of the shortcomings of democracy in the Islamic Republic, but I didn't want to
argue about this, either.

The interrogator got to his feet and declared that it was time for me
to be videotaped. I had been continually reviewing my false confession in my head so that I could recite it on camera as I had two days
earlier to my captors. But I was finding that lies were much harder to
remember than the truth. As the Iranian saying went, *Durugh-gu kam
hâfezeh ast*, "The liar has a short memory."

"OK, I'm ready." I needed to get this over with in order to make it
to somewhere safe. Then I could figure out what to do.

Javan had earlier assured me that because I had agreed to collaborate with him and his colleagues, they would never broadcast the
video—unless I "made trouble" when I got out of prison.

Even if this video aired before I could publicly recant, I hoped that
people familiar with the methods of the Islamic Republic and other
police states would know it was staged, as were the videotaped confessions of many other detainees. But to ensure that my lies wouldn't
sound believable to ordinary viewers, I decided to avoid eye contact
with the camera and to speak haltingly and woodenly—signs of discomfort, as any broadcast journalist would know.

My *bâzju* led me into another room down the hallway, where he
told me to untie my blindfold and sit behind a white Formica table.
On it were a glass of water and a vase holding a plastic flower.

Apparently I was supposed to look comfortable and natural in
this setting. I was wearing my own *roopoosh* and white headscarf. A
woman guard had ordered me to put them on that morning, just as

other prisoners I had seen on Iranian TV were dressed in their personal attire.

I adjusted my headscarf to make sure no stray hairs were showing.

"Let it be," Javan said with a dismissive wave of his hand.

How odd. So now it was OK if I didn't observe proper hejab, whereas the other day his colleague had reprimanded me over a few wisps of hair. My captors must have wanted me to appear on camera as I would if I were taking a stroll in the streets of Tehran.

Javan disappeared behind a green curtain across from me. Jutting out of a hole in the cloth was a camera lens.

"We're rolling," announced another man, presumably the cameraman.

"First take a deep breath," Javan called out, "say *Bismellâh-Al-rahmân-Al-rahim*, then go down the list."

"In the name of Allah, Most Gracious, Most Merciful," I said.

Please forgive me for what I am about to do, I added to myself.

I opened the video by talking about my family, my life in America, and why I came to Iran, as Javan had instructed the night before. Then I moved on to false statements my interrogators had forced me to make, including my confession about Mr. D.

As I spoke, I looked down at my paper frequently, dwelling on each of my notes, trying to avoid the camera as much as possible. I spoke softly, and I intentionally inserted several *ums* and other unnatural pauses.

Javan stopped the camera many times and commanded me to rephrase sentences or to devise completely new ones that were more to his liking. At one point, he told me to talk about the Israeli government, and I deliberately referred to it using the phrase "Zionist regime," as Iranian authorities officially called it. I hoped potential viewers would realize I would not normally use this term and would conclude that I had been speaking under duress.

To close the video, I had to read a statement my interrogator had prepared for me. It went something like, "I apologize for my bad behavior, and I ask for your mercy and forgiveness. I have been under no pressure during this time, and everything I have said was according to my own free will. I am ready and willing to cooperate with you in the future."

My performance had used up three tapes.

"Well done, Miss Saberi," Javan congratulated me, as he emerged from the other side of the curtain with the videotapes in hand.

I wanted to scream curses at him, grab the tapes, and stomp on them.

Instead, I said courteously, "Thank you."

"Thursday and Friday, as you know, are the weekend," he explained, as he walked me, with my eyes covered again, back to the women's ward. "I will show your video to Haj Agha, who because of your cooperation, plans to free you on Saturday. I suggest you use this time in solitary confinement to think about all the awful things you have done."

M y interrogator was right: I had done "awful things"—but not the ones he claimed. Instead, I was ashamed of how I had disintegrated under pressure.

I bowed my forehead to the floor of my cell.

If I got out of here soon, I vowed, I would abandon journalism and writing and never interview anyone ever again. I could become a schoolteacher in Fargo, where I would take care of my parents as they grew old. Or I could give up all my possessions and help those in need.

"If I am really set free on Saturday," I whispered, clasping my hands in prayer, "I promise to serve humanity to the best of my ability for the rest of my life. Please just give me one chance to make up for what I've done."

O ver the next two days, I had no one to speak to but God—and myself. I had never sat alone in one small, enclosed space for so many hours with nothing but my thoughts.

"I would not have moved to Iran if I had known I would someday go through all this," I muttered, as I paced my cell, a few steps one way, then a few steps back. I could have stayed in the United States or at least chosen my mother's native land instead. I had visited Japan a few times, taught English at a school there, and learned some Japanese. But although I adored my mother's family and was fascinated by the country's history and culture, I had felt I could make more of an impact as a journalist in Iran than in Japan.

In fact, Iran seemed to have been part of my destiny, just as my mother's destiny had become tied to Iran in a different way, many years ago.

As a child, I had listened wide-eyed to my mother's account of how she had met my father. She had told me the story only once or twice, with detachment, as if the events leading up to their marriage constituted nothing out of the ordinary.

"Since your father was young," my mother had said, "he had a zest for learning and travel. His family was very poor, but he convinced his father to let him finish school instead of work in their furniture shop at the Tabriz bazaar. A few years after getting a degree in English literature, Reza decided to fly around the world. He made his way to Japan, where he volunteered as an English teacher. That's how he met me, when I attended his class one day. We wanted to get to know each other better, but standing in our way was a considerable obstacle: my parents. They disapproved of Reza merely because having a relationship with a foreigner was considered taboo by traditional-minded Japanese. In spite of this, we went out twice. When my parents found out, they locked me in our home for weeks. In order to show my repentance and be forgiven, I had to have my head shaved.

"Unable to see me, Reza returned to Iran. He kept in touch over the next few months by sending letters through a mutual friend. In one of those letters, I found a one-way plane ticket to Iran. Soon afterward, I secretly left Japan and flew to Tehran, where we got married in

1971. At the time, your father was told he was the tenth Iranian man in the world known to have married a Japanese woman. We moved to the United States two years later. I was eventually offered a job as a pathologist in Fargo, while your father taught part time and wrote a novel. Your brother was four then, and you were two."

Good ol' *safe* Fargo, I said to myself, as I heard the door to my cell open.

One of the guards had brought black tea, a favorite of most Iranians, though I seldom drank caffeine. I didn't want to take it, but she insisted.

Fargo was home to only a few Iranian families when I was a child, I recalled as I poured the tea down the sink and began pacing again. It was through them and my father that I was first exposed to Iranian culture, although back then, I had been more interested in fitting in with my blond-haired, blue-eyed classmates than in learning about my roots.

As I grew older, I felt as if something was missing in my life. I began to search for a way to give it meaning, and in college the path I chose was journalism, with the aspiration of becoming a foreign news correspondent. The career promised the opportunity to learn and to share what I was learning about diverse peoples and international issues. At the same time, I became more curious about both my own heritage and other cultures.

My plans took what at first seemed like a detour my senior year, when a friend organizing the 1997 Miss Fargo Pageant urged me to compete. I hadn't grown up doing pageants, could hardly walk in high heels, and was terrified of wearing a swimsuit on stage, but I was intrigued by the talent competition and the chance to win scholarships. Somehow I won, went on to be crowned Miss North Dakota, and placed in the Top Ten at the Miss America Pageant. The next year, I toured the state as Miss North Dakota, speaking about "Cultural Appreciation." In addition to getting over my stage fright, I earned enough scholarship money to get a master's degree in journalism. I later received a second master's in international relations and was working as a journalist in Houston when I got an offer to report from Iran. I wanted to jump at the opportunity, but my parents were skeptical.

They considered Iran's Islamic regime too unpredictable, especially for a young, single woman who spoke little Farsi and had never visited the country before. Moreover, the United States was preparing for a possible war against Saddam Hussein, and there was speculation that Iran might be Washington's next target. Just one year earlier, in early 2002, President Bush had declared Iran, along with Iraq and North Korea, part of an "Axis of Evil."

Ultimately, my parents gave me their blessing because they knew that just as they had done many years earlier, I was following my heart.

Writing a book had also been in my heart. *"Khâk bar saram,"* I cursed myself in Farsi. "Dirt on my head." Maybe if I hadn't loved Iran so much and tried to write a book to help others understand it, I wouldn't be locked up in this miserable cell.

W*hy hadn't I paid closer attention to the signs that could have warned me of my arrest?* The man and woman filming my friend and me in the park, for example. And recently, my neighbor had told me a plainclothesman had stopped by our apartment complex. She had guessed it was a routine visit, and I had believed her, but maybe it hadn't been.

Then there was Hassan. Our friendship had been strange from the very beginning, namely because American women and Basiji men didn't ordinarily mix.

Although he was no longer an active member of the Basij, as a teenager Hassan had joined the volunteer paramilitary force, which was founded in November 1979 by decree of Ayatollah Khomeini. The aim of this "Army of 20 Million" was to protect the Islamic Republic against domestic and foreign threats. It was thrown into its first great test when Iraqi troops under Saddam Hussein invaded Iran in 1980, sending the neighboring nations into a devastating eight-year war. Hassan often told me he wished he hadn't survived bullets, bombs, and minefields so that he could have become a martyr and earned a key to heaven.*

We had become friends after bumping into each other at an event I was covering. But over time, I began to find his behavior odd. He became very nosy, always wanting to know where I was going, when, and with whom. Once, after he visited me at my apartment, I noticed some of my videotapes of raw news footage were missing. And when I received a few threatening phone calls that I suspected were from intelligence agents, Hassan warned me not to tell anyone, saying that as long as he was in my life, I had nothing to worry about.

Finally, one day in 2006, I told Hassan I wanted to end our friendship because I couldn't trust him anymore. "You will regret this," he warned me with a fierce glint in his eyes.

Two days later, I got a phone call from the Culture Ministry. The official on the line notified me that the ministry had been told to revoke my press pass.

My interrogators had referred to footage on the missing tapes, I remembered, as I sat down on my blankets, and that was one of several things they had mentioned that only Hassan had known about.

Maybe the Intelligence Ministry had sent him to monitor me, and once I had told him good-bye, the authorities didn't replace him with anyone. They couldn't force a translator or minder on me. I was an Iranian American who could easily travel around the country on my own and speak directly with the Iranian people in Farsi.

In any case, I should have realized I might end up here, after witnessing the growing number of other dual nationals, writers, and jour-

---

* Many former and current Basij members are less ideologically driven than Hassan and disapprove of the militia's prominent role in suppressing civil unrest and cracking down on what hard-liners consider un-Islamic behavior. Some Iranians join the Basij just to get a few months knocked off their obligatory military service or to land a secure state job. Others have lost their ideological fervor as they have aged or retired from the Basij.

nalists jailed before me. I had also been foolish to expect justice and rationality from Iran's hard-liners.

And now I was in the grasp of the Intelligence Ministry, which I had read so many horrifying things about.

The ministry, along with the Law Enforcement Forces, the Basij, and the Revolutionary Guards, shared the main responsibility for Iran's internal security. It was heir to the prerevolutionary secret police force, SAVAK, the most feared institution of the shah, which had persecuted many of the people who came to power after the revolution.

In 1984, the new regime created the Intelligence Ministry to sniff out espionage, conspiracies, sabotage, and coup plots, as well as schemes to incite popular unrest. To perform this role, the ministry commonly installed agents, many with a background in the Basij or the Revolutionary Guards, in places such as universities, embassies, and offices, both in Iran and abroad.

The ministry became notorious for intimidation, imprisonment, torture, and periodic executions and assassinations, and it was rarely answerable to others. In 1999, however, it conceded that some of its own staff were responsible for a mysterious chain of murders of Iranian political activists and intellectuals, although it blamed a rogue operation. The victims had been killed through a variety of methods, such as car accidents, stabbings, and shootings.

By the end of Khatami's presidency in 2005, the ministry was somewhat cleansed of radical hard-liners, although many of them were thought to have continued their work in parallel state intelligence units in the judiciary and elsewhere. Several of the hard-liners returned to the ministry after Ahmadinejad took over, purged it of officials deemed insufficiently loyal, and named Gholam Hossein Mohseni-Ezhei the new minister. Mohseni-Ezhei alleged that numerous ordinary Iranians, as well as some moderate ex-officials, were acting as infiltrators and the enemy's fifth column. He was also a main proponent of the idea that Washington was plotting a soft revolution against the regime. His ministry's security-oriented approach helped intensify an atmosphere of fear throughout much of Iranian society.

Now this same Intelligence Ministry was recruiting me. I had to find a way to get out of spying for these people.

I imagined myself released on Saturday and rushing to Bahman. He would help me flee the country, maybe in the dark of night in the trunk of a car—or perhaps he would chop off my hair, disguise me as a Kurdish man with a costume and a fake mustache from one of his films, and send me by donkey across the mountains to Iraq or Turkey.

I must be going insane. But how could I not be? I was trapped in solitary confinement in Evin Prison. At least if my captors had given me a newspaper or book, the act of reading would have transported my mind away from my troubles. I had requested a Koran, but the only one available was in Farsi, which was in a poetic form too complicated for me to comprehend.

And I had no pen, no paper, no human contact—except for the guards. They opened my cell door every few hours to deliver tea or a plate of food, which I hardly touched. Then they would shut the door a few seconds later. Without a clock or watch, my only clues about the time were these brief interruptions; the shifting pale rays of sunlight through the mesh-covered window; and the three daily calls to prayer at dawn, midday, and dusk.

Time had always been precious to me. I was often in a hurry to complete one task and move on to the next, starting from when I was five and insisted on skipping kindergarten so I could enter first grade with my older brother, and continuing through college, which I finished in three years. With so much to learn and the world to explore, I had never wanted to waste a single moment.

But now a few minutes felt like an hour, and a few hours felt like an entire day. To entertain myself, I listened to my heartbeat, but I stopped when I heard my life ticking away. The forced idleness was slowly eroding my mind, body, and soul.

Loneliness. Isolation like I had never experienced. Though I had sometimes spent two or three days writing in my apartment without going outside, now the realization that I could not set foot beyond my cell door whenever I wished made me want to claw my way up the walls. I would rather have been marooned on an island like the one in the American TV series *Lost* than stuck in this tiny cell alone.

Speaking of *Lost*, I would have loved a television.

The guards had one in their quarters around the corner from my cell. At least its constant droning reminded me that life existed somewhere nearby. So did the intermittent whimpering of the prisoner next door. I whispered through the holes in the heater on my wall that she shouldn't worry, everything would turn out all right. But she didn't seem to hear me, and I couldn't raise my voice, out of fear that the guards would notice.

Two or three times, I also heard someone painfully coughing up phlegm and spitting it out. Later, an old woman's cackling shot out from the same direction, so loudly it pierced my eardrums. I wondered if both sounds emanated from the same person and whether she was a detainee. How could these people imprison an old, ill woman? Maybe the more appropriate question was, how could anyone laugh in such a god-awful place? Was I in a madhouse? If I stayed here much longer, I would fit right in.

After two days, on Friday afternoon, my cell door opened to reveal a rotund, middle-aged guard. She was smiling. She was the first person in Evin to express any warmth toward me.

"Do you want to go to *havâ-khori*?" she asked.

This Farsi phrase was unfamiliar to me. Literally, it meant "eating the air." *Was this another way of saying "freedom"?*

"*Havâ-khori?*" I repeated.

"Yes," she replied with a wink. "Get dressed, and I'll take you outside."

I did as she said, and she led me down the corridor to the left, past a telephone on the wall, and through a door into a bare, walled-in, concrete yard. It took several seconds for my eyes to adjust to the bright sunlight and for me to realize this must have been the place where I had unsuccessfully tried to call Bahman five days earlier.

So this was *havâ-khori*. It wasn't freedom, but it was a twenty-minute opportunity to stretch my legs and walk around in a square—over and over and over again. The yard was roughly thirteen paces by thirteen paces. It was surrounded by tall, gray walls, with rails crisscrossing overhead. Without grass, flowers, or trees, it looked more like a cage than a yard.

The shadow of a bird flitted across the pavement. I turned my face upward but saw nothing except bars and clouds. I longed to be even just the shadow of a sparrow. I would soar far, far away.

My poor parents, I thought, as I continued to loop around the slab of concrete. After almost one week without hearing from me, they must have been frantically reaching out to any Iranians they knew who knew me—my close friends, my widowed neighbor, and Bahman. Hopefully by now he had entered my apartment using his set of keys. He would have seen my ransacked belongings, realized I wouldn't go on a trip without emptying the garbage with its leftover tuna, and grown suspicious. Or, if he hadn't been to my apartment, he would have told my parents I had gone missing in Zahedan.

Either way, my father's blood pressure had to now be off the charts, and my mother's skin had probably broken out in hives as it did when I had told her about Hassan. Fortunately, I would be getting out of this hellhole soon, I consoled myself, and then my parents could stop worrying about me.

That night, I ate a little dinner, some bread and canned stew with small chunks of chicken. The meal was edible. Javan had boasted that the prison staff ate the same food as the detainees. I guessed our captors didn't want to give prisoners one more thing to complain about once they were released.

It was the first time since my arrest that I consumed more than a few bites. Not that I had much of an appetite, but I needed to build my strength to escape from the clutches of the Intelligence Ministry after I was freed the next day.

CHAPTER NINE

A clattering sound was coming from outside my cell. The shutter over the small, barred window in the door squeaked open, exposing the pretty eyes of the slim, young guard from my first morning in prison. The woman, whom I had nicknamed Skinny, quickly swiveled around and pattered away.

This wasn't the good news I had been waiting for that Saturday morning, but at least it was one small step toward the outside world. I stood up to look out the window in my door for the first time since I was thrown in solitary confinement one week earlier. All I could see was a few feet of the corridor. On the wall facing my cell hung a poster showing Ayatollah Khomeini's stern face floating amid feathery, white clouds. Below this celestial display was written something to the effect of, "Anyone who imagines that religion is separate from politics is ignorant."

I wondered whether this poster was meant for the guards or for restive prisoners like me with nothing else to look at.

After the Islamic Revolution, Shiite Islam was made the country's official religion, and Islam was decreed the law of the land.* An Islamic government was created whose focal point of power was based on Ayatollah Khomeini's idea of the *velâyat-e faqih*, or rule of the Islamic jurist. This concept held that until the reappearance of the Shiites' Twelfth Imam, who was said to have "disappeared" in the ninth century (meaning that he was not dead but somehow hidden),

---

* Shiite Islam was also the state religion under the Safavid Dynasty, which ruled over the Persian Empire from 1501 to 1722. Shiite clerics had been a key power center since then but did not hold direct political power until the Islamic Revolution.

Islamic society should be governed by a clerical jurist. This was supposed to be the jurist best qualified to interpret God's will and sharia, or Islamic law. It was this doctrine that had allowed Khomeini and his successor, Ayatollah Ali Khamenei, to become supreme leaders with the final say on all matters.

Iran's Islamic government had its critics among both laypeople and clerics. Some wanted to limit the authority of the supreme leader or questioned Khamenei's leadership. Others rejected the *faqih* concept entirely, with some calling for the clergy's complete withdrawal from politics.

The price for expressing such ideas could be high—defrocking, imprisonment, even execution. Clerics were prosecuted by the regime's Special Clerical Court, which was once headed by the current intelligence minister, Mohseni-Ezhei. Perhaps some outspoken critics of the regime had at one time sat in this cell, looking upon this poster with contempt or disinterest.

Another hour or two passed. Lunch was delivered. After a few more hours came tea. It was probably late afternoon, and still, no one had come to free me. I was so despondent, I would have rather talked to my nasty *bâzju* than sit in my cell alone.

This wish was soon granted. Skinny reappeared to take me to the interrogation room.

"Haj Agha watched your video," Javan told me after I sat down with my eyes bound, facing the wall. "He wants you to do it again."

I slumped in my seat.

"This time, do it with more energy," Javan continued. "And try not to look down at your notes so much. You have to appear more natural."

But I don't want to appear natural, I muttered to myself.

"Summarize your notes," he ordered me. "Keep them on a half-sheet of paper. Haj Agha also wants the video to be much shorter."

I had already gone so far down this regrettable path, I figured it would be pointless to object now.

After changing into my own clothes again and sitting behind the same white table in the room with the camera, I began video number two. Like the previous taping, Javan stopped me several times to direct me to make statements the way he wanted. This time, the production took around thirty minutes. He felt it was better than the last one and said he would show it to Haj Agha for his approval.

H aj Agha wasn't satisfied with my second video, either.
"Try to smile once in a while, and use hand gestures," Javan instructed me, back in the interrogation room the next day. "Look like you're having a good time."

I let a sigh slip.

"What's the problem?" he asked.

"Well," I explained, avoiding his eyes, "you told me I would be released yesterday, but I keep having to do these videos."

"Miss Saberi," he said, plainly annoyed, "if you get this right, you'll be freed very soon. If not, you'll have to stay for a long time."

I dragged myself to the taping room and, for the third time in the past five days, began to play the part of a remorseful spy on camera.

At one point during the recording, Javan commanded me to say I had given secret documents to Mr. D.

"But that's not true," I protested. "I told you I didn't give him any secret materials."

"It doesn't matter," the interrogator replied. "Say it anyway. Say that you gave him the document that you copied—the one about the U.S. war in Iraq."

"But—"

"Miss Saberi"—he hurled the words at me—"do you want to waste away here? Not that we mind having you as our guest."

So I said it, trying to sound timorous and submissive as I added this wretched lie to my script.

After my third performance, Javan told me I had to do a fourth—an abridged, fifteen-minute soliloquy. However, I couldn't get through it because I kept messing up. Under the stress, I was forgetting my lines.

"What's wrong with you?" Javan demanded, yanking aside the green curtain as he came out from behind it. "Why are you making so many mistakes and stuttering so much?"

"I'm sorry," I croaked, "but how many times do I have to do this?"

"The sooner you get it right, the sooner you'll go free," he said impatiently. He walked back toward the curtain, calling over his shoulder, "Now show a little energy, and don't forget to smile and use your hands."

I took a deep breath and tried to concentrate. Then I began to speak, with an occasional fake smile here and a contrived hand gesture there.

Javan reemerged wearing a smug grin.

"Now I can tell you're an experienced TV journalist," he remarked, the corners of his eyes crinkling with a despicable delight.

He was about to send me back to my cell when I asked if I could call my father to at least let him know I was alive. He had had a heart attack a few years ago, I explained, and I was very worried about his health. I added that I knew my parents were fretting by now because I was usually in touch with them every day.

Javan clicked a pen in his hand repeatedly as he considered my request. "We'll see," he said. "You might not need to because you'll soon be freed."

Tomorrow, he informed me before passing me off to a woman guard, I was to create a composite computer picture of Mr. D, using a special software program.

It seemed this horrendous ordeal would never end.

All the eyebrows appeared too bushy, too Middle Eastern.

"Do you have any thinner ones?" I asked the man working on the laptop computer, which sat on a table between us. It was Monday, and I had been taken to a different interrogation room, where I had been told to remove my blindfold.

The man was clicking from one eyebrow to the next, trying to find a style that best fit my intentionally vague description of Mr. D. Together, we had already completed my victim's eyes, nose, mouth, chin, and cheeks.

"How are these?" the composite artist asked, clicking on some sparser eyebrows.

"Fine," I said, without paying much attention, and he moved on to the hair. I picked a Western-looking cut.

"How much does this image resemble Mr. D?" asked my *bâzju*, who was peering over our shoulders.

"Maybe 30 percent," I replied, secretly pleased that we seemed unable to match him closely.

The man at the computer appeared embarrassed. "Let's rework it a bit," he said, and he began clicking through various noses.

"So did you see the judge last night?" Javan asked, as he looked on.

T he evening before, the smiling, rotund guard, whom I had heard the other guards calling Haj Khanom, had led me blindfolded and quaking to the prison basement. She left me alone in a room that smelled of cigarettes.

I heard heavy footsteps tread past me and someone shut the door. My chest tightened. What if this was a torture room, buried in the basement where no one could hear my cries for help? A man's husky voice called out, directing me to take off my blindfold. I obeyed and saw two bearded, burly men sitting behind a desk in front of me.

One of them began quietly counting the rest of the days of the week on his fingers: Monday, Tuesday, Wednesday, Thursday, Saturday.

"Don't count the holiday," the second man told him, referring to Tuesday, a national holiday.

The first one swept his hand through the air and said, "Let her get on with her life." Then he signed a few papers and told me to leave.

I hadn't dared to ask any questions. I had only longed for Haj Khanom, who soon took me back to the refuge of my cell.

W as that man a *judge*?" I asked Javan.

"Yes," he replied, noticeably surprised by my question. "Didn't you know?"

"No. I was too frightened to ask him anything," I admitted.

"What did he tell you?"

"Nothing," I said. "Why?"

Javan paused. "Just wondering," he said.

"Wider or narrower?" the composite artist asked, pointing his cursor at a picture of a long, thin nose.

"Wider," I said.

He kept clicking. Fortunately the final drawing still didn't look anything like the person it was supposed to represent.

Something is really going to happen this Saturday, I thought, getting my hopes up again, as my interrogator delivered me to the women's ward without dropping any hints about my future.

CHAPTER TEN

I figured I would be left alone in my cell all day that Tuesday, February 10, the final day of the Ten Days of Dawn. On this date thirty years ago, crowds roused by revolutionary zeal stormed the police and army buildings, and the shah's last forces surrendered. The revolution put an end to the rule of the pro-American shah, whose program of modernization and Westernization had helped alienate powerful religious and political groups. Later that year, revolutionary students who were angered that the deposed shah had been allowed into the United States for cancer treatment invaded the U.S. Embassy in Tehran and took its staff hostage. Shortly afterward, America cut its diplomatic ties with Iran. Since then, the two countries had taken occasional steps toward rapprochement, but for the most part, tensions and mistrust had remained high.

Despite predictions that it would collapse, the new regime had survived. It had withstood external threats, such as the 1980 Iraqi invasion. It had also resisted many internal power struggles and challenges, often ruthlessly crushing any opposition. In the eyes of many Iranian officials, the preservation of the regime—and, as an extension, their own positions in power—justified using almost any means.

Yet although the regime had maintained its power base, divisions among the country's leaders still existed, and the divide between the state and large parts of Iranian society had widened. A lack of reliable polls made it hard to determine public opinion, but it was clear that while many Iranians still believed in the concept of an Islamic Republic, many wanted profound reforms within the ruling system, and still others wanted a whole new government.

As one sign of dissatisfaction with the regime, some Iranians I knew cynically referred to Daheye Fajr, the Ten Days of Dawn, as the rhyming Daheye Zajr, the Ten Days of Torment.

Many other Iranians, however, turned out at rallies held across the nation every year on this date to commemorate the revolution. No doubt my interrogators were doing just that today, I thought, as I rested on my back on the tattered carpet.

I, too, had attended several rallies during the previous years. There I had met some Iranians who seemed to genuinely feel the fervor of the Islamic Revolution, while others admitted they went only because their teachers or government employers were taking roll. I had also heard reports of Iranians being bused in from rural areas or receiving financial incentives for showing up.

I shifted onto my side to give my tailbone a break from the hard floor.

One year ago today, I recalled, I had gone to a rally in central Tehran with a seventeen-year-old acquaintance named Fatemeh. She had told me her family attended every year "to show we are united behind the Islamic Revolution and its principles: independence, freedom, and the Islamic Republic."

Tens of thousands of Iranians were already milling about Freedom Square when we arrived. Some were holding effigies of President Bush, and others were carrying signs saying, "Death to America!"

Fatemeh believed this slogan was aimed not at the American people but at the American government. Washington had supported the shah, she said, was behind the 1953 coup that overthrew Prime Minister Mohammad Mossadegh, and backed Saddam Hussein in the Iran-Iraq War.

I had heard such sentiments many times before, sometimes from ordinary Iranians and frequently from Iranian officials. The latter in particular often added to their list of grievances America's freezing since 1979 of Iranian assets held in the United States, its support for the "Zionist regime," and sanctions. Washington, for its part, accused Iran of actions such as violating human rights, sponsoring terrorism, opposing the Middle East peace process, and pursuing nuclear weapons.

Fatemeh and I stayed at the rally for another hour or so. As we were leaving, we passed a young man shouting, "Death to Australia! Death to Iceland!"

His friend added, "Death to all the countries in the world!" They were both laughing boisterously.

Nearby, a few teenagers in blue jeans were giggling as they sang a rhyme, using the brand names of laundry detergent that were in short supply those days, "Neither Tide! Nor Rika! Death to Am'rika!" Their ditty reminded me that many Iranians ridiculed Tehran's suspicions of Washington by blaming America, tongue in cheek, for whatever went wrong in their lives, whether a car accident, a delayed bus or, as in this case, a lack of everyday products.

I was surprised that these youth were openly poking fun at a main rallying cry of the Islamic Revolution, just after having attended the demonstration. Then again, from what I had learned during my years in Iran, nothing in this country was as straightforward as it appeared. The young Iranians I saw were not old enough to have witnessed the revolution and may have been at the rally only because their school required it.

And although Fatemeh expressed dislike of the U.S. government, she dreamed of one day living and studying in America. So did her older brother, who had stayed home that day to fill out applications for colleges in the United States.

Fatemeh was probably at the rally again today. I wondered whether President Obama's recent election would make the "Death to America" chants less prevalent, or at least less strident, than in previous years.

After all, he had struck a more conciliatory note toward the Islamic Republic than his predecessor had, and Ahmadinejad had sent Obama a letter congratulating him on his election. It was the first time an Iranian president had done such a thing since the Islamic Revolution.

Many Iranian officials, at least in private, had acknowledged that their country could never achieve its full potential without having better relations with Washington—something that most ordinary Iranians also seemed to want.* Many believed this would be more likely with Obama, whose name pronounced in Farsi happened to mean "He's with us" and whose middle name "Hussein" was that of the central figure in Shiite Islam.

I found it strange that my captors had waited until just after Obama's inauguration to detain me. Maybe they were linked to hard-line factions striving to deflect any attempts at engagement, whether for ideological reasons or because they stood to lose politically and financially.

Speculation, I realized, served no use, except to pass my time in solitary confinement. I stared at my cell walls and let my mind run wild until sleep came.

I carved a twelfth line into the heater, praying I wouldn't catch up to the "18" right below it. It was late Wednesday morning, and still, I had no news from my interrogator about whether I would indeed be freed on Saturday. Time dripped slowly. I had begun to feel as if I were in a coffin, that I had died and no one would come for me. Sitting alone in my cell, I started to expect the worst.

What if my captors put me on trial claiming my false confession is true? They say they want me to spy for them, but what if a judge sentences me to death?

Dread filled my chest, and my pulse raced. The room began to shrink, and the walls reeled up and down. I couldn't believe I had ever trusted my captors to free me.

More than anything, I ached for just one chance to tell my family I loved them and to apologize to anyone I had ever wronged.

My lungs were constricting. I had to take a rapid series of breaths. Air. I needed air. I crawled toward the door, hoisted myself up, and mustered all my strength to press the black button on the wall.

---

* In 2002, an Iranian newspaper published a poll showing that around three fourths of respondents favored restoring ties with the United States. After that, pollster Abbas Abdi and two of his colleagues served time in jail.

Click-clack, click-clack, pause. Click-clack, pause. The guard was taking longer than usual to walk down the corridor and open my door.

I needed to get out of here.

Click-clack, pause.

Clank.

At last, my door was opening.

"Could I . . . please . . . *hhhhuuuuuhhh* . . . use the bathroom?" I wheezed, as Skinny slowly swung the door open.

She stepped back and let me pass. I staggered down the corridor, entered the bathroom, and leaned my hands against the wall. My heart was pounding furiously, and each breath became shallower and more ragged. I couldn't seem to get enough oxygen.

I linked my fingers behind my head and tried to inhale deeply.

Calm down, Roxana. You must calm down.

I waited a minute or two, then wobbled out of the bathroom and back toward my cell, steadying myself by pressing against the corridor wall. Skinny watched me with aloofness from her chair at the end of the hallway. When I made it to my cell, she stood up and shut the door behind me.

I had to find a way to remain calm. Perhaps reflecting upon the conversation I had with my father just days before my arrest would help. We had spent over an hour on Skype, chatting about one of his favorite topics, metaphysics.

In his gentle voice, my father had told me that most people dwell in the material reality. This is the physical world in which all things are transient and come and go. But human beings yearn for a world that is higher than this. We cannot prove whether this world really exists, but human aspiration gives reality to that spiritual world, that divine world, that higher plane of existence. One has to go down a path, the path of what my father referred to as enlightenment, to move beyond the physical and mental planes to get in touch with the spiritual or divine world.

I had never considered myself an especially spiritual person, but now I felt compelled to search for solace, understanding, and guidance in something beyond myself. I, too, had to try to transcend my physical surroundings to reach the spiritual plane. But how was that possible?

Sitting on my blankets, I crossed my legs and placed my palms upward on my lap. I closed my eyes and took a few deep breaths. *My body may be imprisoned, but I can transcend this material world. My body is here, but my spirit is free. . . .*

A loud buzzer rang, hurtling me back to cruel reality. It was the bell outside the women's ward. I heard footsteps again, this time scurrying toward my cell. It was Skinny. She had come to tell me my *bâzju* was summoning me.

You'll be allowed to call your father today," Javan told me, after I was led, blindfolded, to him.

I felt a weak smile form across my face. "Thank you. Thank you very much," I said, unable to keep myself from groveling.

"If you want to be freed soon, your parents must not know where you are so that you can collaborate with us in the future," he said. "Tell your father you've been detained for buying alcohol. Tell him the head of an alcohol sales network was arrested and your phone number was among those found in his cell phone, so the police came to your home and arrested you."

Alcohol was illegal for Muslims in the Islamic Republic, but it wasn't hard to find on the black market, and some Iranians even made it at home. The penalty for possession was usually at most a fine. I wasn't sure why my interrogator wanted me to tell this tall tale.

"If your father asks where you are, say you don't know," Javan continued. "Tell him you're fine, and the problem is being resolved."

Why should I lie yet again? I asked myself, as the agent led me up and down two flights of stairs. *Why should I trust him when none of his promises of freedom has materialized?* I had to convey to my father that I was in danger, without infuriating my interrogator.

We reached the outdoor yard, where Javan handed me my cell phone and told me to lift my blindfold. He remained beside me, poised to intervene if I failed to follow his directions.

With a trembling hand, I dialed my parents' home number. It rang once. Then twice. Then three times.

My parents had to be home at this hour. It was the middle of the night in Fargo.

"Hello?" came my father's voice, sounding half-asleep.

"Dad?" I asked in English.

"Yes, Roxana?"

"Dad?" I took a step forward, away from Javan, pretending I needed better reception.

"Roxana, where have you been? Are you OK?"

"I'm OK. Are *you* OK?"

"Both your mother and I are fine."

"Dad, I've been detained for having alcohol in my home," I said, tripping over my words a little. "I was arrested because the guy who sold it to me was caught, and my phone number was in his cell phone."

I paused for a second. "Tell Bahman that the man who was arrested was 'Jaffar,' the same guy I bought alcohol from for my birthday."

Please, Dad, I pleaded internally, *remember to repeat this to Bahman*. Bahman knew I had not purchased alcohol for my birthday and that my nickname for him was Jaffar. Maybe I was making this too complicated.

"OK . . . OK," my father said. He sounded confused. Then he asked me where I was. I obediently lied and said I didn't know, although I added that I thought I was somewhere in Tehran.

"Dad," I said, "tell Mom I'm sorry I missed *ojiisân's* birthday. OK? Don't forget to tell her."

Ojiisân meant "grandfather" in Japanese, and my *ojiisân* had died a few years earlier.

My mother picked up another receiver.

"Roxana!" she cried. "We were so worried about you!"

"Sorry, Mom," I said, "but I'm OK."

"You know," she continued, "Bahman greatly regrets that he didn't answer the phone when you called him."

"He even went to Zahedan to search for you," my father added.

"Really?"

Javan began to motion at me to hang up the phone.

"When are you going to be released?" my father asked.

"Um . . . I'm not sure, but the officials told me the problem is being resolved," I replied hurriedly.

Javan stepped toward me.

"Remember, Dad, tell Bahman the alcohol story."

I had been on the line for only a minute or two, but Javan was now extending his hand to snatch my cell phone from me.

"I have to go. I love you, Mom and Dad," I said, struggling to hold back tears. "And tell Jasper and Bahman I love them, too."

"We love you, too, Roxana," my mother said.

Javan grabbed the phone. "Why did you use the word *story*?" he demanded.

Evidently he understood some English. He must have been translating the English word *story* into the Farsi *dâstân*, which could also mean tale or fable.

"I didn't mean a *false* story," I said, groping through my Farsi vocabulary to explain myself. "In English, a story can mean a *true* story."

"By two P.M., I will find out whether you are lying to me," Javan said through gritted teeth. "I'm going to go listen to the conversation you had with your parents. We recorded *everything*."

He handed me off to Tasbihi, who deposited me at the women's ward with the warning, "If you lied to him, it will cost you dearly."

Back in my cell, I prayed that Javan knew neither Japanese nor that my grandfather was no longer living. I hoped I had never mentioned his death in an e-mail that my captors had monitored. I tried to console myself with the thought that at least my parents now knew I was detained somewhere in Tehran instead of taken hostage by bandits or rebels in Zahedan.

Ages passed before Tasbihi came to take me to the interrogation room. There, he told me to sit down, eyes covered, facing the wall as usual.

"I listened to your conversation," came Javan's voice, milder than before. "I saw that you followed my instructions."

I released a quiet sigh.

"Now I want you to call your parents back and tell them the judge has decided your arrest was a mistake," Javan said. "He has left for the weekend, but he plans to free you on Saturday. Tell them not to tell anyone, including the media, about any of this. Otherwise, we won't free you, and you will be in trouble."

"OK, OK," I said breathlessly. Maybe my first call had been a test, and now that my captors were satisfied, they would truly free me on Saturday.

"And don't add anything else this time," Javan cautioned.

I nodded.

He took me back to the yard, where I called my parents again and dictated the new message to them. Their voices softened with relief. After less than a minute, Javan made me hang up.

That evening, I decided to exercise. During my twelve days in solitary, I had been too preoccupied with the possibility of death to concern myself with my regular workout routine. However, now that I knew my parents were all right and that I would be released in three days, I felt comforted and wanted to leave here healthy.

I started to exercise in place, taking care not to whack the walls of my small cell with my flailing arms and legs. A few sets of jumping jacks, lunges, sit-ups, and push-ups worked up a sweat.

Then a guard let me out of my cell to take a shower in the bathroom down the corridor. Suds from whoever had showered before me were still draining into the toilet hole in the grimy, white-tiled floor.

I had been holding out, pledging to myself I wouldn't bathe properly until I could do so at home. I watched as the water poured over my head, rinsing the grease out of my hair, and ran down my body, much skinnier now than it was before my arrest. My body felt cleansed, but my conscience did not.

Counting down to freedom over the next two days was nerve-racking and interminable. At least my interrogator had given me a newspaper to read, a gift that Skinny had assured me was a sign of a prisoner's impending release. I had never studied a newspaper so closely, and such a dull one at that. *Iran News* was an English-language daily that largely promoted the government's agenda. I reviewed each article several times, even the really dry ones full of grammar mistakes and statistics about Iran's investments in this province or that oil field. I had to confine my reading to the daytime, when the dim sunlight broke through the metal sheet covering my window. At night, the small, yellow bulb, which was always turned on in my cell, emitted only a weak glow.

When I tired of the newspaper, I imagined playing the piano by lightly rapping my fingers on the wall of my cell. First I performed Chopin's Etude in E-major, humming the sweet melody, picturing my college piano professor standing to my right, swaying back and forth with his eyes closed, conducting with his pencil. "And then you go to HERE . . . then you go to *here* . . . then you go to here," he would croon, getting softer and softer as I reached the end of the first passage.

I also attempted Rachmaninoff's Prelude in G-minor, the piece I had performed at Miss America. But Rachmaninoff was too difficult to play on the wall and definitely too complex to hum, so I decided to tap out one of my own compositions. "Vicki's Song," I had titled it. I had written it for a friend who had passed away years earlier in North Dakota. Somehow, each time my fingers ran through the melody, I sensed her presence, listening attentively and smiling fondly. Next, I tried to compose a new piece, but all I came up with was melancholy music.

I moved on to a popular Iranian song my friends had taught me whose refrain, "Kiss me for the last time," made me so sad that I switched to tunes I had memorized as a teenager—"Stand by Me" and "We Will Rock You"—but I couldn't remember more than a few lines of lyrics. I tried my luck with Christmas carols: "Joy to the World," "Deck the Halls," and "Rudolph the Red-Nosed Reindeer," although the names of the other eight reindeer escaped me.

Then there was "The Star-Spangled Banner." Like many Iranians, I hadn't learned Iran's postrevolutionary, ideologically charged national anthem. But I had known the American national anthem by heart since I was a schoolgirl.

So far, I had been singing softly, worried that the guards might overhear and reprimand me. Now I sang so quietly, I could hardly hear myself:

> *O say, can you see, by the dawn's early light,*
> *What so proudly we hail'd at the twilight's last gleaming?*
> *. . .*
> *O say, does that star-spangled banner yet wave*
> *O'er the land of the free and the home of the brave?*

Tears stung the corners of my eyes. These familiar words moved me as never before.

"The land of the free."

Now that I had been deprived of freedom, I valued it more than ever. Freedom to interview people and to write a book about them without being thrown in jail. Freedom to tell my parents my whereabouts. Freedom to use the bathroom when I wanted, to read a book, to have a pen and paper. Freedom to walk without a blindfold and to shut off the lights at night. Freedom from coercion to make a false confession and to spy in exchange for my release. The right to be presumed innocent until proven guilty, to remain silent, to have a lawyer.

I tried to recall the rights of due process and the basic freedoms enshrined in the UN's Universal Declaration of Human Rights. I realized these principles had been breached in various parts of the world, including some Western countries, and that governments such as Iran's often dismissed criticism of their human-rights records as hypocritical and politically motivated. Nevertheless, there was no denying that my captors had totally disregarded my basic rights. Though I knew this had happened to countless others in the Islamic Republic, it still shocked me.

"Joseph! Joseph!" a woman's shrieking arose from the guards' quarters. They must have been watching the series *Hazrat-e Yusuf*, or *The Prophet Joseph*, which played every Friday night on Iranian TV. Joseph was a revered figure not only in Christianity but also in Islam, which saw both Joseph and Jesus as prophets. The show was popular among many Iranians. I had never wanted to see much of anything on Iran's state-run television, but now I pressed my ear to the door. I would have watched practically anything rather than be trapped alone in this cell.

I no longer even had the company of the whimpering woman. Over the past few days, nothing but silence had come from her cell. She must have been freed.

I will also be freed—tomorrow, I thought, as I dragged myself back to my blankets and lay down.

But then what would become of me?

I drew my body up. *Really, what would become of me?*

I knew the answer to this disturbing question. My body would be free, but my conscience would remain imprisoned forever.

I had done so much damage. Even if most people would doubt my false confession if it ever aired, there would always be some who would believe it. It could have terrible implications for Mr. D and for dual nationals and foreign journalists in Iran. And who knew whether my captors might distort or exploit my statements to harm others. My confession could also feed into the animosity between Iran and the United States.

My captors had not touched my body, but I had let them strip me of my dignity and integrity.

Maybe I deserved to remain here. Maybe that would be God's way of punishing me.

PART II

ANGELS
IN
EVIN

در جوار فرشتگان اوین

CHAPTER ELEVEN

Every time the buzzer to the women's ward rang that Saturday, I longed for it to be my freedom bell. Despite what I had told myself the night before, I obviously hadn't convinced myself that I deserved to stay in prison.

I lay on my back all day, pondering what the headlines would be if I ended up staying in Evin and my whereabouts became known. "Former Miss N.D. Jailed in Iran," perhaps. As far as I knew, there were no photos of me in a swimsuit floating around on the Internet. If journalists discovered one, I hoped they wouldn't print it. Hard-liners might use it to claim I was a bad Muslim, which would worsen my case.

Dinner came and went. The sky turned dark.

Finally, the door to my cell opened. It was Haj Khanom. She was smiling as usual. "Gather your things," she said.

I sat up abruptly. "Am I being freed?"

"No," she said, "I'm taking you to meet some new friends."

But I didn't want new friends. I wanted *freedom*.

I sluggishly gathered my blankets, prison uniform, toothbrush, and toothpaste. Then Haj Khanom led me out my cell, around the corner, and down another corridor. This hallway looked like my previous one. I couldn't hear any voices, but I assumed that it, too, held women inmates because Haj Khanom hadn't told me to put on my chador and blindfold, as I had by now learned were required outside the women's ward.

We passed three or four steel doors on our right before Haj Khanom stopped in front of the next one. She opened it and positioned herself in the doorway, blocking my view. "I brought you a new friend," she said jovially to someone. "She's *dorag-eh*" (literally, someone of "two veins," or two origins).

"Where's she from?" came an old woman's voice.

"Why don't you ask her yourself?" Haj Khanom said, stepping aside and motioning me into the cell.

As I entered with my pile of belongings, a tall, olive-skinned woman with slightly graying hair came forward to help me. She smiled warmly, took my blankets from my arms, and deposited them on one side of the cell. I heard the door bang shut behind me.

"I'm Roya,"* the woman said, holding out her hand.

I shook it and introduced myself.

"This is my mother, Zohreh,"* Roya said, gesturing at another woman settled on several layers of blankets on the opposite end of the cell, which was twice the size of my previous one. I guessed from the cobweb of wrinkles that stretched from her neck to her white, scraggly hair that she was around seventy-five or eighty years old. She waved at me and grinned, revealing a mouth with more gaps than teeth. Above her, on the wall, someone had engraved the words *Viva la Libertà*. Perhaps this cell had once upon a time held an Italian prisoner yearning for freedom just as I was.

The elderly woman shouted something at me I couldn't understand. I looked at Roya.

"My mother speaks in a local dialect," she explained. "She never went to school, so she didn't learn much Farsi. She said she's sorry she can't get up to greet you. She has a bad back."

"Oh, that's OK," I said. I stepped over to the old woman, stooped down to shake her hand, then sat on my blankets.

"Where are you from?" Roya asked.

I told her, getting accustomed to the sound of my voice again.

Once more, her mother yelled some unintelligible words at me. She was obviously hard of hearing.

"My mother wants to know why you're in prison," Roya translated.

I wasn't sure how to respond. Javan had said no one should even know I was in Evin. If I told these women the truth, they might inform their interrogators or, once they were freed, others. I could think of only one lie—the one that my *bâzju* had invented.

"Alcohol," I said sheepishly.

When Roya told her mother what I had said, the old woman's grin was replaced with a somber look.

She beckoned to me, and I crawled beside her. Then she cupped her hand over her mouth and whispered loudly into my ear something that resembled Farsi. Spattering spit on my cheek, she said, "Alcohol is worse than murder!"

I turned to see her stern expression crack as she burst out laughing.

I couldn't help but smile. Zohreh was quite a character.

"Why are you two here?" I asked Roya, as I returned to my previous spot.

"We were detained a few weeks ago at the airport, along with a few dozen other women and men," she said. "They're here in Evin, too. We were planning to fly to Iraq to make a pilgrimage to Najaf and Karbala."

These were two holy Shiite Islamic cities, popular pilgrimage destinations for Iranian Shiites. "What was wrong with that?" I asked.

"Well," Roya said, with a soft chortle, "we also wanted to go to Ashraf."

Now I understood why the Iranian authorities had been sensitive about their trip.

Camp Ashraf was the headquarters of the Mujahedin-e Khalq Organization, or People's Holy Warriors, an exiled Iranian group opposed to the Islamic regime. Founded in the 1960s as a leftist-Islamist group battling the shah, the MKO conducted attacks and assassinations against both Iranian and, in the 1970s, American targets. But soon after the revolution, enmity grew between the group and Ayatollah Khomeini and his followers. The MKO killed scores of senior officials, and the regime imprisoned and executed many of the organization's supporters. In the 1980s, the MKO set up a base at Camp Ashraf near Baghdad and fought on Iraq's side in the Iran-Iraq War—turning many Iranians against it. Nevertheless, the organization claimed to have widespread underground backing in Iran.

I had also heard that the group and its umbrella organization, the National Council of Resistance of Iran, enjoyed the support of certain Western officials, some of whom credited it with supplying key information about Iran's nuclear program. And although America and Iran called the MKO a terrorist organization, shortly before my arrest the European Union had dropped the group from its terrorist list—a decision that enraged Tehran.

Despite its violent history, the MKO declared that it voluntarily disarmed in 2003, and it had begun trying to portray itself as a democratic alternative to Iran's Islamic regime. But the group's critics, including former members who complained of abusive and cultlike practices at Camp Ashraf, disputed this.

The Mujahedin-e Khalq was now said to be the best-organized Iranian opposition movement abroad. So far, however, the MKO, along with other opposition groups, had not formed a united front able to pose any serious challenge to Tehran.

Roya told me she was not a member of the Mujahedin, but her sister was. Roya and her mother had been planning to visit her in Iraq, before they were diverted to Evin. This wasn't Roya's first time in jail. She had been incarcerated here twice before—once in the 1980s, when several of her fellow prisoners and her brother, who were members of the MKO, were executed. The second time was a few years ago, when she returned from a visit to Camp Ashraf.

Roya told me our ward was part of Evin's detention center, where inmates usually remained until receiving a sentence. Last time she was here, she was transferred to Evin's regular prison, which housed hundreds of women.

The food there was repulsive, Roya said, and was spiked with camphor to suppress prisoners' sexual drive. Some women inmates suffered from lice, narcotics were just as easy if not easier to get than on the streets, and the guards often treated prisoners much more harshly. But at least in the regular prison, inmates could use the bathroom whenever they wanted and could make phone calls more frequently.

"If you ever get sent there," Roya advised me, "try to room with the murderers."

Many of them had been jailed for killing their husbands, which they felt was the only way to escape their abusive marriages, she explained. The murderers, as well as women who were imprisoned for financial crimes, were the most educated, so they were the best choice of cellmates for political prisoners, who didn't have their own section in the regular prison. The prostitutes and drug dealers should be avoided, Roya counseled.

I had once read that people convicted of narcotics offenses constituted nearly half of Iran's prison inmates. While some international health experts said Tehran had made significant progress in combating drug addiction, critics complained that the authorities were not doing enough to stem the demand for or supply of drugs. Many Iranians even accused the country's leaders of encouraging drug use to make the youth submissive to their rule.

I had also read that some estimates put the number of prostitutes in Iran at three hundred thousand or more. Several observers told me the driving force behind prostitution was economic, while government officials tended to blame the phenomenon primarily on "moral decay." One teenage prostitute I had interviewed in Tehran claimed this moral decay existed among some of the nation's law enforcers and clerics, a few of whom had been her clients.

"What do you think will happen to you?" I asked Roya. "Do you think you could be stuck here for months or even years?"

"I don't know," she said nonchalantly. "My interrogators wanted me to denounce the Mujahedin's beliefs, but I told them I couldn't because I believe in my sister, and I don't want to denounce her beliefs, whatever they may be."

"How do you keep from going crazy here?"

"I pass the time walking back and forth in the cell, reading the Koran, and praying," she said. "And I tell myself that I must be so patient that my patience grows impatient of itself."

I chuckled. My last name meant "one who is patient," clearly a misnomer for me over the previous two weeks.

A shrill cough shot through the air from behind Roya. It was the same hacking sound I had heard from my cell the previous week. Now I realized it had been Zohreh.

Roya stood up and brought her mother some water and cough syrup. Zohreh could have remained free, Roya told me, but had insisted she come here with her daughter. Their captors had acquiesced, but now they regretted their decision and wanted to expel the older woman from Evin. Zohreh had consistently refused. At least she was getting free medical care in prison, Roya laughed.

I felt myself smiling again. I may not have been free, but for the first time after two weeks in solitary confinement, I was having a conversation with someone other than the men who threw me in prison.

I wanted to confide in Roya, to tell her about the atrocious lies I had told in Evin. I no longer cared if I would be blowing my cover. I wanted, I *needed* to trust her.

"Roya," I whispered, uncertain whether even in our cell, we were being listened to or watched, "can I tell you a secret?"

"Sure," she said, sliding across the floor to me.

"I'm not really here because of alcohol."

She raised one eyebrow.

I explained that I was actually a journalist accused of spying, and I told her how awful I felt for submitting to my interrogators' demands to make a false confession.

Roya rested her chin on her hands and studied my face. "You have no choice now but to maintain that what you said is the truth," she said firmly, "or your interrogators won't free you."

At the far end of the courtroom sat an imposing figure: a white-bearded, white-turbaned cleric perusing some files on his vast desk, which stood on an elevated platform about a foot high. Behind him, staring down gravely from two framed photographs on the wall, were Ayatollah Khomeini and his successor, Supreme Leader Ayatollah Khamenei.

It was Sunday, February 15, the day after I had joined Roya and her mother, and I had been brought back to the Revolutionary Court, to a room on the third floor. There I had sat down, mystified about what might happen next.

The cleric looked up, his eyes full of suspicion. "Have you been in contact with foreigners?" he asked in a hostile manner.

"Well, my parents live in America, and I was born and raised there," I said.

"Are you a member of the *monâfeqin*?"

"The *monâfeqin*?" I asked. The cleric was using the regime's way of referring to the MKO. The word meant "hypocrites."

He nodded.

"No, I am not," I said, baffled that this man was opening a new line of questioning when I was supposed to be freed any day now.

He jotted down some notes, then brushed his hand in the air as if shooing away a bothersome fly. "Leave now," he said imperiously.

"But wait," I managed. "What will happen to me next?"

He told me he didn't know. The only information I could get out of him was that he was a judge, although he wouldn't give his name.

My guard took me to wait for a fellow inmate on the second floor, where I sat on a chair to brood over my encounter with the judge. It was impossible for me to figure out who was directing this show in which I felt I was merely a puppet. I had been convinced that Javan and his boss Haj Agha were the ones pulling my strings. But what about the other players: the magistrate, the judge in the basement, the judge I had just seen, maybe even higher-level figures in the Intelligence Ministry and the judiciary? I had no idea how they were connected and who was *their* main puppeteer.

Rattled by these thoughts, I told the guard that my interrogator had said I would be freed the day before, and I asked if I could see the magistrate about it. The guard nodded and flagged down a man I recognized from my previous visit to the courthouse as the magistrate's assistant. From my seat a few feet away, I couldn't hear the guard speaking as he relayed my concern, but I saw the assistant look at me blankly. It seemed he had heard nothing of my release.

I was beginning to feel light-headed. I leaned over a glass table next to my chair to see a haggard face staring back at me. Deprived of a mirror in Evin, it was the first time I was seeing my reflection in more than two weeks. My cheeks were sunken, pouches of stress sagged under my eyes, and my skin had started to break out. I laid my head on the table and closed my eyes.

I lost my appetite again after that. I tried to give my meals to Roya and her mother, but they refused, insisting that I had to eat. So I set some food aside, but after it became infested with ants, I had to throw it all away. I glumly told Roya that if my captors decided not to free me and preferred I never be heard from again, she should someday find a way to inform Bahman that I had once been here.

When Haj Khanom opened our door to deliver dinner on Monday night, Roya announced to her that I had not been eating.

"Why not?" Haj Khanom asked, creasing her brow.

"I'm not hungry," I mumbled.

"Why not?" she asked again.

"I'm a bit distressed."

"About what?"

I told her my interrogator had assured me I would be freed last Saturday.

Haj Khanom smiled warmly. "Don't worry," she said. "*Inshallah*, God willing, you will be freed soon."

Iran, I had learned, was the Land of God Willing. "God willing" was the reply I had received when I asked a Culture Ministry official whether I would get press credentials in 2003. It was also the response given to Bahman whenever he asked for permission to shoot his film. "God willing" was the reply Iranians often gave one another—or themselves—when they couldn't or didn't want to give a direct answer. But I wasn't going to let Haj Khanom get away with such a vague remark.

"Do you really think I might be released soon?" I asked.

She nodded, still smiling, then took a step back into the corridor and closed our door.

Roya was looking at me reassuringly. She told me if anyone in the women's ward knew what was in store for me, it would be Haj Khanom, who was in regular contact with various officials at the detention center.

Feeling a little relieved by these words, I sat on the floor with Roya and her mother and ate a few spoonfuls of baked beans.

Who said you were supposed to be freed last Saturday?" Javan asked, shooting a spine-chilling look at me.

Apparently Haj Khanom had gotten to him in only one day.

I was back in the interrogation room, where I was now facing my interrogator in his trademark black leather jacket. To his right sat Haj Agha, examining me without expression.

"You told me," I replied timidly. "You told me to tell my parents I would be freed on Saturday."

"That didn't mean you would actually be freed on Saturday," Javan said bluntly, as if trying to show off in front of Haj Agha.

Haj Agha cleared his throat and raised his right hand slightly to hush the young agent. "Miss Saberi, I just have a few more questions about your work for Mr. D," he said. "I want you to reflect on these questions over the next week, and then we'll come back for you, and you will go free. But don't even think about changing your story."

I was so scared, I could hardly speak.

"Why is it taking so long?" I quavered.

An impatient look crossed his face. He was about to say something when Javan remarked, "We're busy. You're not the only case we're working on, you know."

I had been wondering what my *bâzju* did all day, whether he studied U.S. policy toward Iran, pored over e-mails monitored by his ministry, or worked undercover, using his deceptively Western image to blend in with unsuspecting young Iranians.

Then Haj Agha spoke, his singsong voice composed: "Well, at first you didn't cooperate, so we couldn't trust you. Now we just need to take care of a few details and the paperwork, and then you'll be all set."

I sat silently as he began to list questions about the fabricated tale of Mr. D. When he finished, he added, "I also want you to think about how you could collaborate with us."

I forced myself to look into his empty eyes.

"Do you think you can gather certain secret information for us?" he asked.

I raised my eyebrows.

"For example, from various Americans and other foreigners you know or whom we will assign you to get to know," he continued.

I pretended to contemplate this request. "What kind of information?" I asked.

"For example, could you secretly take papers from their offices or files off their computers?"

"I can try," I said, attempting to sound convincing.

"So think about that for the next few days," Haj Agha said. "Then we'll bring you back here to talk."

"OK."

"By the way," he continued, "I heard you have new cellmates. You better not have told them why you're in prison. What reason have you given them?"

"That I was arrested because of alcohol," I replied uneasily.

He and Javan exploded into laughter that seared my soul. They were clearly delighted they had converted me into their lying lackey.

T hat evening, our cell door opened to two other detainees. As soon as it shut behind the middle-aged women, they threw their blankets on the floor, hugged Roya and her mother, and started talking excitedly.

Our new cellmates were also relatives of MKO members. They, too, had been arrested at the airport on their way to Camp Ashraf a few weeks earlier. Leila* and Elham* hadn't known each other until they were placed in the same cell on their first night in Evin. Like Roya and her mother, these two women had been accused of aiding their family members in the MKO through financial and other means. Their interrogators had claimed as evidence the cash they were carrying at the time of their arrest, but the women had argued this money was only enough to cover their personal travel expenses.

Over the next couple of days, we had little to do except chat with one another. Roya also taught me the opening sura, or chapter of the Koran, in Arabic. I had known only the first line in Arabic—the same words Javan had made me say to begin the first videotape of my false confession, so my cellmate taught me the rest of it:

> In the name of Allah, Most Gracious, Most Merciful.
> Praise be to Allah, The Cherisher and Sustainer of the Worlds;
> Most Gracious, Most Merciful;
> Master of the Day of Judgment.
> Thee do we worship,
> And Thine aid we seek.
> Show us the straight way,
> The way of those on whom Thou hast bestowed Thy Grace,
> Those whose (portion)
> Is not wrath,
> And who go not astray.

Elham and Leila pitied me. They kept asking me why I hadn't left the country sooner. "Poor girl comes here from the other side of the world," they would say, "and this is how she's treated?"

Leila, the older of our two new cellmates, even made a *nazr*, or a vow made by Muslims to God, for me. She pledged that if I was freed soon, she would do a good deed or religious act whenever she, too, was released.

L eila missed her television, her crossword puzzles, and her freedom, she grumbled. As she trudged back and forth on her blankets one evening later that week, she told us she couldn't conceive of how anyone could survive here for long. She had heard of one woman who had been in detention for nearly eight months.

"Eight months?" I exclaimed.

"Yeah," Leila said. "She was working on some kind of health program when she was arrested along with the Alaei brothers, the AIDS researchers."

I had reported on AIDS in Iran, but I had never interviewed the Alaeis, two Iranian-Kurdish brothers who were world-renowned AIDS physicians. I hadn't realized a woman had been detained along with them.

The Alaeis had spoken very frankly about the realities of HIV-AIDS in Iran. Hard-liners claimed they were part of a U.S.-backed plot to overthrow the Islamic Republic in a soft revolution. One brother had recently been sentenced to three years in prison and the other to six. The rulings were condemned by human-rights activists around the world.

"*Shhh, shhh!*" Leila suddenly hissed, motioning at us to be quiet. She pressed her ear to the barred window in our cell door and whispered, "Do you hear that?"

A sad melody was rising through the air. It was the voice of a woman, singing in a language I could not understand, though her misery was clear.

The singing stopped. The corridors had fallen silent. It was as if all the detainees and even the guards had been hypnotized by the pure, gentle voice.

"That's the woman I was just talking about," Leila told us, leaping away from the cell door as we heard slippered feet approaching.

The door opened. It was Skinny. "Gather your belongings," she ordered all five of us. "Don't talk. Prepare to leave your cell."

Where do you think they're taking us?" I whispered to Elham, as we folded our blankets.

"I heard Skinny tell another guard we're being transferred to the regular prison," she whispered back.

I was stunned. How could I be taken to the regular prison when Haj Agha had told me I was supposed to be freed? And none of us had gone to trial or even met with a lawyer yet.

"Keep quiet!" Skinny said brusquely. "Hurry up. Put on your blindfolds. Let's go."

She passed us off to another woman guard, who herded us out of our cell, with Zohreh lagging behind, hobbling on her cane. As we started down the corridor, I felt someone tug at my chador and heard Skinny say in my ear: "Wait. Not *you*."

My four cellmates shambled away, while Skinny led me in the opposite direction, toward the corridor where I had been held in solitary confinement. Halfway down that hallway, she opened the door of a cell and hustled me in, slamming the door behind me.

I removed my blindfold to be met with four pairs of inquiring eyes looking up at me.

CHAPTER TWELVE

One by one, the four women stood up to introduce themselves. I shook their hands, but I was too flustered to catch their names. I had just begun to get used to my previous cellmates, and now I had to start all over again.

As in my last cell, there was hardly enough room for five women to lie down to sleep. My new cellmates began to rearrange their belongings to clear a small space for me. I would be sleeping next to a woman who appeared to be around my age, despite the gray roots of her dyed brown hair. Her ponytail bounced as she pushed aside her blankets and large collection of books.

I wondered how she had managed to get books—and a television, I noticed, sitting on a chair against one wall.

"Where are you from?" the woman asked, as she plopped down beside me, smiling companionably.

I told her.

She looked surprised to learn of my unusual background. "Why did they bring you here?"

Again I gave the alcohol story.

She nodded slowly.

"What are you here for?" I asked.

"I was working on an exchange program for health experts," she said. "The Iranian authorities claimed I wanted to overthrow the regime in a soft revolution."

This must have been the woman who had been here for eight months, the one who had been sentenced along with the Alaei brothers.

"What did you say your name was?" I asked, as another cellmate, a slim, young woman with short, curly hair, sat down beside her.

"Silva, Silva Harotonian."

Silva. This was one of the people my interrogators insisted I knew, even though I had never heard of her. They must have been trying to somehow link me to her and the Alaeis.

"I heard you've been here for eight months," I said.

"Yes," she replied.

The other woman jabbed her playfully in the ribs. "You're famous," she teased Silva with a grin.

Silva told me she was an Iranian of Armenian descent. Just over one year earlier, she had moved to Armenia, northwest of Iran, where she began working for a U.S.-based nonprofit organization called International Research & Exchanges Board, or IREX. Her job was to help administer a program aimed at giving Iranian maternal and child health-care professionals a chance to visit their counterparts in the United States. While based in Armenia, Silva traveled to Iran several times to discuss the program with Iranian applicants.

Her most recent visit had lasted much longer than she had expected.

In June 2008, security agents showed up at her apartment in Tehran and told her they wanted to ask a few questions. They took her first to the Esteghlal Hotel for interrogation. She was shocked to discover that intelligence agents had been following her for months and videotaping her every move. Silva had assumed the authorities had no problem with her work, especially since the Iranian government had invited IREX staff to visit Iran a few years earlier, though that was under reformist President Khatami.

At the hotel, as day turned to night, she asked to be excused. She had a friend's wedding to attend.

"You won't be going anywhere for a while," her interrogators replied. That night, she found herself in Evin Prison.

Fortunately, one of Silva's friends was with her at the time of her arrest and reported the incident to their mutual friend, a lawyer. That attorney came to Evin searching for Silva but was told she wasn't here. He also went to the Revolutionary Court, but officials there repeatedly claimed that no file existed in her name.

One day at court, the attorney happened to see a folder open to a page with Silva's name on it. "That's the woman I've been looking for!" he shouted gleefully at a judicial official, who was visibly irked by this discovery. "That's Silva Harotonian!"

Like me, Silva was put in solitary confinement while undergoing intense interrogation during her first days in prison.

"They wanted me to confess to things that weren't true," she told me. For example, her interrogators wanted her to say the Alaei brothers headed the program she was administering, but that wasn't the case, so she wouldn't agree to say it.

Eventually, Silva, too, made some sort of videotaped confession under duress, albeit not quite the way her captors had demanded. Only after her interrogation was complete was Silva permitted to get a lawyer, and even then, she was hardly allowed to talk to her legal team before her trial.

The closed-door hearing did not go well. The prosecutor claimed that Silva had several passports, including one from America, and called her a "woman of one thousand faces." In reality, she had only one passport—an Iranian one. She also didn't have ample time to defend herself. Her judge cut her off, she said, because he was hungry and wanted to go to lunch.

He later sentenced Silva to three years in prison. She appealed the decision and was awaiting the appellate court's response, which she expected to receive any day now.

"Why didn't you just make the false confession the way your interrogators wanted?" I asked her. "No one believes those things anyway. You could've been freed and then set the story straight."

Silva pursed her lips, then lowered her eyes. "I'm angry I could lose three years of my freedom," she said, more to herself than to me, "but I'm glad I didn't do what my interrogators wanted."

The other young woman patted her on the back and said, "You did the right thing, Silva."

Silva *had* done the right thing, and I had done the wrong thing. I was too disgusted with myself to continue the conversation, so I told the two women I wanted to go to sleep. They got up and joined our other cellmates across the room. I pulled my blankets around me. Although Silva had been sentenced to three years in prison, at least when she got out of this place, she would have a clear conscience.

I pressed my eyes shut and pretended to fall asleep. My four cellmates had gathered in a circle and were whispering to one another.

"What's she here for?" I heard one ask.

"She said for having alcohol," Silva replied, "but it's doubtful. They don't bring people here for that. Section 209 is for political prisoners."

My belly flipped. Until now, I hadn't realized I was in a section specifically for political prisoners. I vaguely recalled hearing about 209 before, that it was infamous for the worst kinds of torture. Not only was I in Evin, but I was also in one of its most brutal sections.

My parents would never think to search for me here if they really believed the story that I was locked up for buying alcohol. But that didn't matter, I told myself over and over, because as Haj Agha had promised, I was going to be released soon.

M y new cellmates were a motley collection, I learned the next morning, but they all seemed to get along well with one another.

Azar,* a good-humored woman in her fifties, had already spent three months in Evin. She was arrested along with two of her sons for allegedly possessing some antiques that the authorities claimed were state property. Her third son was a cleric from Qom. He was trying to use his connections with various high officials to free his mother and brothers. Iranians widely accepted this *pârti bâzi*, or "playing of connections," as one of the main ways to get things done.

Azar wore her *maqna'e* on her head all day, tied like a bandana to keep her hair off her face. She spent most of her time sitting on her blankets with her legs stretched out, twirling her prayer beads. She suffered from back and leg aches, although these had abated after she lost several pounds during her few months in prison. A Koran was planted beside her, but I never saw her reading it. When a guard asked if she could give it to inmates in another cell, Azar objected. The book's presence, she said, comforted her.

Samira* was the slim woman with short hair who had spoken to Silva and me on my first night in the cell. She was a divorcée in her early thirties who lived with her widowed mother. Samira had been detained two weeks earlier. When I asked why, she replied wryly, "Because I went to my local bakery and shouted, 'We want bread!'"

That seemed harmless enough, I told her. But the authorities, she explained, had thought differently. What she had done was a form of protest associated with a new civil disobedience movement called *Mâ Hastim*, We Exist, which was launched by Shahram Homayoun, an Iranian exile in America. He ran Channel One TV, which openly criticized Iran's Islamic regime and was one of several Farsi-language satellite stations beamed from the United States into Iran.

Many Iranians I knew turned to Farsi-language broadcasts from abroad as a main source of entertainment and news. This was despite a ban on satellite dishes (which were nonetheless ubiquitous), the regime's sporadic efforts to confiscate them, and the frequent jamming of satellite signals.

One satellite channel with many loyal viewers was Voice of America Persian News Network, which was funded by the U.S. government. And BBC Persian TV, which had launched shortly before my arrest, was quickly gaining popularity, much to the chagrin of Iranian hard-liners who accused the two networks of striving to undermine the regime.*

"I will never ask for bread again," Samira told me with a wink. She didn't want to risk her freedom—or her mother's—again.

---

* Many Iranians, however, regard some of the Farsi-language satellite programs as out of touch with reality. Some Iranians prefer English-language foreign news, Iranian newspapers (despite censorship), and the Internet (despite government filters). In 2008, an Iranian judiciary official announced that 5 million Web sites had been filtered in Iran.

Agents had detained Samira's mother because she happened to be at home when they took Samira there to search her apartment. The older woman had been released after a few days. Samira was later told she could also go free until her trial if she promised to never take part in any more We Exist activities, which she agreed to, and if she posted bail. The only problem was that neither she nor her mother owned any property worth 10 million tomans, or about $10,000. So Samira had remained behind bars, anxiously hoping that a generous relative or friend would come to her aid.

Although Samira had gone to college and now worked as a school-teacher, her monthly salary of 400,000 tomans, or roughly $400, was hardly enough to support herself and her mother. Like many of the nation's college graduates, she was grappling with double-digit infla-tion, a lack of good jobs, and a relatively high cost of living. I pitied her for having to stay in jail simply because she could not afford her freedom.

The other woman in my new cell was Vida,* a stout housewife in her midsixties with dark skin and dyed blond hair. She was another member of the group arrested on the way to Camp Ashraf, where Vida had planned to go to see her son. She had already endured a lot of hardship in her life. After the revolution, the Islamic regime executed one of her other sons and her brother, both of whom had links to the Mujahedin-e Khalq.

Vida had a bladder condition that required her to take frequent trips to the bathroom. She was embarrassed, however, to constantly ask the guards to open our door and let her use the toilet, so she often waited restlessly until one of us also felt an urge to go.

As the oldest among us, Vida took it upon herself to act as our mother. She clucked at us if we didn't finish our meals and cleaned up after us when we spilled crumbs on the floor. To pass her time, she hummed Iranian folk songs and, because she was illiterate, she liked to have Silva read poetry and novels to her.

Vida, Azar, and Samira clearly admired Silva. They called her "doctor," even though she wasn't one, and often consulted her about issues related to health and nutrition. They also obediently ate the salad Silva would make for all of us. (Every Tuesday, detainees were allowed to use their own money to buy a few snacks and raw vegetables through a prison official who brought them from Evin's commissary—although goodies deemed too Western, like chips, were not permitted. When my cellmates learned I had brought only a little cash to prison, they kindly shared their treats with me.) As she chopped lettuce and cucumbers with a dull knife borrowed from the guard on duty, Silva would entertain us with stories.

"On the morning of my arrest, I got a manicure for my friend's wedding I was supposed to attend that evening," she recounted. "When I was imprisoned, the guards saw my hands and looked at me as if I was so frivolous. They thought I always painted intricate flowers on my nails."

We giggled, guessing that our conservative captors saw painted nails as one sign of Western materialism and anti-Islamic decadence.

After several months in Evin, Silva was allowed to have a small television. It was continuously humming in the background, even when we fell asleep, as if the women wanted to numb their brains to their surroundings. Like me, Silva had never watched much state-run television before landing in prison, but by now, she had memorized all the programs.

Iran had no private radio or TV channels—only the state broadcaster, the Islamic Republic of Iran Broadcasting. IRIB served as the regime's official voice, and its director was appointed by the supreme leader.

IRIB's communications director, whom I had interviewed for my book, had told me that state TV's main goal was to entertain its viewers so they don't "go and watch [foreign networks like] BBC." IRIB also aimed to educate Iranians and promote Islam, he had said.

Many Iranians, especially in rural areas, relied mostly on domestic television for their news. But I also knew plenty of Iranians who doubted IRIB's impartiality, especially when it came to playing down Iran's domestic difficulties and highlighting the economic problems and crime in much of the rest of the world. IRIB cast America in a particularly bad light, with news stories often depicting it as a country overrun by homeless people and mass murderers.

My cellmates flipped to IRIB's all-news channel only to check the clock in the corner of the screen, the sole way for us to tell time. They preferred to watch foreign TV police dramas, such as the German *Cobra 11*, which were expertly dubbed into Farsi. IRIB often censored such programs, with abrupt edits typically hinting at forbidden scenes of physical contact between actors and actresses. Iranian-made shows were of course also censored, usually long before they reached the editing bay.

Whenever a preaching cleric would appear on the screen, which was fairly often, one of my cellmates would groan and change the channel.

Whenever an actor smoked a cigarette, Samira would start fidgeting her fingers.

And whenever I saw images of green parks, vast fields, or even desolate deserts, I would yearn for the world outside. I missed Fargo and my parents, who must have been extremely worried about why they had no news from me, one week after they had expected me to be freed.

S amira was taken to court on Sunday, February 22, and returned with a light in her eyes that divulged her good news. A relative had finally come through with her bail. I desperately wanted to ask her to find Bahman for me, but I couldn't bring myself to do it. She would be heavily monitored after her release, and contacting anyone for me could put her at further risk.

As Samira hugged us all and said good-bye, I couldn't help but feel envious. I pictured her reuniting with her mother, calling her friends, and sleeping in her own bed.

Silva seemed to read my mind. That night, after Vida and Azar fell asleep, she told me she used to get jealous of her cellmates when they were released. So many women had come and gone from her cell, she said, while she had stayed behind. But after a while, she realized she was genuinely happy for anyone who could leave this prison.

"I have accepted that this experience," she said, gesturing at the walls around us, "is part of my destiny." She paused. "I really believe this."

Maybe my imprisonment was also part of my destiny, I thought, just as moving to Iran had been. In fact, if the Iranian authorities hadn't given me a press pass, I wouldn't have stayed long enough to feel at home in the country and begin writing a book about it. And if I hadn't been introduced to Bahman, who encouraged me to continue with my book, I might have abandoned it and left the country. Then I wouldn't be *here* today. Yes, it was bizarre how all these events had somehow been connected. But for what purpose, and with what meaning?

"How do you keep going?" I asked Silva.

"I pray a lot to Jesus Christ," she said, her face growing solemn. "I feel He is always watching me and always with me."

Like other Iranian Armenians, Silva was Christian. Although Shiite Islam was Iran's official religion and the regime said 99 percent of all Iranians were Muslim, the Islamic Republic officially recognized Christianity, along with Judaism and the ancient Persian religion of Zoroastrianism, as minority religions. While all three were allotted seats in parliament and enjoyed certain freedoms, many religious minorities complained of discrimination and said the regime treated them as second-class citizens.

After a few months in prison, Silva was allowed to have a Bible and a book of Christian prayers. She found solace in these, she told me, as well as in singing.

But I could tell that behind Silva's calm facade, she was struggling to understand why she was here. This confusion was reflected in some words she had scratched into the paint on our cell wall:

Dear God!
I don't understand you.
What do you want from me?
Gratitude or forgiveness?

Silva had fallen victim to Iranian hard-liners who demonized contact with the West, particularly the United States. By claiming that people like her and the Alaei brothers were threats to national security, these hard-liners appeared to be attempting to scare Iranians away from even the most ordinary connections with America. It didn't matter if the accused were simply trying to use these links to help their nation progress.

The following morning, Azar was summoned to court while Silva went to her weekly visit with her mother elsewhere on the prison grounds. Some detainees, Silva had told me, were allowed to get visits from immediate family members, but how long they had to wait for this right to be granted depended on their captors.

Both women returned to the cell at around the same time. Azar was grinning so widely that for the first time, I noticed she was missing a few teeth. Her third son, the cleric, had posted bail for her and her two other sons, and the three would be released shortly. Azar laughed as she told us how one of her jailed sons had commented dryly to the judge: "Prison isn't as bad as I thought. For thirty years, we've been waiting for free electricity and free water. Finally, we've found a place where everything is free!"

I doubted the judge appreciated this remark, which ridiculed a famous statement by Ayatollah Khomeini that water and electricity should be free to the public because Iran was awash in oil money.

Under the Islamic Republic, these services were subsidized but not free, and critics accused the authorities of squandering oil revenues through corruption, reckless spending, and unwise economic policies.

And actually, not everything in prison was free. Inmates had to pay for items such as tissues, shampoo, washcloths, extra underwear, and sanitary napkins.

Silva smiled as she listened to Azar's story, but then a tear escaped from one eye. She wiped it away and apologized. She was upset, she admitted, because that day her aging mother had looked especially downcast and weary as the two spoke, separated by a glass window.

Our cell door opened. It was one of the guards whom my cellmates had named after her orthodontic braces.

"You and you," Braces said, jerking her finger at Vida and me, "get dressed to go to *havâ-khori*."

The four of us exchanged glances. Why was Braces telling only two of us to go outside? Vida and I did as we were told and spent the next twenty minutes plodding around the caged-in yard, brooding over what might be happening to Silva and Azar in the meantime.

When Braces returned us to our cell, the two women and their belongings were gone. Azar, we knew, had been released, but we were concerned about Silva. We presumed she had received a response to her appeal, but we had no idea whether it had been negative, in which case she might have been transferred to the regular prison, or positive, in which case she would have been set free.

We tried to wrest the details from Braces, but she remained tight-lipped.

"Don't make a fuss," was all she said. "She has gone to a better place."

"You mean she's been released?" I pressed her.

She grinned slyly and shut the door.

The swift departure of Samira, Azar, and the bubbly and talkative Silva left our cell quiet and gloomy. Moreover, Silva had taken all her books, which I had begun to read, although her TV was left behind. Soon Vida began to mope. Then she started to cry. When the room had been full of energy and life, time had passed much more easily for her. She wished we would get new cellmates—like the two women she had previously shared a cell with on the other side of ours. They were Baha'is, whose faith was not recognized under the Iranian Constitution, even though its members were thought to make up Iran's largest non-Muslim religious group.

I took Vida's hand and tried to comfort her, but it wasn't easy.

"Trust in God," was all I could say to her—and to myself.

CHAPTER THIRTEEN

The woman who stood in our cell doorway must have been crying for many hours, perhaps even days. Her cheeks were flushed, and her bloodshot eyes were almost swollen shut. It was Wednesday, two days after Azar and Silva left, and our door had just opened to reveal this small and fragile-looking woman in prison garb.

She lingered in the doorway for a few moments with her blankets heaped in her arms, looking bewildered.

"Come in," I said, stepping toward her and introducing myself. Vida did the same.

The newcomer, Nargess,* stumbled forward and dumped her blankets on the floor. When the guard shut the door behind her, she fell onto them and started to weep loudly. I recognized her weeping; it was the same high-pitched wailing I had heard coming from a nearby interrogation room during my first week in prison. This must have been the woman my interrogator had claimed was, like me, accused of espionage.

I soon discovered that Nargess had also been the one whimpering in the cell behind mine during my first days in solitary confinement. Instead of being released as I had thought, she had been transferred to another cell down the hall. In all, she had been in solitary for more than a month.

Vida and I were the first prisoners she had seen since her arrest.

"Are they going to execute me?" Nargess asked with a tremor in her voice. Nargess's interrogator had told her if she didn't confess to being a spy, she would languish in Evin for years or even be executed. Her story sounded painfully familiar.

I assured Nargess she would not be killed, now that she was out of solitary. I was only guessing, though, because nothing was predictable in this prison.

Nargess's face twisted. Then she burst into tears again—this time, tears of relief. She told us that despite threats from her interrogator, she had continued to deny the charge against her. Incensed, he had left her alone for days with no news. He sounded like a tyrant, refusing to set her free although the magistrate she had met on her second day of captivity had ordered her released on bail. Her interrogator had denied her even a single phone call, and she feared that no one knew where she was. At least a family friend was aware that she had been captured. She had been sitting in his car when two plainclothes agents showed up, forced her into their own vehicle, and whisked her here to Evin.

Nargess had never imagined she would one day end up in prison. She said she was a simple businesswoman who had nothing to do with politics, but she had many foreign friends—a fact known by her colleagues, one of whom she suspected had wrongly accused her of espionage.

Nargess told us she had gained sustenance in her solitary cell by reading the Koran for hours on end and praying through the days and nights. And that's what she wanted to do right now. She wanted to thank God for taking her out of her isolation and placing her with us.

She prayed for many hours that day, and when I woke up in the middle of the night, I saw her sitting up on her blankets, praying again.

I envied her for her faith, which had kept her strong and helped her resist the same pressures I had surrendered to, even while I had been pitying her for not recognizing the futility of her weeping. This woman, I realized, loved God so much that she feared disappointing Him more than she feared death.

G et dressed," Haj Khanom told me the next morning. "You have interrogation."

I had been waiting for this day since I had last seen my interrogator and Haj Agha just over one week earlier.

I threw on my chador and blindfold and was led to an interrogation room. There, Haj Agha's stern voice commanded me to uncover my eyes. I saw him sitting at a big desk in front of me, with Javan in his leather jacket dutifully perched behind him to the right.

"We made an exception to come here today—a holiday—because we want to get you out of prison soon," Haj Agha said, full of self-importance. It was Thursday, February 26, one of many religious holidays in Iran and the anniversary of the martyrdom of Imam Reza, the Shiites' revered Eighth Imam.

"Thank you," I said, assuming this was the appropriate response, even though I doubted his motives.

Haj Agha handed me a piece of paper with several questions on it. After this final interrogation, he explained, he would give my file to the magistrate.

"We've asked him to free you because you have cooperated with us and will be working for us, which we'll discuss with you in detail at a later time," Haj Agha continued. "When you go to see him in about ten days, repeat the confession to him and agree to whatever he says."

In about ten days? I was dismayed by the thought that I would have to keep waiting for my freedom and that my family and any friends who realized I had disappeared almost one month earlier would have to agonize even longer. I lowered my eyes and remained silent.

"What is it?" Haj Agha asked.

"Well, I thought I was supposed to be freed by now."

"We've been working on it, but these things take time," he said, as if I should have known better. "Don't worry. We've put in a good word for you with the magistrate.

"And by the way," he added, "don't ask him for an attorney. Lawyers are useless. We make the decisions around here."

During this interrogation, I was to repeat my entire false confession about Mr. D, the details of which had become even hazier in my mind. Then I had to respond to written questions, including several I had been asked in earlier interrogations.

For the first time, I was to write my answers in English, then read each one aloud. Every few sentences, Javan interrupted me, telling me to replace one word or phrase with another he preferred. I hadn't realized he knew English so well. He even informed me that the most accurate translation for the Farsi word *mahramâneh* was not "secret," as I had thought, but "classified."

One new question had to do with whether before my detention I had noticed any signs that the Intelligence Ministry was monitoring me so closely. I told Javan and Haj Agha that I had not, although after my arrest, I had begun to think about the signals I may have missed.

"Like what?" they both asked, intrigued.

I described the woman and man videotaping my friend and me in the park, as well as the plainclothes agent who had come to my apartment complex and asked the manager who lived in which units.

"Yes, that was us," Haj Agha said.

Then I mentioned Hassan.

"No, no," Javan said. "He has nothing to do with us."

I had no way of knowing whether he was telling the truth, but I figured at this point, it didn't really matter.

I returned to the list of questions. I had reached the final one: *Why did you tend to criticize the Islamic Republic in your news reports?*

This was the first time during my incarceration that my captors had made this accusation.

Only once had a Culture Ministry official complained to me about the content of my coverage—back in 2003, during student-led protests that had erupted at the University of Tehran. He had rebuked me for showing images of young men and women demonstrators being chased by baton-swinging vigilantes on motorcycles. The official had also criticized my report for stating that thousands of protestors were in the streets, while failing to mention that millions of Iranians had stayed home.

That day, I had returned to my apartment and repeated the conversation to my boss at the U.S.-based news agency Feature Story News. He wasn't pleased to hear that the Culture Ministry was telling me how to practice journalism.

It was then I understood that to report in the Islamic Republic, I would have to balance the expectations of the regime, my employer, interviewees, and my own conscience to do my job. Doing so had proved challenging, but I had tried my best to be accurate and fair in my reporting. This balancing act was something many journalists contended with in Iran. Local journalists in particular had become experts at it, working within the regime's often arbitrary and unclear boundaries, while still offering a measure of serious discussion and criticism through their work. Others had defied the regime's restrictions on the press and free speech by writing personal blogs or contributing to foreign news Web sites—despite the risk of punishment. Now, sitting in my school desk facing Haj Agha, I admired these brave souls more than ever.

"I aimed to be balanced and to show various views in my reports," I told him. "Besides, a good journalist is supposed to gather diverse perspectives, present them to viewers and readers, and let them draw their own conclusions."

Haj Agha's brow twitched. Apparently he didn't appreciate my lecture on journalism. "But why did you report on sensitive topics such as AIDS in Iran?"

His question made me wonder whether he had ever read, watched, or listened to any of my work. I explained I had said in a 2003 report that AIDS existed in Iran, but the country was leading the region in the fight against it through an enlightened approach. I pointed out that I had also traveled to Thailand to make a documentary about the disease there, and Thai officials had enthusiastically welcomed my coverage.

"Thailand is different," Haj Agha huffed. "They have a huge *sex* industry, while we are an *Islamic* country. There's no need to write about AIDS here."

In reality, the issue of AIDS in Iran was not that simple. According to one UN expert I had interviewed, a country like Iran would not face the threat of a generalized AIDS epidemic for at least another ten years or so. He had added, however, that whether and when the concentrated epidemic found among intravenous drug users and prisoners spread to sex workers, homosexuals, and the youth completely depended on the country's future policies.

Iran's health minister had recently acknowledged there were around eighteen thousand registered cases of Iranians with HIV and that the actual number was likely three times as high, while another ministry official said the figure could be even higher: as many as one hundred thousand. The minister blamed both drugs and—in a rare admission in the Islamic Republic—high-risk sexual behaviors, which could mean unprotected sex outside marriage, prostitution, and homosexuality.

But I saw no use in bringing any of this up to Haj Agha.

"And why did you interview the health minister about the IMOD drug?" he continued.

The Immuno-Modulator Drug was an herbal extract that Iranian researchers had been developing in recent years. Iran's health minister had claimed it would strengthen the body's immune system against HIV infection. I was planning to use my interview with him for my book, I explained.

"IMOD is positive news for Iran," I added. "And Iranian media reported on it, so why couldn't I?"

"They can do that," Haj Agha said. "It's different when you write about it."

I frowned. I was feeling more offended by Haj Agha's accusations about my reporting than I was by the preposterous allegation that I was a spy.

Frustrated, I decided to drop this discussion. I could never prove my point to someone so paranoid. And it was people with this kind of mind-set, I lamented, who held so much power in the Islamic Republic.

After writing my final answer, I handed the papers back to Haj Agha.

Javan stood up to take me back to my cell. "When you collaborate with us in the future," he said with a smirk, "your Farsi will improve enough to write everything in our language."

I forced a nod, retied my blindfold, and got up to follow him out of the room.

"One more thing, Miss Saberi," Haj Agha called after me. I turned around to face the direction of his voice. I couldn't see him, but I sensed his penetrating stare.

"You should remember," he said, in a threatening tone, "if you leave this place and tell anyone about our arrangement, be sure I will sign your death warrant myself."

B ack in my cell, I cast off my chador and sank onto my blankets. After so many unfulfilled promises, it seemed I would really be freed this time, yet I was in no mood to rejoice.

My cellmates asked what had happened that day, but Haj Agha's threats had scared me into silence.

I turned my back to them and stared at the wall. I was vacillating between a feeling of hope that I would finally be freed and the idea that once released, I would have to live in fear of Haj Agha and his henchmen, wherever I happened to be. But mostly, I felt deep shame at the way I was winning my freedom.

Vida and Nargess had gone through three police dramas by the time I came to a realization that I had been struggling to avoid since my first week in prison: I did not want to be freed for telling lies. I wanted to recant my false confession—not after my release but while

I was still in prison.

But how?

If I told Javan, he and Haj Agha would be livid. They would probably throw me back in solitary and keep me cut off from anyone who could help me. I hated that my biggest adversaries were my only lifeline.

S it down," said the bearded man with two rings, motioning at a chair.

The magistrate was at his desk in his office on the second floor of the courthouse, exactly how I had first seen him nearly one month earlier.

I complied. I hadn't expected to be brought here just two days after my last interrogation, much earlier than Haj Agha had predicted. Sitting before the magistrate, whom Haj Agha had described as holding the key to my release, I automatically bowed my head.

"Did your interrogators make some sort of deal with you for your release?" he asked me.

My head snapped up. *What exactly did this man know?*

Then I remembered how, nearly two weeks earlier, my guard had told the magistrate's assistant that my interrogator had promised me I would be freed. The assistant must have informed his boss of this conversation.

"You can trust me," the magistrate said softly.

I didn't understand. This could be another of my captors' tests. If I ignored Haj Agha's warning and told the magistrate that my interrogators made me confess to crimes I did not commit, I might lose my chance at freedom. Besides, all these men were intertwined in one way or another, so how could the magistrate not know the answer to his own question?

"Don't worry," he said. "I won't tell them." He looked at me intensely but without hostility, triggering a tug-of-war in my head.

Maybe I should trust the magistrate. But why? He was the man who had thrown me into solitary and refused me a lawyer.

The magistrate was still looking at me. He appeared patient and disarmingly sincere.

Perhaps if I told him only that my captors demanded I spy for them and not that my confession was false, he would still release me, I thought.

"They . . . ," I began, "they wanted me to spy for them," I blurted out.

The magistrate grimaced.

"Haven't other prisoners been asked to do that?" I asked.

"I've never heard of it. What did they want you to do for them?" he asked, his chair creaking as he leaned forward.

I found it hard to believe he wasn't aware of such arrangements, but I said, "They said I have to spy on foreign diplomats in Iran and on Americans abroad . . . or something like that."

"Weren't you afraid you could be arrested by the U.S. government for that?"

I didn't know what to say. Did this man actually care about my welfare, or was he only pretending? Whose side was he on?

"Well, y-yes," I stammered, "it would be risky, but my interrogators said this was the price of my freedom." I thought it prudent not to admit that once freed, I would have never upheld my end of the bargain.

The magistrate lowered his gaze to his desk and began drumming his pen on a blank notepad, softly and slowly.

Then he looked up at me and said gravely, "You shouldn't have agreed to that."

My body went rigid.

"And you should know," he continued, "that I don't care about any deals they have cut with you. I make my *own* decisions."

"But they told me you would accept whatever they recomm. . . ," I said, my voice trailing off.

"No, it's not like that," he said, shaking his head. "And by the way, don't tell them I asked you about this."

I nodded stiffly, still unable to figure out whether this was all a setup to test my obedience—but to whom?

Then the magistrate asked if I had any property deeds I could put up for bail. I told him my father had an apartment in my name in Tehran and gave him its approximate value. The magistrate wouldn't have been asking me about this, I assumed, if he wasn't planning to release me, though I couldn't be sure.

He waved the guard over to take me away.

I stood up to go, then sat back down. "Could I call my parents and tell them where I am?"

He blinked. "Don't they know?"

I explained that my interrogators had told me to lie to them about where I was.

"Why did you lie?" the magistrate asked.

"They said if I didn't, I wouldn't be freed."

"If they told you to kill someone, would you do that, too?"

I was beginning to think this man might actually have some principles. "No, of course not," I replied.

"So why did you lie?"

"Because I trusted them."

"You shouldn't have trusted them," he said bluntly, and returned to the papers on his desk.

As the guard drove me back to prison, I started to regret that I hadn't also told the magistrate my confession was false. I may have been mistaken, but he seemed to have cared about the truth.

When I arrived at the women's ward, I asked Haj Khanom if I could be taken back to the magistrate. She said that wouldn't be possible. I would have to wait until he summoned me again, whenever that might be.

CHAPTER FOURTEEN

As my cellmates and I were preparing for bed that night, our door swung open again. This time, a thin, young woman in loose-fitting prison pajamas shuffled in. Peeking out between her long bangs, below one eye, was a dark red gash.

"Did they hit you?" the three of us wanted to know, once our new cellmate, Sara, had arranged her blankets in the middle of the floor.

She smiled conspiratorially, her swollen cheek pushing into her left eye.

Sara told us she was arrested early that morning with her fiancé and two of her girlfriends. They had been asleep at their friend's apartment when several plainclothes intelligence agents burst in. The intruders were looking for the owner of the apartment, but because he was absent, they decided to detain the four college students instead.

Sara's fiancé had resisted arrest, so the men started to beat him. Sara reacted by punching one of the agents in the head. In turn, he whacked her in the face with a hard object, leaving the wound beneath her eye.

Eventually the agents collected the four friends and forced them into a van, which was parked so close to the apartment complex's front door that the only way out of the building was into the vehicle.

They had been interrogated all day, Sara explained. Now her two girlfriends were in another cell, while her fiancé had been taken to the men's ward of 209. She chuckled softly as she related this story, as if she found these events quite amusing.

Sara and her fiancé had predicted they might one day end up in prison. They were active in a leftist student group, had taken part in university demonstrations, and several of their classmates had been detained before them.

Imprisonment, I knew, was one risk Iranian students faced for political activism, which had been growing increasingly dangerous—especially after hard-liners expanded their control over universities following Ahmadinejad's 2005 victory. Student activists could also be dealt lesser punishments, such as suspension, expulsion, or the denial of entry to graduate school.

Given the possible costs, only the most daring students continued to openly call for human rights and democracy. Many other young Iranians preferred to follow the political scene from the sidelines or to stay out of it altogether, believing they had little part in determining their country's future.

Nevertheless, Iranian youth remained a large and potentially potent force. Roughly two thirds of the country's 70 million people were under thirty, and around 3.5 million Iranians were enrolled in universities.

As hotbeds of political ideas and activities, Iran's campuses had played a major role in shaping the nation and had often served as launching pads for protests that spread into society. Soon after anti-shah university students helped the revolution succeed, the new regime shut down universities for more than two years to implement its Cultural Revolution, which aimed to purge universities of students and academics with leftist or liberal tendencies and to purify the curricula. The Cultural Revolution also transformed the student movement in Iran, with the Unity Consolidation Office, or UCO, becoming the predominant student organization.

The UCO pledged total support for Ayatollah Khomeini and became a tool for the regime to cleanse universities of opposition. But as a new generation of students emerged in the early 1990s, the group began to shift. Although still loyal to the Islamic Republic's main tenets, it turned against conservatives and transformed into a proponent of civil society, pluralism, and freedom of expression. Many students supported President Khatami and the reformists. Gradually, however, they became disillusioned with the slow pace of reforms.

Iran's student activists could now be divided into four main groupings. The first included Basijis who swore absolute loyalty to the supreme leader and his policies. The second was a democracy-seeking movement led by the UCO, which had split into various factions and included many secular students. The third were modern-thinking Islamists who supported reform within the existing system. And the fourth were leftists, such as Sara, who advocated socialism, particularly Marxism-Leninism.

T he next day, Sunday, March 1, Sara was taken to court and charged with having links to communist opposition groups abroad. So was her fiancé. Their two friends, however, were to be released on bail.

Despite her own discouraging news, Sara wasn't worried. She said she had learned from some classmates what to expect in jail.

"What have you told your interrogators?" I asked.

"It depends on what they ask me," she said. "I try to either tell them the truth, or if I can't, I say nothing at all."

Sara gave me an example of how one of her interrogators pressured her to name other members of her student group. Instead of answering directly, she had said something to the effect of, "We stand for equality and brotherhood. Don't you believe in those values?" He had replied yes. "Then," she had parried, "*you* must be a member, too."

First Roya, then Silva and Nargess, and now this twenty-year-old student had used a variety of methods to resist their captors' demands to lie or to admit to crimes they did not commit. They had stood up to threats and pressures knowing that by telling the truth and proclaiming their innocence, they could jeopardize their chances at freedom.

"Do your parents know where you are?" I asked Sara, wondering if her family, like mine, was in the dark.

"I think so," she said. "My brother was arrested last year and was later released on bail. After that, we decided that in case I was next, he should call me every night at a certain time to make sure I'm OK. If my phone is turned off at that time, he should assume I've been detained."

Sara was concerned, however, that her parents would be terrified their daughter was now reliving their son's ordeal, so that afternoon, she asked the guard on duty if she could call them. Sara's chief interrogator would have to approve, she was told. The rest of the day and all of Monday passed with no reply.

When Haj Khanom brought breakfast to our cell on Tuesday morning, Sara pushed aside the tray and flatly announced: "I want no breakfast, no lunch, and no dinner. I won't take my cold medication. I only want to call my parents, and I refuse to eat anything until I can."

"As you wish," Haj Khanom said, her characteristic smile a little subdued by this outburst. "You can't get what you want here by not eating."

I had never witnessed anyone go on a hunger strike, although I had met and reported on Akbar Ganji, a famous Iranian political dissident who had been freed from Evin in 2006 after fasting for more than seventy days. His strike was highly publicized, and it intensified demands by the international human-rights community for his release. He later went abroad, where he continued to speak out for the movement of democracy in Iran.

But because no one outside Evin knew of Sara's strike, it was difficult to predict how effective the move would be for her.

Sara reduced her daily diet to three cups of tea and three dates, a box of which we purchased each Tuesday. She was already so skinny that her collarbones protruded from her neck, and the rest of us worried she wouldn't last long.

I sat facing the wall with my eyes bound in the interrogation room, where Javan had summoned me one day later that week. I thought he might quiz me about my conversation with the magistrate, but instead, he informed me that my father had started to "make some noise."

I wasn't exactly sure how to interpret the word "noise."

"Really?" I asked. "Does he know where I am?" Even if he didn't know, he must have decided he could no longer stay quiet—ignoring what I had been pressured to tell him by phone nearly three weeks earlier.

The interrogator answered my question with an order: "His noise is not helpful for you. Call him. Don't tell him where you are. Say you're fine and he should remain quiet."

I reflected for a moment on this latest command. My *bâzju* was noticeably irritated. On the one hand, my father's actions might hurt me if my captors decided not to release me in order to demonstrate that they were impervious to outside pressures. On the other hand, media attention, if that's what my father was drumming up, could compel them to free me sooner—that is, if they even admitted to having me in custody.

In any case, my interrogator was telling me to lie once again.

The women I had met over the previous several days had defied *their* interrogators' demands to lie, while I had abided by many orders that were in conflict with my conscience. It may have been late for me to start resisting, but if those women could do it, why couldn't I?

"No," I told Javan meekly.

"What did you say?" he asked.

"No," I repeated, a little louder.

"Why not?" The pitch of his voice had become higher than usual.

"Because," I said, straightening up in my chair, "I don't want to lie anymore."

Javan fell silent. Several seconds went by. He must have been analyzing my unexpected act of noncompliance.

I heard a pen drop onto my desk, followed by the swoosh of a piece of paper. Then came the interrogator's voice, once again under control. "Write: 'I don't want to call my father,' and sign it."

I lifted my blindfold, picked up the pen, and wrote: *I don't want to call my father unless I am allowed to tell him the truth.* Then I signed it.

Javan took the paper and read it. Without another word to me, he instructed a guard to return me to my cell.

You seem very distressed," Nargess remarked.

Vida and Sara had fallen asleep, while I had lain awake, tracing a stain on the ceiling as I thought about the day's events.

I looked at Nargess. She was cradling the Koran in her lap as she often did. Since she had joined our cell, she had begun to appear healthier. Her eyes were no longer puffy from crying, and she had regained some of the weight she had lost in solitary confinement.

"Sit here," Nargess said, patting a folded blanket beside her.

I crawled onto it, and she took my hands in hers.

"Think of me as your sister," she said, gazing into my eyes. "If you want, you can tell me what's bothering you. You can trust me."

So I told her. I told her about my false confession and my desire to recant it, but not to my interrogator. I also implored her not to tell any of this to anyone, fearing that if Haj Agha found out, he might have me killed as he had vowed.

"I don't know what to do," I said to Nargess in a muted voice. "If I tell the truth, I may never be released. But if the only way I can go free is to lie, then freedom has little value. I now know that I was very weak, especially after meeting women like you."

Nargess blushed. "I am glad I didn't succumb to these people's threats to tell lies," she said softly. "Regardless of what they might do to me now, my soul will be at peace." She rubbed my palms gently. "I will pray to God to help you."

Then she released my hands, tenderly ran her fingers across the Koran, and asked, "Do you want me to do an *estekhâre* for you?"

Estekhâre, I had learned years before, was a Muslim tradition of divining answers to questions, in this case, by consulting the Koran. The practice was fairly common in Iran, where many people turned to fortune-tellers for answers to their personal and financial questions and problems.

I had largely regarded fortune-telling as superstitious, but now I was willing to search for clues to my fate through almost any means.

"You know how to do *estekhâre*?" I asked Nargess.

She nodded solemnly.

"OK, please do," I said.

She closed her eyes and wrapped her fingers around the top edge of the Koran. "Look into your heart, and specify your intention or wish," she whispered.

I immediately made two: that no one would ever be harmed because of the falsehoods I had told in this prison and that I would be freed within the week. Then I told Nargess I was ready.

She uttered some incomprehensible verses, opened the Koran without looking, and read the page before her. She shook her head and shut the book delicately. Then she glanced up at me and said, "You made two wishes."

I was astounded. "How did you know?"

Nargess smiled as if the answer to my question was obvious. "The Koran said so," she said. "Make another wish—this time, only one."

I paused, deliberating over whether instead of making a wish, I should ask a question. "May I pose a question instead?" I asked Nargess.

"Sure."

I raised myself to the balls of my feet and hugged my knees. A minute or two passed as a multitude of possible questions rattled around in my head. My entire dilemma, I realized, rested on whether I should let my lies persist or put a stop to them while I was still in jail. In short, should I risk my freedom to pursue the truth?

"I'm ready," I whispered.

She recited some more verses, opened the Koran again, ran her eyes over the page on the left side, and read the last sentence to herself. She nodded slowly, as if turning over the words in her mind, then reread it.

Finally, she looked up and said with conviction: "Do it. Even if you suffer, in the end you will prevail."

Those were not the words I had wanted to hear. I had wanted Nargess to say something like, "Stick to your story until you are free."

Yet I knew in my heart that what she told me was right—painfully but beautifully right.

Tears started to roll down my cheeks as I realized that I had given up the truth on account of fear of man and fear of death. Yes, I wanted to live, but what kind of life was worth living? The one in which I would have a clear conscience; the one in which I did what I thought was right—even under pressure. At last, I understood that I *had* to tell the truth—even if it cost me my freedom, even if it cost me my life.

Sara had started to look rather sickly. As the days passed that week, she still hadn't received permission to make her phone call. She seemed determined, however, to persevere with her hunger strike until her wish was granted.

Sara was headstrong in other ways, too. She refused to walk around the prison yard, despite the fact that the twenty- to thirty-minute sessions four times a week were our only chance to go outside. The yard was insulting, Sara declared, and it existed only so that prison officials could announce to the world they were humane enough to give us an opportunity for outdoor exercise.

She didn't have the energy to walk, anyway. After she had stopped eating, she spent all day lying on her blankets, watching TV from two feet away, straining her nearsighted eyes because her interrogators had confiscated her glasses.

The more weight Sara lost, the more disgusted at our captors I became. A simple phone call to her family, which should have been every detainee's right, was a privilege that Sara was prepared to starve herself to obtain.

Yet the weaker she grew, the stronger her resolve to continue became, as if she was deriving fortitude from this act of resistance.

As I witnessed Sara's hunger strike, I mulled over starting something similar. Unlike Sara, my goal wasn't to gain permission to call my family, although I had recently requested that from my interrogator. Instead, I wanted to punish myself for having yielded to my captors' demands. I brushed aside the thought that this frame of mind was unhealthy, and the day after Sara began fasting, I, too, decided to stop eating.

I wasn't actually starting a "strike," so I didn't formally announce my intention to the guards as Sara had. I simply began to decline my meals. The guards noticed, of course, but did not attempt to change my mind.

Because I had never thought about how to try to live without food, I decided to follow Sara's daily regime of three cups of tea and three dates, which my father had once told me were the most nourishing food to have if you were ever stranded in the desert with nothing else to eat.

My initial three days were the most difficult. First my stomach growled wildly, demanding to know why I was withholding its nutrition. Then it began to ache, pleading with me to soothe it. By the fourth day, Saturday, it had begun to adjust to its deprivations and, except for an occasional grumble, had resigned itself to quietly awaiting its unknown future.

I looked away whenever Nargess and Vida ate their meals, but I couldn't escape the aroma, which made me fantasize about the home-cooked Iranian food I used to eat, the last time on Christmas Eve on my trip to Qom. I had spent that night at the home of a man I had met at a seminary just that morning. He, his wife, and their three children lived in a middle-class neighborhood down the street from the local mosque. The family had treated me with traditional Iranian hospitality: a tour of the town followed by a dinner of *qorme sabzi*—a popular stew of greens, meat, and beans served over rice— and fresh baklava from a nearby bakery for dessert. Like many Iranian housewives, my hostess was a superb cook. She had had plenty of practice in the kitchen since her marriage at age thirteen, the same age as her youngest daughter.

"I wish I had lived an independent life like you," the woman had told me that night, as she rolled out a thin mattress for me on the Persian carpet next to her three girls. "I'm only thirty-eight, but I feel old."

She hoped her daughters would have more options than she did. One aspired to be a dentist; another, a physician; and the third, an engineer.

The family had dropped me off at the train station the next day, after making me promise to return someday to travel with them to their small cottage in the north of Iran, where we would pick the most succulent wild berries. Just the thought now made my mouth water.

Nargess flung herself on the floor, crying, "Thank God! Thank God!"

She had just come back that Saturday, March 7, from court, where she had wept before her magistrate, swearing that she was not a spy and had never done anything even remotely political. In between sobs, she had explained with heartfelt sincerity how she had gone on pilgrimages to Mecca *x* number of times and made donations to *y* mosque, and how could such a devout Muslim ever be a spy?

The magistrate had decided, as he had once before, to release Nargess on bail, and she had been permitted to call her family for the first time since her arrest several weeks earlier. The court would hold on to the deed to her home until her trial, whenever that might take place—

if ever—giving it the power to keep her under constant threat of re-arrest, the same situation faced by my former cellmates who had been freed on bail. But for now, none of this was important to Nargess.

The magistrate was an understanding and fair man, she main-tained, much more decent than her chief interrogator, who hadn't wanted to release her. When I asked her to describe the magistrate's appearance, she said his right hand was embellished with two large rings.

Saturday was a good day for Sara, too. Her interrogator had al-lowed her to call her parents, but only after she broke her strike with a meal and only if she told them she was fine. She did as directed, then tried to comfort her grieving mother by making up the prediction that she would be released in a couple of weeks. Despite these fibs, Sara was happy to have spoken to her parents, and she returned to our cell with an exultant grin.

I tried to share in my cellmates' joy but couldn't. For them, free-dom seemed within reach. But for me, there was only uncertainty.

I was starting to fall apart. My nerves had become raw from lack of food and nothing but silence from my interrogator. My lower lip quivered, and a lump grew in my throat. The last thing I wanted to do was spoil my cellmates' high spirits, so I pressed the black button by our door and waited as Glasses, the guard who had been on duty the night of my arrest, appeared.

Once in the bathroom, I shut the door. I leaned my back against the wall, buried my face in my hands, and released my tears—tears of helplessness, of guilt, of a profound longing for my family. I tried to muffle my weeping by pulling my shirt over my mouth, but after a few seconds, I couldn't hold back anymore. I cried and cried and cried. My reservoir of tears, which had released only a few trickles during my five weeks in prison, now came pouring out. With each sob, my pent-up anxiety, fear, and fury came gushing down my cheeks, finally giving expression to my anguish.

"The sound of your crying is pealing throughout the corridor," I heard a woman snap at me. I lifted my head. Glasses had opened the bathroom door and was leaning in, glaring down at me from behind her thick lenses. "People here already have enough to be sad about without hearing your sobbing."

"Sorry," I said, not bothering to dry my tears. "I didn't want to cry in front of my cellmates."

Glasses scrunched her lips to one side of her broad, white face and stared pensively at me for a moment, as if pondering what to do with the mess she had been unfortunate to encounter on her shift.

I was waiting for her to bark at me for breaking down. But instead, she said softly, "If you're going to cry, at least do it in the next room."

The next room was the size of one cell, where two big potted plants, a large trash bin, and a water fountain sat on a dirty tiled floor. That was where my fellow prisoners and I were allowed to fill our plastic water bottles and throw out our garbage—tasks we often competed over to break the monotony of our daily lives. Whenever we could, we would delay returning to our cells for a few extra seconds to press our noses into the green leaves and inhale deeply, taking in a pure form of life that, contrary to our bleak surroundings, would help sustain and never harm us.

I straightened up and let Glasses lead me. Here, too, she stood in the doorway, watching as I squatted down and resumed my crying, heedless of her presence.

After a minute or two, she asked, "What's wrong?"

I used my sleeve to wipe my nose and looked up at her. "Do some prisoners stay here for years?" I asked, struggling to get the words out.

She hesitated, then said, "Not usually, but sometimes."

This reply set off a new round of bawling.

"Why doesn't my interrogator let me tell my parents where I am?" I sniffled.

She cocked her head to one side. "He *must*."

"He *hasn't*."

Glasses dropped her gaze from me to her slippers, as if she didn't know what to say. She almost seemed sympathetic.

She let me sit there for a few more minutes, until my eyes dried.

Wake up," Skinny told me the following morning. "You're going to court."

It was Sunday, March 8, the day that Haj Agha had said I would be sent to the magistrate's office, where, if I wanted to be freed, I should repeat my confession and agree to everything the magistrate said.

I tried to hurry as I splashed water on my face and put on my chador, but I was dragging after more than four days of having eaten virtually nothing.

"I'll pray for you," Nargess said, as Skinny led me out the door.

A male guard loaded me into a van, where he handcuffed me to a young woman prisoner I hadn't seen before. My wrists had become so small that I could have easily wriggled free. Two male prisoners sat in front of us, also shackled together.

"Don't speak to one another," the guard ordered from the passenger seat, before we headed out the prison gate and toward the Revolutionary Court.

"Please give me the strength to tell the truth," I murmured to myself with my eyes closed, "whatever the result might be."

The guard began to say something to me, but the driver, who must have glimpsed at me in his rearview mirror, interrupted him and said, "Let her be. She's not talking to anyone. She's praying."

With my free hand, I drew my chador over my face and continued, whispering over and over, "Please give me the strength to tell the truth, whatever the result might be."

When we arrived at the court about thirty minutes later, the guard unlocked our handcuffs and led us to the second floor. As we neared the Security Division, a balding man approached me.

"Miss Saberi?" he asked.

"Yes?" I said, stunned that anyone other than the guards and officials would recognize me.

"I'm your attorney, Abdolsamad Khorramshahi."

This was news to me. I had never seen or heard of him. Perhaps Javan had cunningly appointed a regime attorney for me—if this man was even an attorney. With his outdated suit, stooped shoulders, and stubble on his chin, the only thing that gave him the aura of a lawyer was his leather briefcase.

My guard admonished the man for talking to me and took the other woman prisoner and me into the magistrate's office. She and I sat in the first row of chairs in front of the magistrate's desk. Khorramshahi followed and sat down a few rows behind us.

The magistrate greeted him warmly enough and remarked that he was surprised to have heard he was representing me. "Don't you usually cover social cases instead of political ones?" the magistrate called out.

I glanced back at Khorramshahi, who was just smiling politely. Then I resumed my prayer.

"Please help me tell the truth today," I whispered. " 'Even if you may suffer, in the end you will prevail.' "

"What are you praying?" the magistrate asked, evidently having noticed the movement of my lips.

"Something in English," I said quietly.

"What is it?"

"I was saying, 'Please help me tell the truth today.' "

He gave me a puzzled look, then began to leaf through a file on his desk.

For the next half hour or so, I waited as the magistrate interrogated my fellow prisoner by having her write down answers to his written questions. Through the few words they exchanged, I gathered that the woman had been in solitary confinement for twenty days and was charged with propaganda against Islam. After the questions finished, the magistrate told her she would be freed on bail that day. She thanked him, and the guard took her to sit in the hallway.

It was my turn.

The magistrate asked me why I had once spoken to the Japanese ambassador to Tehran at a dinner party, why I had traveled to Lebanon, and why I had tried to assist my jailed acquaintance—all questions repeated from my interrogations five weeks earlier. He also wanted to know why I had interviewed various political figures in Iran. I explained that I was writing a book and that these people were among the approximately sixty Iranians I had interviewed to try to depict for foreigners a balanced and colorful view of Iranian society.

The magistrate also asked whether I had had any classified documents, and I answered that as far as I was aware, I never did.

After I wrote each answer, he would read it, then write down a new question on another sheet and hand it to me. At one point, the magistrate interrupted himself.

"How is the state of Ohio?" he asked, without altering his tone.

He was looking at me with what appeared to be complete earnestness.

"I hear it's a beautiful place," I said. "It borders the Great Lakes."

The magistrate nodded and began to write his next question. Then, without shifting his gaze to me, he asked, "Could you get me a visa?"

I had no way of telling whether he was joking.

"Sure, if you set me free," I said, only to see what his response might be.

"That's what we're working on today," he replied, as he passed the next sheet to me.

So I really was supposed to be released soon. He had asked me about a deed for bail last time, and now he was talking about my freedom. He had set Nargess free, and he seemed more believable and powerful than Haj Agha and Javan. *Should I still recant?* I asked myself, as I read the next question: *Who was Mr. D, and what was your connection to him?*

I sat motionless for a moment, my pen hovering inches above the paper. If I wrote the truth, I could remain locked up for years. But if I continued to cooperate as Haj Agha and Javan had instructed, I would be freed.

In sum: Truth = Prison. Lies = Freedom.

CHAPTER FIFTEEN

I took a deep breath and exhaled slowly.

Then I pressed my pen to the paper and wrote:

> *Neither Mr. D nor anyone else has asked me to gather informa-*
> *tion for them. I have never done so, and I have never received any*
> *money to do so. What I said in my interrogation about Mr. D was*
> *false because whenever I told my interrogators the truth—that I*
> *was not a spy and was simply writing a book about Iran, and that*
> *this was a personal project not funded by any individual, institu-*
> *tion, or government—they told me they didn't believe me and that*
> *I wasn't cooperating.*

I paused to gather my thoughts. Although I was simply trying to tell the truth, I still feared criticizing my interrogators too harshly or mentioning their threats against my life and the lives of my family. After all, the agents worked with the magistrate and whoever else was making the decisions.

> *I deduced from my interrogators' words that I would not be freed*
> *unless I told this false story. But now I would rather tell the*
> *truth and risk staying in prison than win my release by telling*
> *lies. Mr. D is innocent, and I am not a spy.*

I handed my paper to the magistrate. He read my answer without expression. Then he lifted his eyes, peered into mine, and asked, "Why should I believe this?"

"I made up that story based on the questions my interrogators asked me," I explained. "Out of fear, I agreed to state those lies. But I regret it."

Tears had begun to run down my cheeks. Without speaking, the magistrate held out a tissue box, as if he was used to dealing with distraught prisoners. I took a tissue, wiped my face, and steadied myself.

"The last time I saw you," I continued, "I got the feeling that the truth was important to you. God knows what I'm telling you now is the truth."

The magistrate was still staring at me, his thumb rotating his two hefty rings. "But *I* don't know what God knows," he remarked.

I smiled faintly. "That's all right. It's enough for me that *I* know that God knows."

The magistrate gave me a slow nod, but I couldn't tell what he was thinking. Then he picked up his phone, dialed a number, and told whoever had answered, "She's changing her story now." He hung up, turned toward me, and carried on with his questions.

Finally, at what felt like midafternoon, the questions ended. They must have taken at least three or four hours.

Only after the interrogation was complete did the magistrate allow me to speak to Khorramshahi for a few minutes.

"Who found you for me?" I asked the lawyer with suspicion.

"Bahman," he said in a low, guarded voice. "One of your mutual friends recommended me to him."

I still didn't know whether to trust this man, and it was disquieting to have heard he didn't usually cover political cases, but when he told me to sign a form retaining him as my lawyer, I did as he said. I didn't want to lose what might be my only opportunity to get an attorney.

I told Khorramshahi I had just recanted a false confession about spying that I had made under duress and that my captors had videotaped me making many untrue statements. He seemed a bit hard of hearing, so I raised my voice and repeated everything. I then asked him to go to my apartment, find the deed (even if I wouldn't be freed on bail any time soon), and take out the garbage. "You can get the keys from Bahman," I added.

"*Shhh!*" he hissed. "Don't say his name loudly here."

I couldn't discern whether Khorramshahi meant that talking about Bahman would put Bahman, me, or the lawyer himself in danger, even though my interrogators already knew about the two of us.

"It's time for you to go," the magistrate said, motioning at the guard to take me away.

"Please tell my parents where I am," I told Khorramshahi before getting up.

"They know. They know," he assured me.

The guard led me to the hallway and sat me down next to the other woman detainee. She and I were to wait here for the two male prisoners who had come to court with us. The guard again ordered us not to speak to each other, then positioned himself on a chair a few seats away.

"What crime are you accused of?" the woman whispered.

I glanced at the guard. He had busied himself with talking to another guard.

"Spying," I replied.

The woman's eyes bulged.

"Are you Roxana?" asked another woman in civilian clothes who had sat down beside us. The detainee introduced her as her sister.

"How do you know me?" I asked, astonished.

"You're all over Voice of America Persian TV," she replied, smiling broadly.

On the way back to Evin, the detainee's sister joined us in the van. Oddly, the guard handcuffed me to her. She offered me a cracker from her bag, and I accepted. Now that I had recanted, I had decided to eat again. It was the most delicious snack I had ever tasted.

Looking out the window, I took in scenes I had been too unsettled to notice on my way to court. Pedestrians were scurrying along the streets and weaving through lines of slow-moving traffic. Many were carrying shopping bags, full of what I assumed were gifts and new outfits for the upcoming New Year's holidays. Nowruz, the Iranian New Year, was on March 21—less than two weeks away.

The touch of warm fingers drew my attention back to the van. It was the fettered hand of the detainee's sister, who had reached out to grasp mine.

"Don't worry," she whispered to me, her eyes straight ahead. "By Nowruz, you will be free. We promise you. We feel it." She repeated this several times, with a knowing smile upon her lips.

The way my handcuff was angled, it was cutting into my wrist, carving a red dent into my flesh. But the young woman's firm grip and uplifting words, though hard to believe, were like an anesthetic numbing me to any pain. She kept clutching my hand, our palms wet with sweat, until we reached Evin.

When I arrived at my cell, I felt much lighter. I had no idea whether retracting my confession that day meant I would be stuck in jail for many years, but I no longer cared. My parents knew where I was, and the media were covering my story, which made my execution highly unlikely. Plus, my interrogators could never expect me to spy for them now. And most important, I had told the truth at last. Though still incarcerated, I now felt liberated, as if I had transformed into the sparrow's shadow and finally set myself free.

My cellmates sensed my happiness without my saying a word. As soon as I shed my chador, they stood up and one by one, embraced me.

I didn't know why I had been given my own clothes, but they felt good against my skin. Haj Khanom had led me into the corridor that evening, handed me a large garbage bag containing my jeans, T-shirt, *roopoosh*, and white headscarf, and told me to get dressed.

She gave no reason for this, but I had obeyed. I had learned that if the guards didn't inform us of our destinations, it was an exercise in futility to ask.

Javan was waiting for me outside the women's ward. He led me to a Peykan and told me to get in. Then we set off, with another car following closely behind.

The streets of the city blurred past me. To my surprise, we were driving toward Sadr Highway, the freeway leading to my neighborhood.

"Where are we going?" I asked.

"We're taking you home so you can give us the cash you have left from Mr. D."

I broke into a cold sweat. Apparently Javan had not yet learned of my recantation. If he found out, he might try to convince the magistrate, who had possibly believed me, that my confession was not false but true. So I sat wordlessly until we pulled into my alley, which was once again deserted.

As Javan and I stepped out of the Peykan, three men I recognized, including Tasbihi and the Mailman, descended from the second car. This was none other than the gang that had ransacked my apartment on the day of my arrest.

Javan handed me my keys and told me to open the door to the building. He didn't warn me to act naturally in case we came upon any neighbors. For some reason, just like the last time, no one was in sight—not even Gholam, the building caretaker.

Shoes of all sizes were strewn in front of the unit next to mine. My neighbors must have been having one of their big family gettogethers. Laughter and children's chatter leaked into the hallway. I pictured the look of fright on their faces if they happened to open the door and see me standing there with four plainclothes agents. I snickered wryly to myself, amazed that I had become used to the presence of such men.

My apartment had never looked so welcoming. It also appeared that someone had been here since my arrest. The notepads and books in my living room had been neatly stacked, and there was no smell of tuna.

"Find us the money and the rest of those documents you told us you got from the Center for Strategic Research," Javan ordered.

I had thought he already had all those papers from their first raid. *So he had been bluffing.*

It took a few minutes to gather them because they were scattered throughout my closet. I looked at each one as I handed them to my *bâzju*. I saw that none was marked as classified.

"Give me the one on the U.S. war in Iraq," he said.

I had thought he had that one, too. When I found it, I noticed that it was not marked as classified, either. "See, there's no classified stamp on it," I said joyfully, as I gave it to Javan. "It's not classified."

He glared at me and snatched it from my hands.

"But this is very good news!" I exclaimed. "It's just as I told you at the beginning, I don't have any classified files."

"Just give me the money you got from Mr. D," he said bitterly.

I opened the drawer to my desk and pulled out an envelope in which I had stored extra cash. Javan made me count it—just over $2,000. Then he took me to the living room, where his three associates were lounging on my furniture. He placed a pen and a sheaf of paper on the counter separating the living room from the kitchen.

"Write the following," he said. "'This $2,100 is what is remaining of the $15,000 I received from Mr. D for the information I collected for him.'"

I hesitated. I had been hoping to get out of this mess without having to tell Javan I had withdrawn my ridiculous confession just hours earlier. I still feared his wrath.

I picked up the pen and started writing: *This $2,100 is what is remaining of the $15,000 I received from* . . . I couldn't do this. I set down the pen, looked down, and crossed my arms.

"What happened, Miss Saberi?" my *bâzju* asked, his eyes digging into me.

I opened my mouth. Then I closed it again. I licked my lips and said softly, "I can't write that."

"Why not?"

Courage is the first step to victory, whispered a voice within me.

I propped my arms on the counter and slowly raised my head to look at him.

"Because it's not true. Mr. D never asked me to do anything for him and never gave me any money, and I never gave him any information. It was all a lie. I am not a spy. And I told all of this to the magistrate today."

Javan tried to cover his shock with a shaky laugh. The other agents were staring at us, dumbfounded.

"Why did you tell a lie?" Javan asked.

"Because when I told you the truth—that I was just writing a book on my own—you said you didn't believe me and that I wasn't 'cooperating.' You pressured me to lie and promised me freedom only if I acted according to your demands."

"So why are you telling the truth now?" he asked.

"Because the Koran told me if you tell the truth, you may suffer, but in the end you will prevail."

A stony silence fell over the room. A few seconds passed until the silence was broken by the squealing of the children next door.

Javan began to grin. I had never seen his mouth open wider than necessary to speak, sneer, or grimace.

"We knew from the very beginning that it was a lie," he declared.

His words struck me like a blow to the stomach, and I had to take a step back from the counter. Javan was essentially telling me that my captors had known all along I wasn't a spy. And yet they had coerced me into making an appalling false confession, forced me to repeat it four times on camera, and perpetuated it while locking me up for more than five weeks.

And then I, too, started to smile. I smiled because I finally realized what a ludicrous game these people had been playing with me from the start.

"I have decided," I announced, "that I would rather die than be released based on these lies."

Javan's grin instantly receded. He extended the pen toward me and said, "Then write that down: You are ready to be executed."

"I refuse to write that," I said emphatically.

He tittered, as if I was embarrassing him—the star interrogator—in front of his colleagues. I was no longer going to be the "OK, whatever-you-say girl." Finally, I had drawn the line.

"Fine then," he said, having regained his characteristic steadiness. "Then write that your entire confession was a lie."

"OK," I replied, "I will." I tore off the sheet of paper, ripped it up, and turned to a new page.

The story about Mr. D was false, I wrote, then for the first time mentioned that I had been coerced. *I made it up under pressure because my interrogators had told me it was the only way I would be freed.* I also explained that I had been told I had classified documents, but it was now very clear I did not.

I signed the paper and handed it to Javan.

He read it, then said darkly: "Don't think that the world will care if you stay in jail. There's so much other news for them to cover. You're not even worthy of a tiny paragraph in the newspaper."

I kept quiet, not wanting to dignify his spiteful remark with a response. The other three men stood up to leave. I asked them if I could bring back to Evin a photo of my family, a little Iranian money, and a few books. They agreed, as long as they found the books acceptable. So I picked out two thick volumes of *The Story of Civilization* by Will Durant, my Bible, and the Koran in English.

In the car on the way back to Evin, I reflected on Javan's words: "We knew from the very beginning that it was a lie."

I wondered how often my captors and their colleagues deliberately made false accusations against other prisoners, too. Maybe they were not really paranoid but only pretended to be in order to support their spurious allegations against people like me.

And if the authorities had known I wasn't a spy, why did they detain me in the first place?

My captors had told me they knew I was leaving the country soon, and they may have wanted a return on the money and energy they had invested in monitoring me all these years. They had also seemed to resent the fact that I had interviewed numerous Iranians for a book I had been hoping to publish overseas, out of their censoring range. But instead of simply warning me not to write it, they had extracted a false confession they could someday use to pressure me to spy for them. They could also use my confession to reinforce their claim that America had planted spies throughout Iran and to bolster their argument for more restrictions on society in the name of protecting national security. In addition, my captors could use my detention to solidify their support among anti-American hard-liners and to scare other dual nationals, writers, and journalists in Iran, as well as Iranians advocating better relations with the West.

The more I considered these various possibilities, the more I believed that what I had witnessed over the previous several weeks boiled down to an issue of power: Certain people in power were exploiting that power to suppress individuals who they feared were threatening it.

Call your parents," a man commanded me, "and tell them you're fine."

Early that morning, I had been instructed to put on my chador to go to court again. I was surprised to hear I was returning there so soon, just one day after I had recanted. Blindfolded, I had been led downstairs, where a man whose voice I didn't recognize gave me my cell phone.

"Inform your parents you are going to court today and that you'll be freed in two to three days," he was telling me. "Say nothing more."

This was hard to believe. Would my captors really free me after I had retracted my false confession?

I lifted my blindfold to dial my parents' number.

My father answered. "Roxana, are you OK?"

"Yeah, Dad, I'm OK," I said. "They told me to tell you I'm going to be taken to court today and that I'm supposed to be freed in two to three days." Then, without heeding the guard's order, I added, "But I'm not sure if that's true."

"But we also heard that you will be freed soon."

"Really?" I still couldn't believe this news. "I'm not sure about that, Dad. I made some statements during my interrogation that were not true, but yesterday I finally told the truth. Dad, if you ever see or hear anything, even if it's from my own mouth, don't believe it, OK?"

I hoped he understood I was referring to my videotaped false confession. I knew my captors wouldn't like what I was saying, but this no longer concerned me.

"OK," he said. "But don't worry. We are doing as much as we can to help you, and the State Department has called for your release."

"The State Department?" I hadn't realized my case had reached that level. It was comforting to know I had such support, but I also hated to think that my detention may have created new tensions between the two countries when the possibility of rapprochement had been looking more likely.

"Are they torturing you there, Roxana?"

"No, but it's very . . ." I tried to think of the appropriate words: ". . . spiritually and psychologically challenging."

The guard was gesturing at me to hang up.

"I have to go, Dad."

"Roxana, just remember: They can never hurt your soul."

"You're right, Dad," I said, choking up. "I love you all. Don't worry about me. I'll be fine."

As soon as I handed my cell phone to the guard, he demanded to know why I hadn't followed his instructions.

"I only told my father the truth," I replied.

"*Hmmph*," he said. "In any case, your interrogator and Haj Agha said they apologized that it took so long for you to be freed, but they did their best."

I nodded. *So I truly was going to be freed?*

The guard led me to a van outside Section 209, where several male prisoners were waiting. None of them was handcuffed, and this time, for the first time, neither was I.

The weather had become a little warmer, and the guard in the passenger seat let us crack open the windows when we got onto the highway. A polluted wind blew against my face, making me squint.

M y chador made a squeaking sound as I sank into a plastic-covered seat. The guard had brought me to the Security Division at court, but instead of going to the magistrate's office, I had been dropped off in a spacious room on the right. There, I had stood before a man sitting alone behind a desk, stroking his graying beard.

Without speaking, he had motioned at me to sit on one of the many cushioned chairs encircling the room. They smelled stale and looked old, even though they were still wrapped in plastic, as if they had just come from the store. I had picked one as far as possible from the desk, figuring I should observe the personal space of a male official in the Islamic Republic.

The bearded man had begun paging through some papers when a younger, slender man with a dark beard entered, took a seat just in front of the desk, and shot a stinging glance at me with his beady eyes.

Then, without any introduction, the older man started grilling me about where I had grown up, why I had come to Iran, whom I had reported for while in Iran, why I had "a tendency to write antiregime reports" (though he didn't give me any examples), and several questions about the book I was writing.

I answered, although I couldn't comprehend what my lawyer was for when he was absent for yet another interrogation. The list of questions continued for some minutes until the older man brought up the tale of Mr. D.

My confession about Mr. D was false, I explained, adding that I had been told I had to make it in order to be freed.

The younger man raised one eyebrow, then spoke for the first time. "Why are you changing your story now?" he asked in a challenging voice.

"Because I later realized how harmful the implications of my false confession could be," I explained. "It could hurt U.S.-Iran relations, other dual nationals, or journalists like me."

"Are you willing to take a lie-detector test?" he asked.

"Yes, please!" I said, ecstatic to hear this might be an option. "I have been ready since day one."

He laughed hollowly.

"Well," the older man began, "I was going to free you, but I decided not to anymore."

"Why not?"

"Because last night, your lawyer did two interviews with the media," he replied casually. "Lawyers always complicate things. They make statements to publicize themselves."

"I don't know whether Mr. Khorramshahi did interviews," I said, "but even if he did, why should I be punished for it?"

He ignored my question and continued, "Did you speak to him yesterday when you were with Mr. Sobhani?"

Sobhani must have been the magistrate. "Yes," I said.

"I knew it," the older man gloated, then announced, "I haven't decided yet how long I will keep you in prison—maybe a few months, maybe one or two years."

I was confused. That morning I had been told I was going to be freed, and now I was hearing just the opposite. But whoever this man was, he seemed to be more influential than anyone else I had encountered during my imprisonment. And if the size of his office was any indication of his position, he must have been higher ranking than Sobhani.

"Whenever I decide to free you," he went on, "I probably won't let you leave the country for a while, until the media frenzy over your case has died down."

I knew that if he kept me in Iran, the Intelligence Ministry could continue to monitor and intimidate me. Still, being out of prison and prohibited from going abroad would be better than sitting behind bars.

Then the younger man spoke up again. "Are you ready to go on camera to criticize the U.S.?"

I winced.

"She wouldn't agree to that," the man behind the desk said dryly. "She's an *American*."

"I am an American *and* an Iranian," I pointed out. "I love both countries."

The younger man scoffed at this remark and made a grandiose gesture at his colleague. "Don't you know who this man is?"

I had never seen him before, I replied.

"This is Mr. *Haddad*," he said proudly.

"Sorry," I said, "I haven't heard of you."

The younger man continued, admiringly, "Mr. Haddad is the man whom university students like to criticize for jailing their classmates."

Haddad shrugged, as if this accomplishment was all in a day's work. "Miss Saberi probably never had anything to do with these things."

"You're right," I said. "I didn't. So are you Mr. Sobhani's superior?"

"Yes, you could say that," Haddad replied, puffing up his chest a little. "Anyway, we're all somehow connected." Then he abruptly added, "Now leave."

"Wait," I said. I didn't want to go before telling Haddad what I was thinking. "You and your colleagues seem bothered that I was writing a book, but I was trying to make it as balanced as possible. I was discussing both the opportunities and the challenges in Iranian society. There is no country in the world that has only opportunities and no challenges. If I had written about Iran like that, outsiders wouldn't believe it. You may think my research and reporting are reason enough to keep me in jail, but what I said here today was the complete truth."

Haddad listened calmly, but when he began speaking, a cloud passed over his face: "Why is it that the U.S. has Guantánamo Bay and Abu Ghraib, yet when we imprison an American woman for one month, the world cries out, 'violation of human rights'?"

By referring to these places, Haddad seemed to be taking his resentment against America out on me. Iran and other Muslim countries had been particularly outraged by graphic reports of U.S. soldiers abusing detainees at Iraq's Abu Ghraib prison in 2004. Tehran often brought up these reports, as well as allegations of torture at the American detention camp at Guantánamo Bay, when it accused Washington of hypocrisy.

"And why is it," he went on, "that America intervenes in other countries' internal affairs? Why does America oppress so many people and nations—which always happen to be Muslim?"

"I don't agree with everything the U.S. government does," I said. "But I am not responsible for America's policies or actions. I have nothing to do with them."

Haddad pressed his lips into a tight line. Instead of responding, he returned to the papers on his desk and again told me to leave.

I felt there was nothing more I could say to these men. The only way I could have changed their minds about me was to change their minds about America, and that was impossible.

As the van took us back to Evin, my fellow prisoners joked with one another. It was clear that they were all going to be released. But my hopes, which I had cautiously allowed to rise that morning, were now shattered.

Free, not free; free, not free; free, and now, according to what the seemingly influential Haddad had told me, not free—possibly for two years.

B ack in my cell, I told my cellmates about my encounter with Haddad. Sara had heard of him and his assistant, Heidarifard, who was likely the younger man in the office that day. She explained that both were radical hard-liners. Haddad was Tehran's deputy prosecutor for security affairs. He worked under Saeed Mortazavi, the infamous hard-line prosecutor general of Tehran, who was said to get his orders from the supreme leader. Human-rights activists criticized Mortazavi for imprisoning many activists, students, and bloggers, and they accused him of involvement in the death of journalist Zahra Kazemi, a charge he denied.

Mortazavi, I had heard, was also known as the Torturer of Tehran and the Butcher of the Press.

CHAPTER SIXTEEN

A bearded man handed me a sheet of paper and told me to sign it. It was hard for me to make sense of, so Braces read it aloud. It went something like, *You, Roxana Saberi, will be freed on 5 billion rials bail.*

I wasn't sure I had understood and asked her to read it again. It was the day after I had met Haddad, and she had brought me to the ground floor of Section 209, into this man's office.

Braces reread the paper for me, confirming what I thought she had said.

"Really?" I asked her.

"Yes," she replied, her teeth sparkling as she grinned.

It was impossible for me to decipher what was going on behind the scenes and outside this prison. But this time I was not only being told I would be freed. I was also being asked to *sign a form* officially notifying me of my impending release.

I would have to give the court a deed to property worth 5 billion rials, or around $500,000. My father's apartment wasn't worth that much, but maybe the court would agree to reduce my bail.

I signed the paper quickly. I couldn't wait to tell my cellmates.

In my cell once more, I had not yet removed my chador when Braces again appeared at the door. I had a meeting with my attorney to discuss my bail, she informed me. "But tell him," she added, as she escorted me out of the women's ward, "that it has been raised to 10 billion rials."

I struggled to keep track of the zeros as I calculated the amount in dollars in my head. "That's around one million dollars!" I exclaimed. I had never heard of such a high bail in Iran. Neither had Braces.

Khorramshahi was waiting for me when a male guard took me to a small building just inside the prison gate and into a room filled with several cubicles, where lawyers were meeting with their clients. I sat down across from Khorramshahi at a small, white table.

"Have you gone to my home to get my deed yet?" I asked him.

He shook his head.

"Why not?"

He hunched toward me and said in a barely audible voice, "The authorities might monitor me."

My shoulders wilted. If my lawyer was too afraid to pick up my deed, who would?

"But now I really need you to get it for me," I said, then described what had transpired that morning. Khorramshahi agreed to see if the court would accept only the deed to my apartment as bail, although I would have to wait a few days while he traveled out of town to meet with another client.

The guard soon informed us my time was up. I asked for Khorramshahi's cell phone number, but he didn't have a pen and had to borrow one from a lawyer in the booth behind us.

"By the way," I said, as I was leaving, "I met Mr. Haddad yesterday."

"You did?"

"Yeah, and he told me he was going to keep me in jail because you had done media interviews about me."

"But I didn't do any interviews," Khorramshahi said, looking befuddled.

If that was the case, Haddad had been lying to me. It was a good thing I wouldn't have to deal with him anymore because I was going to get out of here soon.

To celebrate my impending freedom, I decided to attempt to beautify myself. After all, I was to be freed by the next week, the start of the Nowruz holidays, thirteen days of joy that Iranians traditionally spent visiting relatives and friends. To prepare for the festivities, they often cleaned their homes from top to bottom and flocked to barber shops and beauty salons. I had caught a glimpse of myself in a mirror in the courthouse elevator earlier that week and noticed that I had sprouted a monobrow.

Although I didn't care if I even grew a beard in this odious place, I realized if I didn't make it to a beauty salon before the holidays, I would look pretty hairy for the New Year. The guards prohibited tweezers, but Sara had filched a piece of black thread a few days earlier, when Haj Khanom had given her a needle and some thread to patch a hole in her prison uniform. Now Sara unwrapped it from a folded tissue and got to work. As she used the thread to deftly grasp and rip out the hairs between my eyebrows, I hardly felt any pain—unlike the first time I had experienced threading, just after I had moved to Iran.

Back then, I hadn't paid much attention to my facial hair, and although nature had bestowed less upon me than upon the average Iranian woman, my Iranian girlfriends told me I had to do something about it. They had taken me to a local beauty salon, where I had entered a different realm of Iranian society. In that male-free zone, women were able to take off their hejab and relax as they transformed their appearances through haircuts, manicures, pedicures, waxing, cosmetic makeovers, and threading.

My beautician had bent over me and attacked me with her heavy string, stinging my face so badly that my eyes watered. As I dried my tears, she had laughed and tried to console me with a popular saying among Iranian women, *Bekosh o khoshgel-am kon*, "Kill me, but make me beautiful." Beautiful for their husbands, beautiful for parties behind closed doors where women often removed their hejab, and beautiful for passersby whose eyes fell upon their uncovered faces.

After two or three minutes, Sara sat back, inspected my brow, and said with a satisfied smile, "You're all finished."

I asked the Koran about your release," Nargess whispered to me that evening, with the Koran lying open before her as usual.

"And?" I asked, crouching down next to her.

"It said you will be freed in more than a month but less than a year."

That was impossible, I told her, because I was to be released on bail within the next few days.

"No," Nargess countered. "The Koran says more than a month but less than a year."

I thanked her but fell asleep that night wishing her prophecy would be trumped by that of the two sisters who had earlier predicted I would be released by Nowruz.

Vida, Sara, and I peeked out the barred window in our door to catch sight of Nargess dressed in her own clothes and headscarf, winking good-bye at us. It was Wednesday, March 11, and she was going home.

"Remember," she had told me before leaving, "I will always be your sister."

The next day, Vida was unexpectedly and suddenly removed from our cell. Sara and I were left to debate whether she had been freed or transferred to the regular prison, where she might meet other relatives of MKO members.

The two of us tried to keep ourselves occupied over the next few days by exercising in our cell and watching TV shows I had never wanted to see when I was free, such as police serials, violent movies, and *The Prophet Joseph*. When we were lucky, IRIB would broadcast the South Korean series *Jumong*, whose pretty protagonist and archer-prince had become the latest TV hit among Iranians. European soccer matches and reruns of *Dr. Quinn, Medicine Woman* were on after midnight, so we stayed up for them, then slept until noon. This schedule had the added benefit of shortening the longest and worst period of the day: the time between waking up to find ourselves still trapped in Evin, and nightfall.

To keep our minds from wasting away from so much TV, we also passed hours discussing politics, economics, and Iranian society. Sara represented a new generation of young, educated Iranian women who had been exposed to a broad range of ideas. In recent years, women had come to make up around 65 percent of Iran's university entrants. Women's-rights activists found this trend encouraging, but some conservatives deemed it disruptive to society, and under Ahmadinejad, the government began imposing gender quotas on university entrants.

Critics claimed the quotas were largely motivated by a fear that educated women would make greater political, social, and economic demands than uneducated women and therefore, be harder to control. They also argued that gender quotas at universities intensified the discrimination women already faced in other areas.

Iranian women generally enjoyed more rights—such as the freedom to drive, own businesses, and keep their own names at marriage—than many of their counterparts elsewhere in the Middle East. They held some political positions, raced cars competitively, and worked as firefighters. Nonetheless, the regime's interpretations of Islamic law helped to limit other rights. For example, a woman was entitled to only half the inheritance that a man could get, and her testimony in court had half the weight of a man's. A man could have up to four wives, and men could obtain a divorce much more easily than could women. A grassroots campaign had been endeavoring to collect one million signatures to push for changing such laws, even though the authorities had threatened and imprisoned many of its volunteers.

Sara told me her fiancé fully supported her continued studies and would hate to have her stay at home doing housework all day. As she spoke about him, she squeezed her blankets against her chest, as if she were embracing him.

I thought Sara might be released soon. She had already agreed to her interrogator's demand that once freed, she limit her activities as a student activist. She wasn't a student leader, anyway, and her captors didn't consider her much of a catch. They were probably only waiting for her wound to disappear so that she wouldn't return to classes with evidence of their skirmish. The gash had begun to heal nicely, first turning green, then yellow, and now subsiding.

A distant thumping sound, as if someone was getting beaten, was reaching our cell.

Sara scrambled to her feet, turned down the volume on the TV, and pressed her ear to the window in our door.

"Do you hear that?" she whispered to me.

A man was crying out, somewhere beyond the women's ward, "I'm not a spy! I'm not a spy! I won't confess!"

Sara whirled around. The cut on her left cheekbone had again become inflamed.

"That's my fiancé!" she cried. "I recognize his voice!"

Her eyes bolted around the cell until they fell upon an aluminum can of juice. She emptied the contents into the sink and twisted the can, tearing it in half. Then she lightly scraped the sharp edge against one of her wrists.

"What are you doing?" I exclaimed.

Sara said she was prepared to slit her wrist, if that's what it took to get her interrogator's permission to see her fiancé. She asked a guard on duty to talk to her interrogator about this. Several minutes passed, and no answer came.

"I know it was my dear," Sara kept uttering to herself, as she rocked back and forth, clutching her blankets, "I know it was."

As evening fell, she became withdrawn, and her eyes grew vacant as she stared at the TV. By bedtime, she had resigned herself to waiting. That night, she moaned her fiancé's name again and again in her sleep.

Sara didn't have to wait long. The following day, Monday, March 16, she was allowed to see her fiancé. She was relieved to discover that he had not been the one whose cries we had heard through our door, although we both pitied the unfortunate soul who had been suffering. The whole episode made me thankful that at least Bahman, too, was not in jail, though I feared my captors may have harassed him in other ways.

Meanwhile, I was starting to get nervous about my own situation. The last workday before the Iranian New Year would be in two days, and the court would then close for several days. If Khorramshahi didn't deliver my deed by then, I would be spending my holidays in Evin.

On Wednesday morning, Sara was taken to court, while a guard we prisoners had named Cheeks, for her chubby face, informed me that I had another meeting with my attorney. She accompanied me to the building where I had met Khorramshahi the previous time and slid into the seat beside me, across the table from him. She must have been assigned to monitor our conversation.

Khorramshahi greeted me, then told me the Swiss Embassy, which represented U.S. interests in Iran, had been asking for consular access to see me in Evin, but the Iranian authorities had not yet granted the request.

I couldn't see why the Swiss would want to visit me here when I was on the verge of going home.

"Have you picked up the deed from my apartment yet?" I asked Khorramshahi.

"No," he said.

He still must have been too scared to go there.

Khorramshahi lowered his eyes and said, "I'm under a lot of pressure, a *lot* of pressure."

I waited for him to elaborate, but he didn't, perhaps because Cheeks was listening to our every word. I was beginning to think that despite what seemed like his good intentions and kind disposition, my lawyer was too intimidated to fully act in my interests. The court or Intelligence Ministry must have been threatening him somehow.

"By the way," Khorramshahi continued, "I asked the magistrate about reducing your bail, but he said your file hasn't been returned to him yet."

"I don't get it," I said. "I have already signed a form that allows me to be released on bail."

Khorramshahi wrinkled his forehead. "You did?"

"Yes," I replied, growing impatient. "I told you that last time."

I felt my anger bubbling beneath the surface. "If these people don't free me soon, it is to punish me for recanting my confession, and I will go on a hunger strike," I declared.

"No, no," Khorramshahi said, shaking his head. "You mustn't do that."

I gave him a prickly stare.

"By the way," he went on, "what's the charge against you?"

"Don't you know yet?" I asked, astounded.

"I haven't been able to see your file."

Actually, I wasn't sure of the formal charge against me, either. The only time I had been informed of any charges was on my second day of imprisonment, and back then, I was accused of acting against national security.

"They say I'm a spy," I said.

He lifted his shoulders. "What's the most they'd give you for spying, anyway? One year?"

I was alarmed that my lawyer didn't seem to know that espionage could carry the death penalty.

"But I can't stay here one more month, let alone a year," I protested. "I'm innocent. Why should I have even been imprisoned in the first place?"

"You must continue to have hope," Khorramshahi chided me. "I have a client who has been here for several years, and still, each time I see her, she tells me, 'Mr. Khorramshahi, you must always have hope.'"

"That's easy for you to say," I lashed back. "You are free. I am in prison!"

Cheeks told me I had to go. I had wanted to discuss my case with

Khorramshahi, now that I had heard the disappointing news about my bail, but we had neither the time nor the privacy.

As I stood up to leave, Khorramshahi said, "Please keep eating."

"I'll think about it," I replied curtly.

You used to be so good-tempered," Cheeks said to me, as we walked outside, back to Section 209. "What happened to you?"

"Wouldn't you be angry if one day you were told you're free, and the next day you were told, 'Well, maybe not'?" I retorted.

"Well, yes," she conceded. "But you must eat."

I didn't feel like responding and looked up at the sky. It was an unusually clear day in Tehran—unlike those days so polluted that schools would be canceled and my all-women's gym wouldn't allow people to run on the treadmills, warning it was hazardous to their health.

I could even see the Alborz Mountains. I had spent many days hiking and picnicking with friends in the parks that dotted those slopes, and I had also gone downhill skiing at a popular resort about an hour away. Over the Nowruz holidays, those mountains would be swarming with families and young men and women, packing every patch of green space available. But I, it seemed, would be spending my Iranian New Year in a prison cell.

"Where did you sign the form for bail that you mentioned?" Cheeks asked.

I told her about the bearded man on the ground floor of 209. She said she knew who he was, an official named Mr. Jaffari, so I asked if I could see him, and she agreed.

When I told Jaffari that my lawyer had no news about my bail, he looked baffled. He picked up his phone and began speaking in a hushed tone to someone on the other end. After a minute or two, he hung up and told me he had just checked with a colleague at the Revolutionary Court.

"The magistrate wanted to free you on bail," Jaffari explained, "but Mr. Haddad reversed the decision."

Cheeks said something to me on our way back to the women's ward, but I was too disheartened to listen. I just wanted to talk to Sara. She seemed to understand how things worked here, and I needed to ask what she thought all this meant. Now that I was no longer going to be freed on bail, what would happen to me?

My cell was empty. Sara and her belongings were gone. A plastic plate with a few pieces of rice lay in the garbage can under the sink. Sara must have been released.

I sat against one wall and began to thump my head lightly on it, as if this would untangle the web of thoughts that my mind was furiously spinning.

I assumed there was a good chance my case would go to trial, where Haddad had said he might have me sentenced to two years. But most other detained dual nationals I had heard of had been freed without trials. Why couldn't I, too, have been released on bail? My captors must have been irate that I had frustrated their plans after initially agreeing to cooperate. In addition to no longer being able to force me to spy for them, they couldn't broadcast the video of my false confession with any credibility, now that I had retracted it to the authorities, to my lawyer, and implicitly, to my father. I couldn't help thinking that if I had waited to withdraw my confession until after my release, as some previous prisoners had done, I would most likely have been freed by now.

In any case, I wouldn't learn anything until after the Nowruz holidays, which, including the weekends, would last roughly two and a half weeks.

I wanted to pray, but I couldn't. *If God was just, where was His justice?* I was starting to question my pledge to myself to suffer any consequences of telling the truth.

Something shiny on the other side of the cell caught my eye. I crept across the room to find a glass bottle containing Sara's cold medication. I snatched up the container and stashed it in the plastic bag

I used to store my shampoo and toothpaste. Maybe the bottle would come in handy later, I thought. I didn't really want to kill myself, but I imagined bleeding just enough so I would still be alive when the guards would find me, realize the hassle of keeping me here, and set me free.

I turned on the television but lay still without watching it. A few tears dribbled down my cheeks. They itched, but I let them stay there.

The sky grew dark, and a faraway sound of fireworks began to reach my ears, reminding me that the day before had been Chahâr Shanbeh Suri. On the last Tuesday of the Iranian year, Iranians poured out of their homes to ignite fireworks and jump over small fires set in the streets and yards, a pre-Islamic, Zoroastrian ritual intended to bring good health in the coming year. Some folks must have been using up their leftover fireworks that evening.

People out there were living normal lives, but I could only sit in this rotten cell.

I curled my arm under my head and stared at the family photograph I had brought from home. My brother, who was twenty-five when this picture was taken in 2001, looked skinny. That was one year before he had joined the army in search of discipline and personal development, after he had dropped out of a master's degree program in physics. I wondered how he would have acted if he had been captured by the Taliban in Afghanistan. He probably would have been brave.

Jasper had spent a few years after college devouring books about great leaders in history, trying to learn from their strengths and weaknesses. He had become so conscientious about his own morality and ethics that when I gave him some computer software copied cheaply in Iran, where copyright laws didn't apply to foreign works, he had refused to accept it.

If Jasper saw me sulking here today, he would probably quote Confucius: "They sought to act virtuously, and they did so; and what was there for them to repine about?"

I drew myself up. I opened my Bible to the Gospel according to

Matthew and began desperately searching for any verses that could soothe me. Eventually I came to Jesus' Sermon on the Mount:

> So do not start worrying: 'Where will my food come from? Or my drink? Or my clothes?' . . . Instead, be concerned above everything else with the Kingdom of God and with what he requires of you, and he will provide you with all these other things.

I had read this passage before, back when I was free, but I had never reflected on what these words might mean for me.

I can *think* about tomorrow, but I don't need to *worry* about it. Instead, I must focus on what is required of me *today*: to remember God in whatever I do and to not allow the unjust or cruel to bother my mind or soul. I will stop longing for either the past or the world beyond these walls and promise myself not to cry again until the day I am released—whenever that might be—and then, I will cry tears of joy.

I heard the door to my cell creak open. I raised my head to see Haj Khanom.

"Get your things together," she said. "You're going to meet some new friends."

CHAPTER SEVENTEEN

I'm Mahvash," said a petite woman with graying hair and kind eyes, as she helped me with my blankets.

"And I'm Fariba," said another woman, who appeared to be in her midforties. She smiled and held out her hand.

Haj Khanom had dropped me off in a cell next to my previous one, which my former cellmate Vida had told me she had shared with two Baha'i women.

Mahvash and Fariba had often spotted me through the barred window in their door walking back and forth down the corridor, they told me, as I sat down on my blankets beside them. They had heard I was from America and wanted me to teach them some English. I readily agreed. If I was going to be cooped up in Evin, at least I could do something worthwhile for others.

My new cell looked as though its occupants had been living here for a while. The two women had built up a large supply of blankets, which were spread out like a carpet over half the floor. A row of books lined part of one wall, and a family photo was leaning against them. This cell, like my last one, had a television.

"How long have you two been here?" I asked.

The women exchanged glances, as if they had heard this question many times before.

"One year," Mahvash declared.

"Ten months," Fariba said.

I shuddered. And yet they were still smiling.

I had read that Baha'is in Iran had been persecuted and dis-

criminated against since their faith was founded by a man named
Bahá'u'lláh in nineteenth-century Persia. Critics around the world
accused the Islamic Republic of systematically violating the rights
of Baha'is, whom the regime considered heretics because according
to Islamic principles, Islam was the last revealed religion, and therefore, no religion after it was legitimate. Even so, Iranian officials often
denied that Baha'is and the country's other religious minorities were
treated unfairly or punished for their religious beliefs.

Mahvash told me she had been held in solitary confinement for six
months. Fariba, who was arrested on the same day as five Baha'i men,
was in solitary for four months. During that time, the seven Baha'is
had almost no contact with their families and, like many other prisoners in solitary, were allowed to read only the Koran. When Fariba and
Mahvash were finally placed in a cell together, they jabbered to each
other for forty-eight hours straight.

The seven Baha'is had been targeted because they were the members of a national-level body that tended to the needs of Iran's Baha'is
who, according to the community, numbered more than three hundred thousand.

After the Islamic Revolution, some Baha'i leaders had vanished or
were executed, and many Baha'is were attacked, arrested, and pressured to renounce their faith. Executions gradually halted, and the
number of imprisonments diminished, but Baha'is continued to be
barred from government posts and blocked or expelled from universities. The Baha'i community eventually set up its own unofficial
university, which Mahvash directed and where Fariba had earned a
degree in psychology.

"Considering you face so many limits in Iran, why didn't you just
leave the country?" I asked the two women, aware that many other
religious minorities had emigrated since the revolution. "You could've
easily been granted asylum."

"We love Iran and want to serve not only Baha'is here but also the
entire nation," Mahvash replied. Fariba agreed.

They and their five colleagues faced charges such as insulting religious sanctities and espionage for Israel, an allegation my cellmates said stemmed solely from the fact that their world headquarters was located there. These two charges could result in the death penalty.

Despite the gravity of these accusations, the prisoners had never been allowed to see their attorneys, Abdolfattah Soltani and Shirin Ebadi. I had read that Ebadi, a human-rights activist and Nobel Peace Prize winner, had received threats on her life for defending the group.

Far from posing a threat to the state, Mahvash told me, Iran's Baha'is were nonviolent and politically impartial, and they denied involvement in any subversive acts against the regime. The seven leaders had even agreed to their captors' demand to dissolve the national and local ad hoc Baha'i groups in Iran, but they remained imprisoned, along with nearly thirty other Baha'is throughout the country.

"We are willing to cooperate with the country's authorities," Mahvash said, "but we draw a line when it comes to our spiritual duty."

"For example," Fariba explained, "the regime doesn't want us to introduce our religion to others, but we feel it's our duty to share the tenets of our faith with those who are interested."

As the two women spoke, they began to prepare a salad. Fariba washed some carrots and cucumbers they had bought, and Mahvash started to peel them with a blunt knife. The women seemed so tranquil, as if they were making a salad in the comfort of their own kitchens.

"How can you two remain so calm here?" I asked.

"We believe it's natural for new religions such as ours to face challenges like this," Mahvash explained, without looking up from the cucumbers. "We are trying to turn this challenge into an opportunity."

"Opportunity?" I asked, surprised. "What opportunity?"

Mahvash raised her eyes and smiled at what must have been a perplexed look on my face.

"We trust in God to do what is best for our community," she said. "If He thinks we can serve our faith better by remaining here, we accept it."

"But if you leave everything up to God and fate," I said, "what room is left for a person's choice of action?"

Fariba shook her head. "We don't leave *everything* up to God," she said. "We choose what we do and say here, and these choices are very important. We always try to keep in mind the repercussions that our actions in prison might have for Baha'is throughout the world."

"In other words," Mahvash explained, "we do what we think is right. By doing so, we are taking one step toward God, and we believe He will then take ten steps toward us."

Her words reminded me of a famous saying in Farsi, *Az to harakat, az khodâ barakat*, which roughly meant "God helps those who help themselves."

"And what are *you* accused of?" Mahvash asked me, as she began to slice the carrots.

I explained, telling her and Fariba how I had retracted my false confession and how Haddad had decided to keep me imprisoned. When I was finished, they told me that even after sharing their cell with numerous other women, they had never heard of anything quite like it.

"Recanting took a lot of courage," Mahvash said, "even more than if you hadn't given a false confession to begin with."

"It means a lot to hear that," I said, grateful for her reassuring words.

She started to divide the salad into three plastic containers.

"Please don't serve me any," I told her.

"Why not?"

"Because I'm going on a hunger strike starting tonight."

The two women looked at each other and then at me. "Why?" they asked together.

"Because I'm angry that I'm stuck in prison for having told the truth."

"We generally don't believe in hunger strikes," Fariba said.

"And the court will be closed for days because of the holidays," Mahvash added, "so your strike won't have much influence on any officials, if that's what you're aiming for."

It would be better, they said, if I waited until the holidays were over, and then, if I was still determined, to begin. Their argument seemed rational, so I ate salad and dinner that night. My appetite was also whetted by the company of my two new friends.

I wasn't sure when or where Mahvash and Fariba expected to use their new English vocabulary, but over the next few days, I began teaching them phrases they would need to know in order to shop, cook, and travel, as well as expressions they didn't really need to know, like how to swear.

The women jotted down the new words with a pen their interrogator had given them after they had spent several months in prison. Haj Khanom warned she would confiscate this treasure if they used it to write anything other than vocabulary and to do crossword and Sudoku puzzles, which they found in the newspapers they received every few days. The guards usually gave them one of three papers: the hard-line *Keyhan*, the government-owned *Iran*, and less often, the moderate *Ettela'at*.

In addition to English classes, which became part of our daily routine, we exercised in our cell for two hours a day and read books. Sticking to a schedule made the time pass faster and helped us feel as if we were making the most of our situation.

At various times of day, my two cellmates would say their prayers, and I would say mine. At my request, they taught me a few Baha'i hymns, such as "Holy, Holy, the Lord our God, Lord of the angels and the spirit."

We were careful to sing softly, especially after I was scolded for singing "Silent Night" in the shower loudly enough for the male guards in the outer hallway to overhear me.[*]

I had never experienced the beauty of song as I did when my cellmates and I hummed these simple Baha'i hymns. It didn't matter that

---

[*] A woman's voice, according to some religious conservatives, is provocative and can arouse untoward sexual thoughts in men. In the Islamic Republic, a woman is usually not allowed to sing solos in public unless she performs for an all-female audience and is accompanied by an all-female band.

our voices were a bit off-key. When we sang together, I felt myself retreat temporarily from our grim environment to a place of inner peace.

A few days into this routine fell the Iranian New Year.

I had spent my previous Nowruz with Bahman and his mother in Iran's Kurdistan province; the one before that, with friends, also in Kurdistan; the one before that, in Tehran; the one before that, . . . It was now my seventh Nowruz in Iran, and my first in prison.

The celebration of Nowruz stretched back thousands of years. When Iran's revolutionaries came to power in 1979, some of them tried to stamp out pre-Islamic traditions such as Nowruz, which were seen as challenges to Islamicizing the country. In official documents, where possible, references to Iran were replaced with references to Islam, and allusions to the Persian Empire founded by Cyrus the Great in the sixth century B.C. largely disappeared from schoolbooks.

But many Iranians resisted such efforts to disregard Persian culture. Just as Mohammad Reza Shah and his father had alienated some Iranians by downplaying the Islamic aspect of their national identity, the Islamic regime began to realize that by slighting pre-Islamic Iranian culture, it would lose much of the national support it needed, especially during the Iran-Iraq War. To bolster national unity against the Iraqi invaders, regime leaders started to revive Iranian nationalism. They made sure, however, to link it to Shiite Islamic convictions and regime ideology.

Since 1980, in observation of the holiday, the supreme leader had given an annual speech to the nation on Nowruz. In the meantime, Nowruz rituals had remained important even among the most religious families. Following tradition, they set their tables with seven symbolic items starting with the Farsi letter *seen*, for example a *seeb*, or apple, representing elements sacred to ancient Zoroastrians, such as plants and water.

During the previous several days, Fariba and Mahvash had collected a few such objects—an apple they had bought, some greens that had sprouted from rotten carrots, and a few coins they had set aside. They placed these on a thin plastic cloth on the floor.

Next to the cloth they set a copy of the works of Hafez, the venerated fourteenth-century Persian poet. His *Divan* was found in the homes of many Iranians, who often used it to tell fortunes by reading randomly picked poems.

With only an hour or two left until the New Year, Mahvash and Fariba asked the *Divan* to predict their futures. One poem they read included these couplets:

> *One day the lost Joseph will return to Canaan, grieve not.*
> *The hut of sorrows will become a rose garden, grieve not.*
> *This grief-stricken heart will recover, do not worry.*
> *And this agitated mind will find its peace, grieve not.*

Just then, the door to our cell opened, and a woman in her thirties with disheveled, long, black hair lumbered in. She was hunched over with her eyes half closed, looking as if she might collapse at any instant.

We rushed to help our new cellmate with her blankets and delicately laid her down on them. Her name was Parisa,* she murmured, and she had been in solitary confinement since she and her brother were arrested a few days earlier. She hadn't eaten a thing the entire time.

We offered Parisa some fruit. She hesitated, then agreed. So we propped her up against the wall, and she began to eat—listlessly at first, but with every bite, a little more energetically. When she finished, she lay down again, raised her head on a folded blanket, and told us her story.

Parisa was an office assistant who, like my former cellmate Samira, had been a supporter of the We Exist movement, led by Channel One in Los Angeles. She had told the prison guards she had no appetite, but in reality, she had deliberately refrained from consuming anything except tea. As a result, her sugar levels, blood pressure, and pulse were spiraling out of control, exacerbating her diabetes.

Mahvash, Fariba, and I listened, then shared our stories with Parisa. I began to tell her who I was, but she said she already knew. She had seen my photograph in various reports on satellite TV, though she hadn't heard about the accusation of espionage. It seemed the Iranian authorities had not yet announced it. When I told her I had retracted a false confession about spying for the United States, her mouth fell open and she shook her head slowly.

"You should've waited to recant until after you were released," Parisa said. "They'll never free you now."

"Whatever happens," I told her, unshaken by her words, "I have begun to accept the consequences of my decision."

Our television had started to announce the countdown to the New Year. As festive music played from the TV set, we hugged and kissed one another. Then, to brighten our moods, we decided to tell some jokes.

Actually, I told the jokes, and the other three women listened. Ironically, I was the only one who seemed to know any, even though all my jokes were Iranian. Over the years, I had heard dozens of jokes about Iran's politics, nuclear energy, and gas rationing. Many of them also stereotyped the country's ethnic minorities and other people from areas outside Tehran. For example, Esfehanis were supposedly stingy and Azeris dull-witted, while Rashtis were said to allow their wives more freedom than did most Iranian men. Some Iranians justifiably found these kinds of jokes offensive, while others considered them part of the humor that was key to getting by in Iran.

I told a joke Bahman had once shared with me. It poked a little fun at Kurds, but I figured if a Kurd could tell it, so could I.

"How do you torture a Kurd?" I asked.

My cellmates raised their shoulders.

"Put him in a pair of tight jeans for two days."

They cracked up. Kurdish men often wore baggy pants as part of their traditional attire.

At my audience's request, I went on to the next joke.

"One day, three intelligence agents—one from America, another from Russia, and a third from Iran—entered a competition," I said. "The goal was to find a *khar* [donkey] and come back with it as quickly as possible. The first to return was the American agent, who presented a donkey to the judge with the words, 'Here you go. Here's a donkey.'

"A few hours later, the Russian agent arrived. 'Here you go,' he said to the judge. 'Here's a donkey.'

"After a few days, the Iranian agent showed up with a rabbit. 'Here you go,' he said. 'Here's a donkey.'

"The judge was confused. 'But that's a *khar-gush* [rabbit],' he said, 'not a *khar* [donkey].'

"'It certainly is a *khar*,' the Iranian agent argued. 'Just ask him what he is, and he'll tell you.'

"And indeed, when asked, the rabbit replied he was a donkey."

With this, my cellmates burst out laughing. "You're just like the rabbit, Roxana!" whooped one of them, slapping me on the back.

"Quiet down in here!" someone called from the doorway. It was Braces. She frowned at us, then slammed the door.

We must have appeared to be getting along too well, because early the next week, Mahvash and Fariba were transferred to another cell.

I woke up several times each night to feel Parisa's pulse and make sure she was still breathing.

She had stopped eating again, and she was becoming more and more feeble. The guards hardly checked in on her, and I sensed they relied on me to tell them if she seemed on the brink of death.

One day I joined her at the dispensary, where the doctor expressed alarm at her deteriorating condition and said he would schedule an off-site hospital visit. Compared to Parisa, my health concerns were insignificant, but I shared them with the doctor anyway. I had menstruated three of the past five weeks, my heart had begun to palpitate violently a few times a day since my hyperventilation episode in solitary, and my skin had broken out in a rash from my synthetic prison-issue sweatshirt. After listening to my complaints, the doctor offered pills for my irregular periods, told me to read the Koran to calm my heart, and decided that my skin had to heal naturally.

I then asked if he would permit me to get dental floss, a hairbrush to replace the flimsy plastic comb the guards gave to prisoners, and a soft blanket to cushion my sore tailbone. The doctor said the first two items were banned in 209, and as for the third, inmates simply had to get used to the cement floor.

The next day, the prison authorities took Parisa to a hospital outside Evin. While there, she fainted and had to be brought back in a wheelchair.

Parisa relished the fact that she was creating a headache for her captors. She even hid her medication under her tongue when the guards brought it to her twice a day, then spat it out once they left. She wasn't concerned about her health, she told me. She would rather die than stay locked up in Evin.

When Parisa grew too frail to walk down the corridor to the dispensary, the doctor had to come to our cell to examine her. Another day, she received a visit from a man our guards told us was the director of the detention center. He told Parisa to start eating. She said she would try and then asked if she could call her parents.

I took the opportunity to inquire if I, too, could call home. A few days earlier, I had asked Haj Khanom to pass this request on to my interrogator, but she said he had gone on a trip for the holidays and couldn't be reached. The director said he would think about our requests and get back to us soon.

The following day, Tuesday, March 24, Parisa was allowed to call her mother after agreeing to eat a few bites of food, and I was taken by a male agent to call my parents, this time from a phone in a hallway. My hand shook as I raised my blindfold and dialed my parents' number. I knew I would have at most a couple of minutes to speak to them, and I had to spit out everything I wanted to say before the agent would make me hang up.

My father answered.

"Dad," I said, speaking in Farsi as the agent had directed, "I don't have much time. Please, just listen."

I explained how the deputy prosecutor had decided not to free me and how he had warned that I might have to stay in prison for up to two years. I wasn't sure if I would be put on trial, I told my father, but I wanted a second lawyer. My father suggested Mohammad Dadkhah, whose name sounded familiar. I agreed.

Then I announced I was beginning to lose hope and was thinking of starting a hunger strike.

As soon as I spoke these words, I saw the agent's shoulders tense in his reflection on the telephone's glass panel.

"Never mind what those people are telling you," my father said, trying to console me. "We're trying everything we can to get you out of prison. Please don't go on a hunger strike. It can be very dangerous for your health."

The agent had raised his hand over the hang-up button and was angrily gesturing at me to say good-bye.

"Dad, I have to go now," I said quickly. "I love you."

"Why did you tell him you want to go on a hunger strike?" the man fumed as he led me back to the women's ward. "Your case is already politically sensitive. You will only make matters worse."

Parisa's captors apparently didn't want a dead diabetic on their hands. They decided to free her at the end of March, after the prison doctor gave her a checkup in front of them and she had failed the exam with flying colors. As a condition of her release, she agreed, as Samira had, to sign a statement promising to never again take part in any We Exist activities. However, her brother, who was also a supporter of the group, had to remain behind bars.

After Parisa left, I was hoping to get another cellmate, but Haj Khanom said that depended on my interrogator, who was still out of town. Perhaps he had taken his family to Persepolis, the ceremonial capital of ancient Persia's Achaemenian Empire. The site in southwestern Iran was a popular destination for many Iranians, even the most conservative.

These days on my own were much easier than my first two weeks in solitary confinement. Not only did my parents now know where I was, but also I had my books, and I was finding words within them that were helping me put my circumstances into perspective. For example, when reading Will Durant, certain passages took on a special meaning for me, such as one about Girolamo Savonarola, a fifteenth-century Italian priest. While his destruction of precious manuscripts and Renaissance art was deplorable, his experience in captivity struck a chord with me:

> Savonarola, high-strung and exhausted, soon collapsed under torture, and gave whatever replies were suggested to him. Recovering, he retracted the confession; tortured again, he yielded again. After three ordeals his spirit broke, and he signed a confused confession. . . .

Alongside Will Durant, I reread *Man's Search for Meaning*, a Farsi copy of which Fariba had left with me. Since reading this book in college, I had forgotten what Viktor Frankl, a Holocaust survivor, had written about "the last of the human freedoms"—the ability to "choose one's attitude in any given set of circumstances . . ." Some of my former cellmates had exercised this ability by refusing to be robbed of their dignity, morality, and inner freedom, despite their difficult conditions. The women I most admired had used the adversities they faced for their own improvement while setting examples for others, both in and out of prison.

I was also calmer this time in solitary because I realized that with the country more or less shut down for the holidays, I could do nothing to alter my situation. I was still intent on starting my hunger strike after the holidays, but only if I became certain that my case would be going to trial. It felt good to have a plan.

The sound of several women clapping and whistling from what seemed like somewhere fairly close by caught my attention one early afternoon.

The cheering became louder and louder, taking me back to one night nearly two years earlier, when I attended a friend's wedding reception on the outskirts of Tehran. The location was so inconspicuous that the two women who had come with me drove past the building twice before we could find it. From the street, we couldn't hear any music, and all we could see was an old warehouse. But when we passed through the gates, pulled off the sweatpants we had worn under our dresses, and walked into the building, we entered another world. A live band was playing Iranian music, and unlike another friend's wedding I had attended where the genders were kept apart, here dozens of sweaty men and women were exuberantly dancing together under colorful, flickering lights. I joined them when the band started playing a song I liked.

All of a sudden, the music stopped. The guests looked at the band, puzzled, but when they followed the musicians' eyes toward the door, they understood: Three plainclothesmen had entered.

Then chaos broke out.

"Women, put on your hejab!" word rippled through the crowd. The female guests began a high-heeled stampede toward the cloakroom, where most of us had turned in our hejab. The woman working behind the counter hurriedly handed me my *roopoosh*, while the bride's mother cried out, "I can't find my headscarf!" Another woman had an extra one and gave it to her.

The three uninvited guests, it turned out, had come to break up the party, which they deemed un-Islamic. At least, I thought to myself, no alcohol had been served.

By the time I came out of the cloakroom, the hosts had drawn a thick curtain across the hall. The women were on one side, the men on the other. Peering through a hole in the curtain, one guest reported that the musicians had packed up their equipment and disappeared. So had the two wedding video cameramen. Minutes passed. No one knew what might happen next. If we were unlucky, we would be detained and given lashings, as one of my friends had after she was caught at a mixed-gender dance party.

A little girl started crying. Her mother cuddled her and said, "It's OK, *azizam*, it's just a game."

All at once, a woman started singing. Another began clapping. The clapping spread as the bride stood up and began to dance. The Islamic regime could control these women's lives in public, but they were not going to let it ruin their party.

About an hour later, the plainclothesmen left. We presumed the hosts had paid them off. The women removed their hejab again, the curtain was pulled to the side, and the festivities recommenced.

Whate's the cheering about?" I asked Skinny when she opened my door to give me lunch.

"It's the women from the regular prison," she said. "They've been allowed to gather in their yard today to celebrate the holidays."

I took the food from her. "Are they dancing out there?"

"I don't know," Skinny replied. "Do you know how to dance Iranian style?"

"Yes," I said, recalling my many attempts to imitate my girlfriends' moves on the dance floor, "but I'm not very good."

D uring these days, the guards would linger a little longer at my door when they brought me meals.

In all, there were six women guards in Section 209. My cellmates and I had nicknamed them Haj Khanom, Skinny, Braces, Glasses, Grumpy, and Cheeks. They worked twenty-four-hour shifts every other day. That way, three women were usually on duty most of the time.

Sometimes the guards asked about my family, and I asked about theirs, but they divulged little personal information—not even their own names, as if they had been instructed against it.

All I had learned about their private lives was that Braces had trained in the martial arts, and although she looked younger than I, she had a son in his twenties. Skinny, at twenty-six, was the youngest of the six, planned to quit her job in a year, and like many Iranians, had had a nose job.

Haj Khanom had studied at a *howzeh*, or religious seminary. Having worked at Evin for more than a decade, she was the veteran among her colleagues. She was always the most likely to treat inmates as ordinary human beings, the only guard who would guide blindfolded prisoners by the hand instead of tugging at our chadors or grabbing our arms. And when my lips grew so chapped that they bled when I opened my mouth to eat, Haj Khanom sold me some foreign-made lip balm. She wouldn't, however, fulfill my requests for deodorant, a T-shirt, and a bra, all of which, she told me, were forbidden in 209.

From what I had witnessed, the other guards were usually civil but not always kind to prisoners. On one occasion, I heard a guard rail at a woman who had been crying uncontrollably after months in solitary confinement. On another, a guard berated one of my former cellmates for rinsing her hair on an off–shower day. (We were allowed to shower and wash our clothes by hand on three specific days of the week.)

For the most part, however, the guards were not rude to me. Maybe they saw me more as a foreigner than as an Iranian, and many Iranians were inclined to treat foreigners as guests.

Still, the guards seemed to think that I, along with the rest of the detainees, was guilty of some crime. If we weren't, why would we be in prison?

A few of them seemed to enjoy their position of authority, such as the power to open and close our cell doors at will and being our only route to the world beyond our cells. For anything we wanted, from a phone call to a visit to the bathroom or the doctor, we had to go through them first. The guards also liked to take advantage of our short exercise periods in the yard to search every nook and cranny of our cells for prohibited pens or notes we may have taken. They frequently conducted body searches and, at any time of day or night, peeked through the peepholes in our doors, to the point that we sensed their presence whether or not they were watching us.

Perhaps by reigning over us, the guards believed they were serving God, Islam, and the regime. I guessed that they, like the interrogators, came from a religiously conservative, lower-middle-class background, or they wouldn't be working in a place like Evin. None of the women wore makeup or nail polish, at least not to work. They must have prayed regularly because they were never available during prayer time, and they wouldn't allow even one lock of hair to peep out of their hejab.

The women likely felt lucky to have found an occupation with a steady income and plenty of job security. And even though I despised the profession they had chosen, I certainly didn't hate them.

The walls of my cell were to be repainted, presumably to cover the etchings left behind by former inmates, to prevent them from passing on words of solace or guidance that could help new prisoners when they needed it most.

So after I had spent four days alone, Skinny was moving me into another cell in a corridor that she said had previously housed male prisoners.

To my joy, there I was reunited with Fariba and Mahvash. Fariba left to scrub the filthy bathroom, which the male inmates evidently had seldom cleaned, while Mahvash and I hugged each other with delight. She had heard from Haj Khanom that my interrogator was furious to discover I had been placed with the two Baha'is without his permission, but for some reason, he was letting us get back together. From this news, I gathered that Javan had returned from vacation. It was early April, the Nowruz holidays had just ended, and the country was now back at work.

Mahvash showed me a recent newspaper article she had saved. It stated that a U.S. official had handed a letter to an Iranian diplomat in The Hague on the sidelines of a major conference on Afghanistan. The letter requested Tehran's intercession in a few individuals' cases that were of interest to America. The report was so vague that Mahvash and I couldn't figure out who these individuals were, though I guessed the list might include Iranian-American student Esha Momeni, who had been released from Evin but was barred from leaving Iran; retired FBI agent Robert Levinson, missing since his visit to Iran in 2007 . . . and maybe even me.

The encounter between the American and Iranian officials was a rare diplomatic exchange for the two countries, although it seemed to be in line with reports I had been seeing lately on IRIB that suggested a thawing of tensions between Washington and Tehran. President Obama had sent a goodwill message to the people and government of Iran for Nowruz, and various Iranian officials were hinting at the possibility of better relations with the United States. I couldn't help but wonder how this might affect my situation, if at all.

I woke up on Monday, April 6, with the taste of french fries in my mouth. In prison, we had never been served this Western delicacy, but the night before, I had dreamed of them. I had entered a large room full of my high-school classmates and walked past them toward the far end, where I spotted my parents sitting at a round table with their backs to me. They must have heard me coming because they turned their heads, saw me, and smiled. Then, without a word, they offered me a plate of fries. I put a few in my mouth and chewed. They were delicious, crispy on the outside and soft on the inside, warm and fresh with a pinch of salt.

"Your parents are going to do something for you," Mahvash said, after I described my dream to her. Fariba nodded in agreement.

The two women were in good spirits that morning, just as they were every Monday around this time. On this day of the week, their families were allowed to visit them, usually from behind a glass window, but on rare occasions, face-to-face. After breakfast, Glasses came to fetch them. They stepped out of the cell, looking back at me guiltily, as if it was their fault I couldn't share in their pleasure of weekly family visits because I had no family members in Iran (though I could have seen Bahman had we had a temporary marriage).

"I'm OK," I told them, smiling encouragingly. "Have a good time."

I was reading a book when, a half hour later, one of the guards opened the cell door and instructed me to get dressed for a meeting.

"With whom?" I asked, surprised.

"I don't know," she replied.

I assumed it was with my lawyer again. Once dressed, I was loaded into a car. This time, however, instead of being driven to the right, in the direction of the building where I had last met Khorramshahi, I was taken to the left, toward another building in the prison compound. A male guard led me inside and down a flight of stairs to the basement. There I spotted Mahvash, Fariba, and five men in prison uniforms, presumably their Baha'i colleagues. I realized they must have just finished their family visitation, and I was in the building set aside for such visits. My two cellmates raised their eyebrows at me.

"I don't know why I'm here," I mouthed.

The guard guided me past them and into a large hall where

prisoners were sitting with their families at round plastic tables that looked like cheap patio furniture. We walked past them to the far end of the hall, where Tasbihi was waiting for me, one hand grasping his prayer beads, the other, the knob of a closed door behind him.

His face expressionless, he twisted the knob and pushed the door open.

There, in the middle of a small room, stood my mother and father.

CHAPTER EIGHTEEN

For a few moments, I couldn't move.

The first words that left my mouth were, "You came all this way to see me?"

And the first thought that raced through my mind was, *What if the authorities harm my parents?*

They rushed forward and wrapped their arms around me. I wanted them to never let go.

"I'm so sorry," I said, my voice muffled by their clothes as I tried to hold back tears. "I caused so much trouble for you."

"It's not your fault, Roxana," my father said tenderly.

"We had to come because we're the only ones allowed to see you," my mother added, as she planted a wet kiss on my cheek.

Tasbihi told us to sit down on a couch. My parents sat on either side of me and took my hands in theirs. The agent positioned himself across from us and ordered us to speak loudly. As far as I knew, Tasbihi didn't understand English, so I assumed our voices were being recorded by a device that must have been hidden, perhaps under the coffee table in front of us.

"What's your name?" my father asked Tasbihi courteously.

"It's not important," came the curt reply. *Poor Dad*, I thought, as I caressed his hand. He didn't know that these types of people never introduced themselves by name, and if they did, they used pseudonyms. My father had made only four short trips to this country over the past few decades, and I presumed he wasn't completely familiar with the ways of the Islamic Republic. At least he knew not to wear a tie, seen by the regime as a symbol of the Western decadence of the shah's era.

My mother was dressed in a long, shapeless, dark jacket. Her graying bangs jutted out of her purple headscarf. She looked as foreign to hejab as she must have felt here. I had always wanted my mother to visit me in Iran but certainly never under these circumstances. She had consistently made excuses for not coming—Tehran had too much pollution, too much traffic . . . Now, deprived of North Dakota's clean air, she must have been suffering from headaches, and her allergies were probably acting up.

"After your last phone call, we decided to come," my mother explained. My father said they had been distressed by the tone of my voice and my threat to go on a hunger strike.

"Speak up," Tasbihi interjected.

My father, whose voice was naturally soft, strained to speak a little louder. He explained how he and my mother had landed in Tehran two nights earlier. Bahman had picked them up at the airport. I tried to picture this scene—my boyfriend and my parents meeting for the first time, brought together by my imprisonment.

Bahman had taken my mother and father to my apartment, where they were now staying, and my widowed neighbor had been keeping them company and cooking their meals.

"Are you sure you'll be OK here?" I asked my father, hinting at my concern for my parents' safety.

"The Iranian ambassador to the UN has ensured our well-being," he replied.

These words soothed me. It made sense that the regime wouldn't allow my parents to be detained or killed in one of those mysterious car accidents in Iran, now that my case had gained a measure of international attention.

"How long do you plan to stay?" I asked them.

"Until you are freed," my father said, cupping his hands over mine. My mother added that she had been granted leave from work for several weeks and that Jasper had decided to put off his wedding until I was released.

"But that might not happen for a long time," I explained. "I'm not even sure if I'm supposed to be freed on bail or put on trial."

My parents didn't know either, and neither did Khorramshahi.

"Speak louder," Tasbihi reminded us.

"If I do go on trial," I said, raising my volume a notch, "I need to talk to the lawyer first. My file contains certain things that are not true. I made some false statements under pressure, and I have to speak to him about it."

My parents nodded. Then I asked if they had found a second lawyer for me.

"No," my father replied. "Mr. Khorramshahi objects."

"What?" I asked. "Why?"

"He says he can't work with anyone else," my father explained.

"And we went to his office and saw that he has many news articles about his work posted on the wall," my mother added. "He has represented a lot of important cases. He's also a nice man."

I knew he was nice, I told my mother, but I needed more than nice. I needed someone who had more experience with cases like mine.

My parents began telling me about steps that people around the world were taking to push for my release. Along with the U.S. government and Swiss Embassy, the Japanese Embassy had become involved. The Committee to Protect Journalists had collected more than ten thousand signatures over one weekend on a Facebook petition that was sent to President Ahmadinejad through the Iranian mission to the United Nations. North Dakota's governor and congressional delegation had been speaking out on my behalf, some local churches were including prayers for me in their services, and many friends were raising awareness about my story in the media.

"People in many countries are behind you, Roxana," my mother said.

I felt amazed, humbled, and a little embarrassed that so many people were going through such efforts on my behalf. Yet I also felt somewhat detached from these events. They were taking place so far away that they seemed much less real than my surroundings.

Tasbihi interrupted to inform us our time was up and I would have to return to my cell.

I still had much to say. "Please bring me some books from my apartment: *Plutarch's Lives*, Gandhi, my French-English dictionary," I rattled off, thinking of books that my captors would allow. "If you can, buy one of those Tolstoy novels in English—the longer the better—and bring that, too.

"And tell Bahman," I continued, "that I miss him. But I want him to go on with his work, and I don't want to be an obstacle to his goals."

My father leaned over and whispered to me it would be better not to talk about Bahman here, but my mother mentioned he was waiting outside Evin with Khorramshahi. Both had wanted to come in; the prison officials had refused. She also told me that several weeks earlier, Khorramshahi had come to Evin looking for me, and he was told I wasn't here.

"Time to go, Miss Saberi," Tasbihi said impatiently, standing up.

My father hugged me, and I found his ear perfectly positioned for me to whisper what I didn't want the agent to hear. "I was pressured to lie in a video about spying for the U.S.," I told him.

"I know," he whispered back. Khorramshahi had already informed him.

"We plan to come here every Monday," my mother said, as Tasbihi led me out of the room.

My parents flashed reassuring smiles at me, but beneath those smiles I saw anxiety and sorrow.

I waved back at them, then followed Tasbihi into the large hall. I had thought I wouldn't see my parents for a long while. At one time, I wasn't sure if I would ever see them again. But for some reason, when I returned to my cell, I felt an emptiness that hadn't existed just minutes earlier.

M y father broke the news to me when I was allowed to call him on Thursday: I was to go on trial the next week for espionage. So this was what I got for telling the truth.

I hadn't even spoken to Khorramshahi about my file yet, I reminded my father. He told me not to worry, that my lawyer would ask for a postponement.

Iran's conservative judiciary, I knew, was headed by Ayatollah Mahmoud Hashemi Shahroudi, an Iraqi-born Shiite cleric who had been appointed by the supreme leader. I had read that Shahroudi had pushed for a few judicial reforms, but hard-liners like Tehran prosecutor Mortazavi and his deputy Haddad were working under him. Maybe Shahroudi didn't have much control over them. In any case, I had no doubt my trial would be closed and without a jury.

I began to pray for a fair judge. It was my only hope.

K horramshahi was crouching over a far table, taking notes from a thick dossier, when I saw him at court that Sunday, April 12.

He looked up, smiled, and greeted me. We sat down on two chairs, with my guard standing beside us listening. Khorramshahi told me he had been reading my file. It was the first time he had been allowed to see it. "Your trial is set for tomorrow," he informed me. "But I will request a delay."

"Good," I said, "because most of that file is lies, and I need time to discuss it with you."

Then I told him I would like to get a second lawyer, reasoning that two could be more effective than one.

Khorramshahi's face tightened. "If you do, I will quit."

"Why?"

"Because I only work alone."

I didn't know what to say. I couldn't start all over with another lawyer, whom the authorities might prevent from seeing my file, or me—or both. I also didn't know if Khorramshahi would share what little he knew about my case with a new lawyer.

"You know," he continued, repeating a statement he had made in our last meeting, "I'm under a lot of pressure, a *lot* of pressure."

Just then, a bearded man entered the room and informed us that the judge, Mr. Moqiseh, was ready to see us. He didn't explain what the meeting was for, but Khorramshahi and I followed him into the next room.

I recognized this place right away. This was the courtroom where I had been brought two weeks after my arrest, and the man sitting behind the raised desk at the opposite end was the white-bearded, white-turbaned judge who had asked if I had been in contact with foreigners. I swayed a bit. I had a bad feeling about this.

The cleric motioned at Khorramshahi and me to sit down several feet away from his desk, in the first of two rows of chairs facing him.

"You are charged with espionage," he said matter-of-factly, barely giving me a glance. "What do you have to say to defend yourself?"

I looked at Khorramshahi to see if he would respond. He was staring straight ahead, as if he expected me to speak. I looked back at the judge. "I am not a spy, but I made a false confession saying I was."

"How do I know it was false?" he asked skeptically.

"I was pressured to make those statements and was promised freedom in return."

The judge looked at me with hate-filled eyes. "How could you agree to spy for the U.S.?" he demanded. "Don't you care about the Islamic Republic?"

"But I'm not a spy!" I protested. "I gave a false confession!"

I couldn't believe this. He seemed to have made up his mind that I was guilty without even questioning me. Guilty until proven innocent—though I suspected few people were ever proven innocent here.

Khorramshahi cut in to ask if we could postpone the trial. The judge wanted to know how much time we needed.

"Two weeks," Khorramshahi replied.

"That's fine," the cleric said. "Just write your request for me." Then he ordered us to leave.

After I returned to my cell, I skipped lunch and dinner. When Mahvash and Fariba asked why I wasn't eating, I told them my judge appeared completely biased against me, and I saw no way out of my predicament other than to finally start a hunger strike.

"Keep faith," they told me. "God is watching over you."

PART III

ON TRIAL

CHAPTER NINETEEN

I didn't realize that writing a book was against the law in Iran," I told the judge the next day.

His upper lip curled back into a sneer. "It's not," he retorted.

"Well, that's what I was doing," I said.

That morning, Judge Moqiseh had summoned Khorramshahi and me back to the courtroom, and we had submitted our request for a delay of my trial. To our surprise, the judge had then told us to sit down, as three men paraded in.

First came the guard who had brought me to court. He took a chair on the right side of the room. Following him was an unfamiliar man whose pudgy, hairless face made him appear younger than he probably was, maybe in his early forties. I assumed from the confident way "Baby Face" carried himself that he wasn't just a prison guard.

Finally, a slender, bearded man tottered in. It was Heidarifard, the beady-eyed assistant to Deputy Prosecutor Haddad, both of whom I had met five weeks earlier. Heidarifard was carrying several heavy-looking dossiers. He dropped them on a desk to the judge's right and sat down there.

Then he opened a file and began to read aloud. The sentences were long and complicated, making me wonder whether I should request a translator for my trial in two weeks' time. But I quickly dismissed this thought. Any translator the judge would give me would be one I couldn't trust. It would be safer to rely on my own Farsi skills.

"You are accused," Heidarifard was now saying, "of acting against national security by way of espionage for the United States."

"Do you accept this charge?" Judge Moqiseh asked me, looking down from his elevated desk.

"I accept that *he* says it's the charge against me," I replied, nodding at Heidarifard.

That was enough for Heidarifard to launch into a list of accusations against me. He read off some statements I had made in my false confession, including that I had received $15,000 from Mr. D for using my book as a cover to gather information on Iran for him, and asserted that, as proof, the prosecution had $2,100 found in my apartment.

The judge asked what I had to say in my defense.

I looked at Khorramshahi. His lips were tightly closed, and he appeared engrossed in taking notes in a notepad on his lap. I interrupted to ask if he was going to respond, and he whispered that I should instead. When I asked again, he repeated that I should speak and that I should trust him because he knew what was best for me.

So I took a deep breath, then said: "I was pressured to fabricate the story about Mr. D based on the leading questions my interrogators asked me. I did it after they claimed they didn't believe the truth—that I was just researching and interviewing people for a book I was writing about Iran and that it was a personal project paid for out of my own pocket."

"But why would you interview U.S. officials for a book on Iranian society?" Heidarifard challenged.

I couldn't comprehend why we were delving into these subjects now. I guessed that in Iran, pretrial proceedings often went something like this.

I explained that U.S.-Iran relations and U.S. policy toward Iran affected Iranian society in various ways.

"And why did you interview a Hezbollah member in Lebanon?" Heidarifard asked, his voice brimming with sarcasm. "Should we assume that was also for your book?"

"It was for a news report."

"Right," he continued, clearly not caring for my answer. "Let's get back to Mr. D. You knew him, and you gave him information."

"I didn't give Mr. D anything," I objected. "He never asked me to do anything for him, and he never gave me any money."

Heidarifard grunted. "Let me remind you that you admitted in your interrogation that you received $15,000 for giving him information."

As he spoke, a chill rippled up my spine. Something about the way he kept grilling me felt very wrong.

Then it hit me.

This wasn't just a pretrial hearing. This was the trial itself. The judge had refused to grant me a delay, but he hadn't even announced that the trial had begun. My lawyer had said nothing, and I was totally unprepared. Yet I felt I had no choice but to continue on my own.

"Those were all lies," I said, "which I stated under—"

"But you wrote about it *here!*" Heidarifard exclaimed, brandishing a stack of papers. They must have been the false confession I had made up with Javan several weeks earlier.

"I stated those falsehoods under pressure," I said, growing frustrated. "I was told that if I cooperated—"

"What else did she write?" the judge asked, leaning over to see Heidarifard's papers.

Heidarifard opened another file and read aloud, "Miss Saberi wrote, 'I was recently chosen as a fellow for the Aspen Institute's Middle East Leadership Initiative.'" Then he turned to the judge and said under his breath, just loud enough for me to hear, "Everyone knows the Aspen Institute aims at the soft overthrow of the Islamic Republic. And as you may recall, the Alaei brothers went to a seminar organized by the institute."

Heidarifard took a sip of water and continued to read: "'I have not yet attended any of Aspen's seminars. I am not going to get any funding from the institute, and fellows were even supposed to pay for their own airfare to the seminars. We were expected to set up community service projects in our own countries after that.'"

"*Community service,*" Heidarifard repeated. "We all know what that is code for."

Code for an instrument of the soft overthrow of the regime, I supposed he meant.

"What kind of community service projects?" the judge asked me, with one eyebrow raised.

"I was told they can include, for example, setting up soccer teams for kids," I replied, "or programs to tackle pover—"

Heidarifard silenced me with another grunt, then returned to the previous dossier and skimmed a few pages. "'Mr. D wanted me to interview top officials, members of the Revolutionary Guards, and people in decision-making institutions.'"

He set down the file and turned toward the judge, who had tipped his chin upward and was peering down at me with disgust.

My false confession was clearly being used as "evidence" of espionage. "What you have been reading," I began, "is—"

Heidarifard interrupted with a few more sentences of the Mr. D tale. When he paused, I tried to defend myself, but the judge broke in with another question. Then when I tried to reply, Heidarifard cut me off again.

Exasperated, I threw my hands in the air and asked, "Does it even *matter* what I say here?"

Judge Moqiseh flinched. "Of course, of course," he said, leaning forward as if suddenly interested.

"Then why do you both keep cutting me off?"

"Go ahead," the judge said with a nod.

"Thank you," I said. "I was trying to say that the confession was false, I made it because I was threatened with many years in prison if I didn't and promised freedom if I did. I recanted it after I realized it is better to tell the truth late than never, and the Koran told me to tell the truth because even if you suffer, in the end you will prevail."

"Uh-huh!" Khorramshahi said in approval, the only sound he had uttered so far.

Heidarifard flared his nostrils and pursed his lips. Then he began flicking through the pages of another file. After a few seconds, he looked up and said, "Saberi also met with the American journalist Mr. C when he was in Tehran."

"Is it illegal to meet with an American journalist?" I asked. "We just had coffee together."

Judge Moqiseh asked what we had discussed. I told him we had talked briefly about the upcoming presidential election in Iran. As I was speaking, his eyes glazed over.

When I was finished, the judge waved something in the air. From where I was sitting, it appeared to be the research article on the U.S. war in Iraq. Without speaking, he wagged it at me for a few seconds. Then he announced, "This is one of *many* classified documents you had."

"That is not classified," I countered. "It's not marked as classified. There's no classified stamp on it. I didn't have any classified documents."

"But down here," Moqiseh said, pointing to something scrawled by hand on the cover of the article, "it says *mim*." *Mim* was the letter *m* in Farsi.

"What does that mean?" I asked.

"*Mim* for *mahramâneh*," he replied, stating the Farsi word for classified.

I couldn't see from where I was sitting. When the judge allowed me to step forward, I saw a small handwritten letter that looked like a *mim*.

"I've never heard of an article being marked classified with one handwritten letter," I said.

Besides, I wanted to exclaim, *how could I know that my captors didn't write it themselves? And "mim" could stand for many things.* I looked back at Khorramshahi. He was sitting mutely, observing the scene. I wished he would step in.

"You must have read this document," Moqiseh continued, ignoring my comment and flipping through the typed pages.

I noticed that none of them had any classified markings, either.

The judge instructed me to go back to my seat. Then he turned the article over and pointed to some notes scribbled on the back. I must have used it as scratch paper at some point.

"*Kolli naghshe keshidi poshtesh*," he declared. "You plotted out an entire scheme on the back."

I couldn't believe my ears. "That is not some kind of plot," I seethed. "And even if that thing really were classified as you say, and if I really were a spy as you claim, I'd have to be a pretty stupid spy to keep a classified paper with some secret plan written on the back of it in my apartment."

Someone snickered. I looked to my right. It was the prison guard. When he saw me watching him, he immediately recovered his somber expression.

The judge held up a fat, green folder. I could see through its partially transparent cover that it contained some pamphlets. "This is *full* of classified documents retrieved from your apartment," he proclaimed.

"But as far as I know, I never had any classified documents," I said, even though the conviction in Moqiseh's voice was starting to make me doubt myself.

He pulled a few articles out of the folder and asked where I had received them. They, too, had no classified stamps on them. I said they looked like ones I had received at the Center for Strategic Research. He asked what I had done at the center, and I told him.

"Miss Saberi also confessed that she passed classified documents on to the Americans," Heidarifard added. "In fact, her trips to the United States were to deliver classified information, not to see her parents."

"That's not true," I protested. "I didn't pass *anything* on to *anyone*."

Then Baby Face spoke up for the first time. "Your Honor, we questioned Mr. V, who admitted to giving several classified documents to Miss Saberi."

I felt the hair on my arms stand on end. Mr. V was an Iranian acquaintance I had lost touch with some time ago. His name had come up in an early interrogation session, but I never dreamed that my captors would pressure him to falsely testify against me. He had once given me some research articles to read, but he had never said that any was classified.

"Mr. V said he gave Miss Saberi classified documents because he was captivated by her, and she promised to marry him if he gave her certain information," Baby Face continued.

I didn't know whether to laugh or cry. The story was sheer nonsense, but I felt extremely sorry for Mr. V, who must have been under incredible pressure to agree to tell such a tale.

"Moreover," Baby Face said, "Miss Saberi's confession about Mr. D was true, and she acknowledged on video and in writing that she wasn't under any pressure. She even ate the meals her interrogators provided to her."

Then he turned up his nose at Khorramshahi and said, "We also request that you prohibit Saberi's lawyer from doing any more media interviews. This is a security-related case, and his interviews threaten our national security."

Khorramshahi shot to his feet. "But Your Honor," he said, objecting for the first time, "I only talked to the media to deny false statements, such as those news reports claiming that Miss Saberi is on a hunger strike, but she isn't."

Actually, I hadn't eaten a thing since the previous morning.

"We can all see her health is fine," the judge said, swiping dismissively in my direction. "There is no need for you to talk to the media."

"But . . ." Khorramshahi sputtered. He finally seemed to be getting a little riled up.

"And the BBC and Voice of America are our redlines," Baby Face said, meaning the often ambiguous lines that, according to regime officials, should not be crossed.

The judge sided with Baby Face and ordered Khorramshahi to abstain from interviews with all media except Iran's state-run news services.

Khorramshahi sat down, looking defeated.

"Excuse me, sir," I said to the judge. "May I respond to that man's accusations?" I asked, referring to Baby Face.

"Go ahead."

"First of all," I said, shooting Baby Face a fiery glare, "I apologize for having eaten food in prison. I didn't eat much during those first few days, but I thought it wouldn't be a bad idea to consume a little to remain alive. Secondly, I never promised Mr. V I would marry him. And he is not the type of person to go around handing out classified materials. Thirdly, my interrogators certainly wouldn't have agreed to free me if I had stated, 'I am under pressure,' when I made my false confession."

"A *true* confession!" Baby Face interjected.

"No. A *false* one."

"It was true, Your Honor," he said.

This man was starting to aggravate me. "Who are *you*, anyway?" I lashed out.

The judge laughed lightly and answered for Baby Face, "He's a representative from the Intelligence Ministry."

"Then *you* must know my confession was false," I said to the agent, "because when I told your colleague, my *bâzju*, that I had withdrawn it, he said he had known from the very beginning it wasn't true."

"If that's the case, we can ask your *bâzju*," the judge said with a smirk.

"As if he would admit the same thing to you," I muttered, then went on: "My interrogators pressured me to say I was using my book as a cover to spy for the U.S. government. There was no truth to this, but I agreed to say it because they promised to release me if I 'cooperated.'"

"By 'cooperate,'" the judge said, "they meant confessing to your crime."

"They meant confessing to a crime I did not commit," I countered. "And they also meant . . . something *else*."

I hadn't been planning to say these words, which would likely turn the judge even more against me. But they just spilled out of my mouth. And even though I hadn't explicitly stated that my captors had required I spy for them, everyone in the room seemed to understand exactly what I was getting at.

Khorramshahi straightened up briskly in his seat. I turned to see him bite his lower lip, the same signal my father used to give me as a child when I had misbehaved.

A heavy silence followed. I surveyed the room. Every man had lowered his eyes, as if waiting for someone else to speak first. I had obviously broached a subject that was off-limits.

At last, the judge spoke. "Miss Saberi's work here is finished," he said coldly, as he looked past me to Khorramshahi. "You have two days to write her defense argument."

I wondered what Khorramshahi would write. We had never been given time to discuss my case. On the way out of the courtroom, I asked him if he could cross-examine the "witness," Mr. V, but he said that was not permissible, just as he was barred from studying the so-called evidence against me. The guard separated us before I could ask Khorramshahi anything else.

On the way back to Evin, my stomach rumbled loudly, but I didn't feel hungry. It was early afternoon, and I had missed the chance to have my weekly visit with my parents. I would have to put in a request to my *bâzju* to see if I could at least call them.

I rested my head on the back of the seat and shut my eyes. The trial was so short, it seemed to have lasted only about half an hour. Although I hadn't expected much, I never thought it would be so unjust and that I would have to present my own defense as my lawyer merely took notes. But I suspected the day's events didn't really matter. The judge must have made his ruling before the trial had even begun.

I tossed and turned on the cement floor for hours that night, long after Mahvash and Fariba had fallen asleep. My blindfold, which I tied on every night to block out our cell's bright fluorescent light, kept slipping. Finally, sometime after dawn, I dozed off into a vivid dream.

Several people are gathered on a narrow street, talking excitedly and pointing at something on the other side of the road. As I near them, I see the object of their attention: a black dog with golden specks that is growling and foaming at the mouth.

The dog is standing beside a lanky man who is deliriously laughing and wildly flapping his arms up and down, as if he thinks he is a bird. He must have been bitten by the rabid dog and become infected.

A knot winds tightly in my belly. I walk on with my head down, hoping that if I don't look at the dog, it won't notice me. I pass the crowd and am about to breathe a sigh of relief when I feel the dog's eyes rise in my direction. The next instant, the animal is chasing after me. I try to run, but it swiftly catches up to me, pounces, and hooks its fangs into my sleeve. The dog is dangling from my outstretched left arm, like a swing from a tree branch.

"Please!" I cry. "Somebody help me!"

A man whose face I can't see breaks from the crowd and runs toward me. The dog drops to the ground and saunters away, leaving four holes punched into my sleeve.

"Take off your coat," the man instructs me, "so I can examine your arm."

Even though the day is sunny and windless, and no snow is in sight, I am wearing a heavy winter coat. The man carefully helps me remove it. I avert my eyes. I can't bear to see the injury.

"Amazing!" he marvels, as he holds up my arm for me to see.

Miraculously, it shows no trace of injury. No blood, no bruises, no fang marks. My coat was so thick that the dog's teeth failed to pierce all the way through it and into my skin.

The coat, I now realize, is my father's. He gave it to me two years earlier to take to one of his relatives in Iran.

I f you eat something, you can call your parents," Tasbihi told me the next morning, apparently having heard from the guards that I wasn't taking any meals. "If you don't, you can't."

I figured if this was the price to talk to my parents, I could eat something small for the first time in nearly two days. I returned to my cell and ate two dates. Then Tasbihi brought me back to the hallway outside the women's ward.

"If you eat lunch, you can *see* your parents," he now said. "If you don't, you can't."

I agreed, ate lunch, and then, with Tasbihi towering over me, called my parents and told them to come to Evin.

In the car on the short ride to the visitation building, Tasbihi instructed me to pass on a message to my mother and father. "Tell them to stop talking to the news media because it's not in your interests," he said. "But there's no need to tell them we told you this."

I was pleased to learn that my parents had been doing media interviews while in Iran. The Iranian authorities definitely seemed bothered by news coverage of my case, and contrary to what Tasbihi was now saying, I had begun to believe this media attention was helping more than hurting me. When my parents had remained quiet during the first month of my imprisonment, the authorities had dragged their feet. I had concluded that silence wouldn't push my captors to release me any faster.

Tasbihi ordered me to walk behind him when we entered the visitation building, but I skipped ahead to my mother when I saw her waiting in the large hall. I hugged her and whispered quickly in her ear, "This man wants me to tell you not to talk to the media anymore, but you must continue. If I cough during our visit, it means I'm lying."

She smiled and nodded.

Tasbihi took us to the same private visitation room where we had met the week before. It appeared my parents and I were getting special treatment, perhaps because of all the media reports about my case or because we could be monitored more easily here.

After we sat down on the couch, I told my parents how badly the trial had gone the previous day, although I intentionally kept my descriptions vague in front of Tasbihi.

"We know," my father said. "Mr. Khorramshahi told us about it."

I said I wanted Khorramshahi to show me the defense argument before he delivered it to the court, so I, too, could have a say about what was written. But my father told me the attorney had already presented it to the judge. I was stunned he had written it in less than a day, and without even talking to me or letting me know what he was arguing on my behalf.

From time to time, Tasbihi shot glances at me, evidently anxious for me to do his bidding.

So I took my parents' hands in mine and said, "It seems (ahem, ahem) that it would be better for you two not to talk to the media (cough, cough) because it could be harmful for me."

My parents nodded, and we moved on to other subjects. As we talked, I randomly threw in a few more coughs so that Tasbihi wouldn't catch on to my code. My mother began to look confused.

"I don't get it, Roxana," she said, squeezing my hand. "Do you want us to do media interviews or not?"

"Um (ahem, ahem)," I stammered, "it's better that you don't. It could hurt my case."

Before long, Tasbihi told me I had to return to my cell. As I kissed my father good-bye, I whispered to him: "Keep quiet until my ruling is given. If the sentence is bad, and it probably will be, then talk to the media again."

Even though I had, in a way, passed on Tasbihi's message about the media, my captors still were not satisfied, as I learned the very next evening.

It was Wednesday, April 15—weeks since I had last found myself sitting at the school desk in the dreadful interrogation room, facing the wall, blindfolded and unaware of how many men were behind me.

"How is everything?" came Tasbihi's voice. "Is the food OK?"

My body relaxed a little. Of all the agents I had encountered, he seemed to be the least villainous, a follower and not a leader, even though he was still one of *them*.

"Fine," I replied abruptly. I didn't know why I had been brought here, and I wasn't about to let this turn into another interrogation.

"How about *havâ-khori*? Is your outdoor exercise adequate?"

I paused. "Well, I shouldn't have any extra privileges that other detainees don't have."

"And you're feeling well?"

I was starting to wonder whether my voice was being recorded to be broadcast later to make it seem as if I was having the time of my life in Evin Prison.

"Excuse me," I said, "but I thought my interrogation had finished."

"Yes, it has," Tasbihi acknowledged.

"Then what am I doing here?"

He didn't respond.

"Hello, Miss Saberi."

My body froze. Except for my heart, which was now hammering in my chest.

I recognized this voice all too well. I hadn't heard from Javan for more than a month, when I had informed him that I had withdrawn my false confession. Even though I had finally stood up to him that evening, traces of fear remained.

"I'm not very happy with you," he declared.

The words from the Bible, "Do not be afraid of those who kill the body but cannot kill the soul," began to whirl around in my head. *Do not be afraid of those who kill the body but cannot kill the soul.*

"I'm not very happy with you, either," I replied.

A hush came over the room. Then Javan cleared his throat quietly and said: "You should know that the media are reporting a lot about you. It is not to your benefit that your case has become so political."

I heard him stand up, click toward me, and throw what sounded like a heap of papers on my desk.

"Look at these," he ordered.

I raised my blindfold above my eyes and, without lowering my chin, glimpsed at a pile of papers. On top was a BBC news article in Farsi, printed off the Internet. I lifted my eyes and stared at the wall.

"Don't you want to read these?" Javan asked, still standing beside me.

I didn't say a word. I wanted to refuse him any serious reaction or dialogue. At last, I had learned that engaging in conversation gave interrogators like him an opening to do what they were trained for: to offend, intimidate, and lie; to wear down an inmate's mind; and to provoke the prisoner with the aim of sparking an instinctively defensive and wordy outburst.

"Yeah, it would take you a while to read them," Javan said condescendingly, "so I will read them for you."

Out of the corner of my eye, I saw him shuffling through the papers without lifting them off my desk. "BBC, VOA, CNN, the Associated Press," he said. "I've highlighted the important parts for you in yellow."

He stopped at one article and began to read it aloud: "Roxana's father said her lawyer met with her for the first time today. The lawyer said she showed no signs of physical torture but initially appeared very depressed. After they talked a little, her mood improved."

Javan leafed through more pages, occasionally reading out the names of groups, such as the U.S.-based Council on American-Islamic Relations, which had spoken out for me.

"And then there's this one," he said scornfully. "The European Union has issued a statement on your behalf." He paused. "You're not European. What do *you* have to do with the European Union?"

I sat silently, trying to conceal my elation. This was the first time I truly understood the extent of the international media coverage and efforts to release me.

"Why don't you say something?" Javan asked.

"*You* can speak," I replied quietly. "I'll listen."

"Why? Don't you want to talk?"

I shrugged.

"Fine," he said, starting to sound annoyed. He continued reading: "Secretary of State Hillary Clinton announced the U.S. will 'use any means' to free you. Do you know what that means?"

I doubted Clinton had really made that comment, but still, I didn't make a sound.

Javan kept thumbing through the pages and reciting the headlines. At one point, I glanced down to see a photograph of former President Khatami and me. The picture was from 2005, when journalists had jostled to pose next to him at a dinner he had held for us just before he left office. I hoped hard-liners wouldn't criticize him for having stood in this snapshot with me, flashing his trademark smile.

"Don't you want to talk to me anymore?" Javan asked, now attempting to seem hurt.

I shrugged again. I knew what he was trying to do. The same man who had earlier told me I wasn't worth a single paragraph in a newspaper now wanted to scare me into thinking that all this coverage was bad for me. But this display of news articles was building me up, not breaking me down. I no longer felt so alone. Friends and strangers were standing with me, and I didn't have to face my captors by myself anymore. This outpouring of support humbled me even more than before and left me in awe of the goodness of human nature.

"Can't you at least say yes or no?" Javan asked, sounding a tad unhinged.

I felt strangely pleased to have frustrated him.

He sighed loudly and clicked back to his seat behind me. "Do you need anything else?" he asked off-handedly, as if he didn't really care but was obliged to ask.

"Yes," I said, finally speaking up. "I would like the same right I have seen granted to some other prisoners: to call my parents once a week on a set day without having to ask you for permission every time."

Javan paused. "We'll see. Anything else?"

"Yes, I would like some dental floss."

"We can't allow that," he replied. "Do you know why?"

"Because you think prisoners will kill themselves with it."

"Yes, there was an incident some time ago . . ."

"Well, if someone really wanted to kill herself, she could use the straps of her blindfold," I pointed out.

"Not possible. The cloth isn't strong enough."

I wondered how he had figured that out. "What about a bra? Why is that prohibited?"

Javan started to say something but stopped himself. A few moments passed before he and two other men in the room broke out in coarse, full-throated laughter. I felt my cheeks redden. I probably shouldn't have mentioned this feminine undergarment to men in the Islamic Republic, especially to this category of men. Then again, these people had spoken so explicitly about sex in one of my interrogation sessions. Couldn't they handle the word *bra*?

"What about a pen?" I asked, trying to change the subject.

The men regained their composure.

"What do you want it for?" Javan asked.

I wanted to mark important points in my books, I told him, without adding that I also needed it to take notes on my case in the margins, where I hoped the guards wouldn't think to look.

"We'll see."

I heard two men stand up and leave. Tasbihi ordered me to lower my blindfold before I got up and walked toward the door to return to my cell.

"Wait," he said to me. "Is there anything you want to say?"

"No."

"Are you *sure*?" he tried again.

"It seems you want me to tell my parents not to talk to the media," I said. "I have already told them. What else can I do to convince them?"

M ahvash and Fariba shrieked with laughter when I told them I had asked my *bâzju* for a bra. "Roxana," Mahvash cried, "I can't believe you said that to him!"

I was back in my cell, where I had recounted for my cellmates my latest run-in with Javan. I had also told them how heartened I was to discover that the support for me was so widespread.

A couple of the groups Javan had mentioned as calling for my release were tied to Iranians living abroad. I felt lucky to have the backing of these people, who I knew because of my research on "brain drain" in Iran included some of the best and brightest Iranians in the world.

Each year, a large number of well-educated Iranians emigrated, although estimates were highly disputed and ranged from 50,000 to at least 150,000 annually. One U.S. study found that Iranian Americans were the most educated ethnic group in America and held five times the number of doctorates than the national average.

Iran had experienced three main waves of emigration in recent decades—one beginning in the mid-1950s, the second in the lead-up to and aftermath of the Islamic Revolution, and the third starting in the mid-1990s. Some emigrants were asylum-seekers claiming they were fleeing persecution for their political activities, religious beliefs, or taboo behaviors such as homosexuality. Many others were young people in pursuit of education and economic welfare.

Though I had met some Iranians who said they would get too homesick to stay overseas for long, several of my friends had left for good during my six years in Iran. Perhaps some of them were among

those in the Iranian diaspora spreading news about my detention—
that is, if they weren't too afraid their families would face repercussions back home.

J udge Moqiseh's assistant handed me the verdict.
      It was Saturday, April 18, and I had been brought back to the
courthouse, where Khorramshahi and I were now sitting before the
turbaned judge.

The ruling was fairly long, and I knew it would take me several
minutes to read, so I asked my lawyer to summarize it. As he went
through the two typed pages, I looked over his shoulder. I was trying
to find a number—one, two, however many years I was supposed to
remain in jail. I couldn't spot any figures on the first page, so I decided
to wait for Khorramshahi to speak.

He slowly finished the first page and moved on to the second, his
eyes widening as he progressed. He shook his head, went back to the
beginning, and read the entire two pages again. Then he began shaking his head again, this time clucking his tongue softly on the roof of
his mouth. I shifted in my seat, started bobbing my foot up and down,
and exhaled noisily. Still, Khorramshahi said nothing.

"Well?" I asked impatiently. "What's the verdict?"

Without looking at me, Khorramshahi murmured, "Eight years."

CHAPTER TWENTY

W hat?" I asked. Maybe I hadn't heard my lawyer correctly. "Did you say eight years?"

He gave me a ghost of a nod.

Eight years. Much more severe than I had anticipated. Yet despite my shock, I felt a grin spread slowly across my face. After a farce of a trial, what else should I have expected but a joke of a ruling? "That is hilarious," I said.

Khorramshahi didn't seem to hear me. He had slouched in his chair and was gazing straight ahead.

"It's a *shoo*," he whispered, more to himself than to me.

"A what?" I asked. I didn't know this word in Farsi.

"A *shoo*."

"What's a *shoo*?"

"Show, show," Khorramshahi said, pronouncing the word in English.

"Ohh." He must have meant he saw my ruling as purely political.

"You've had enough time to read it," Judge Moqiseh barked. "Now sign it."

"I refuse to sign this," I said vehemently.

The judge frowned. "Why?"

With nothing to lose now, I figured I might as well tell him, though I hardly knew where to begin. "Because you didn't give me a chance to discuss my case with my attorney, and he saw my file only one day before the trial. I didn't even realize the trial had begun until several minutes after it started, you didn't grant us the delay you promised, and my coerced false confession was used against me."

By the time I finished speaking, the judge's face had grown contorted. "Fine, don't sign it," he said. Then he nodded at Khorramshahi. "Mr. Khorramshahi, as her attorney, you sign it."

I whipped my head toward him. "Don't sign it," I ordered.

Khorramshahi looked at me apologetically. His pen was poised above the blank space at the end of page two.

"I have to," he whispered. Then he signed it.

"Why don't you sign it, too?" the judge asked me, his voice now oozing with artificial kindness.

"Because I object to this entire process."

He scowled. "Then just sign that you have an objection."

That sounded acceptable to me.

I object, I wrote next to Khorramshahi's signature. Then I signed my name.

Before leaving the courtroom, Khorramshahi showed me a copy of the brief defense he had turned in after my trial. The prison guard was telling me I had to leave, so Khorramshahi quickly explained that he had argued I didn't have any classified materials, my confession was false, and I was simply writing a book. I was about to hand the paper back when I noticed he had written I had conducted around six hundred interviews for my book.

"It was sixty," I pointed out, "not six hundred."

"Oops," he said. "Typo. Not important."

The guard gestured at me to leave. I stood up. "What do you want me to tell Bahman?" Khorramshahi asked, with creases in his brow. "He's waiting outside the building. He's very worried about you."

"Tell him and my family not to worry," I replied. "Tell them all I love them and that I'm fine."

As I was led out of the courthouse, I scanned the parking lot with blazing eyes, yearning to find Bahman. But he was nowhere to be seen.

"Get in the car," my guard ordered me. Reluctantly, I obeyed, and he fastened my handcuffs. The driver started the engine, and our car began to pull out of the lot.

I wanted to see Bahman with such a painful intensity that my whole body drooped with disappointment.

Something moved outside my window. I yanked my head up to see Bahman. He was alone, his eyes darting left and right, evidently searching for me. Just then, he caught sight of me and started waving frantically.

The car lurched forward, and Bahman fell behind. I whirled around to see him through the rear window with a bruised, helpless look on his face. My handcuffs clinked as I raised my fingers to my lips, blew him a kiss, and mouthed, "I love you."

Bahman began to beat his head with his hands and run after our car, but he couldn't keep up. When we turned onto another street, he disappeared.

His image played over and over in my mind on the way back to Evin. He had put himself in a great deal of danger by showing up before at Evin and now at court, and seeing him for the first time after all these weeks stirred emotions that I had been trying to repress to better cope with prison.

I couldn't imagine how he, my family, and my friends would handle the news of my conviction and sentence.

M ahvash and Fariba were doing sit-ups when I returned. They sprang to their feet when they saw me.

"We prayed for you all morning," Mahvash said cheerfully.

"And when we opened Hafez for you," Fariba added, "we turned to a very, very good poem."

I chuckled and told them the verdict.

"Oh, Roxana!" they cried in unison, their voices full of sympathy.

I smiled. "I'm fine."

They stared at me as if I had gone a little crazy.

"Really," I assured them, "I'm fine. In fact, I've never felt closer to God in my life."

Khorramshahi hadn't believed me, either, when I had told him the same thing that morning. He could not have realized that I had finally found confidence in God, who must have truly known what He was doing. I was thankful for the ruling. It was proof of my captors' rage over my refusal to cooperate, and I felt proud for having stood up to them. I also believed my eight-year sentence could create an even bigger international uproar than if I had been given only one or two years, and it had erased any inkling in my mind that I might be treated fairly. I now had no doubts about the path I had to take: one of all-out resistance.

"Now the whole world will recognize the judicial process I experienced for what it is," I had told Khorramshahi, "a sham."

That night, I confided my plan to my cellmates.

Judge Moqiseh had given my lawyer twenty days to submit a request to appeal the verdict. In the meantime, I would expand my defense team, a wish that Khorramshahi had this time respected without threatening to take himself off the case. I had told him before leaving the courthouse that I wanted to work with Shirin Ebadi and her colleague Abdolfattah Soltani, who were representing the Baha'is. Both attorneys had spent time behind bars for their work, but once freed, they had continued to take on tough, politically charged cases. Lawyers like them, I believed, would be brave enough to stand up for my rights, too.

Khorramshahi said that Ebadi was out of the country but he would approach Soltani, although he preferred Saleh Nikbakht. I had heard this lawyer's name before but knew nothing about him, so I told Khorramshahi to focus on retaining Soltani.

Yet although I was relieved to be getting a second attorney, I had come to realize that I couldn't rely on anyone, not even additional lawyers, to win my release.

The appellate court certainly wouldn't reduce my eight years to nothing, I predicted. That would make officials in the judiciary and Intelligence Ministry look bad. At best, the court would give me a couple of years in prison, and then I would have to appeal again, but to the Supreme Court. And who knew how long that process might take or what the result would be.

I now understood that I had to depend above all on myself—on my ability to control not only my attitude but also my body. I would go on a hunger strike—this time, with unwavering determination. It was the only weapon available to me to pressure the Iranian authorities in the next, critical stage of my case. This action could attract more outside attention. It was also a form of protest that seemed completely justified after the verdict I had received.

But if I began right away, the authorities might not allow me to see my parents or Soltani. I decided to wait until I met them and then launch the strike.

T oday was the Western media's turn to speak out against the eight-year sentence of Roxana Saberi, who was convicted of spying for the United States," I was surprised to hear the TV anchor say on Sunday night. This was the first time I was hearing news about my case on IRIB.

My cellmates and I had switched on the nightly newscast because of what an intelligence agent had alluded to earlier that day. He had taken me into an interrogation room and asked whether I had watched the news the night before. I shook my head. He kept asking how scared I was after receiving an eight-year sentence, and I kept repeating a Farsi saying, *Har chi khodâ salâh bedoone,* or "Whatever God deems advisable." I had gleaned from this encounter that IRIB had reported on my verdict the previous night, probably in a way that the agent thought would intimidate me.

Tonight, a roughly three-minute report followed the anchor's introduction, showing snippets from Western TV reports about my sentencing and a sound bite from a European friend named Coco, who had once lived in Iran, declaring that it was unfortunate I had become a political pawn. The story also included samples of my old TV reports, as well as clips from a foreign network's interview with my parents. According to the Farsi voice-overs, my father had said something like, "She was tricked into making untrue statements," and my mother followed with, "She is really ill, really weak. I am worried about her." I caught my breath when President Obama appeared, saying something about his concern for my well-being.

I turned to Mahvash and Fariba. Their eyes were as wide as mine must have been.

The broadcast left me with conflicting emotions. I was shaken by an eerie feeling that I had just watched a report about someone else, not about me. Maybe this was what people meant when they said they felt they had witnessed their own funerals. But I was also uplifted by the realization that my verdict had been widely criticized, and I was proud of my parents for defending me so openly. My father's statement suggesting I had been pressured to make a false confession was exactly what I had wanted the world to know. He was acting like my spokesman, defending me against the lies Iran's propaganda machine was churning out. I recalled my dream about the rabid dog. My father's winter coat was protecting me.

I could see the anguish in my parents' faces from across the hall, where they were waiting when I entered the visitation building. My father was speaking to an elderly woman who must have been another prisoner's mother. Inmates' family members, I had learned, got to know one another during their visits to prison and court, creating a growing network of people united in their resentment against their loved ones' captors.

Javan had taken the place of Tasbihi that Monday, two days after my conviction, to monitor my weekly visit with my parents. He was wearing a long-sleeve shirt without his leather jacket—the weather was getting too warm for it. He had also put on some pounds since I had last seen him, about a month and a half earlier. Perhaps he had overindulged in his New Year's pastries.

Javan greeted my mother and father civilly, then led us into the private visitation room and motioned courteously for them to sit down. I hoped they wouldn't be fooled by this pretense of geniality. Javan obviously wanted something from them, but what that was, I could not yet ascertain.

I had planned to spend my precious few minutes with my parents discussing my case, but before I could speak, Javan pulled a chair up to my father and began talking to him in Farsi. The agent claimed he didn't understand any English and ordered me to speak only in Farsi, although he would allow me to translate for my mother, who understood only a few phrases of the language. Before I could disclose that Javan's English was in fact very good, he launched into a lecture that ended up lasting what seemed like twenty minutes. His main points were these:

1. The Islamic Republic had gone its own way for the past thirty years and did not care what the foreign media said about it.

2. Interviews with the news media had no effect on the regime's decisions and furthermore could harm instead of help me.

3. Therefore, my father should tell the Western media to cut back their coverage of me.

4. My parents should also remember that they were in Iran as Iranian citizens, and "God forbid a problem might arise" for them while they were here.

As Javan spoke, I began to clench my teeth. This man was doing nothing less than threatening my parents to stay silent. He had held a great deal of power over me, and now he wanted to rule over my parents, too.

I looked at my father. He was listening politely. His composure amazed me, although I worried that he would be intimidated by Javan's threats. I wanted to erupt at my *bâzju*, but I reminded myself of what I had recently read in the book of Proverbs, "If you stay calm, you are wise . . ." *The wise remain calm,* I said to myself. *I, too, must remain calm.*

"It would be better to remain patient," Javan was now telling my father. "I am only delivering the message that was given to me from above."

With these words, I couldn't keep quiet anymore. "Dad," I butted in, as I took my father's hand in mine, "don't listen to a thing he's saying. Keep talking to the media."

Javan furrowed his brow at me. I did the same to him. I no longer cared about angering him or whether what I was about to say would be recorded. "If you don't want the media to report about me," I exploded, "tell them yourselves. *You* can reach out to the Western media, and you have plenty of your *own* news organizations to get your messages across."

For a second, he glared at me from under his arched eyebrows. But soon he slipped on his mask of impassivity, turned to my father, and said: "It means *more* coming from you and your wife. If you talk to the media, talk to the local, Iranian media."

"Everyone knows that the local media are censored," I growled.

"I'm not talking to you," Javan said testily. "I'm talking to your father. I can tell he is much more *logical* than you."

I looked at my father again. He still appeared calm and attentive.

Then, he spoke. "I understand your message," he told the agent softly, "but we gave you a chance. We waited for the verdict, and we saw what happened."

"No," Javan said forcefully. "*We* are giving *you* a chance."

He continued to speak. I pretended to translate for my mother. I whispered to her that this man had been my main interrogator, lying came naturally to him, he actually knew English quite well, and she must tell my father to ignore what he was saying and to keep my story alive. She nodded.

While I was talking to her, I overheard Javan tell my father I was guilty of the accusations against me. My father replied steadily that he knew his daughter was not a spy.

"How do you know?" the agent asked.

"Because we raised her, and we know her character," my father answered, speaking as serenely as if he were giving one of his presentations on Persian poetry. "She is not a spy."

"But we even have a video of her conceding that she's a spy," the agent said. "We could air it."

"Go ahead and show it," I dared him. I turned to my father and said, "Dad, if they do, it's full of lies that I stated under pressure. Deny them."

Javan glared at me again. "You were under no pressure here."

"What about being threatened that I would stay in prison until I was an 'old lady' or even that I could be killed?"

"No one ever said that," Javan snapped. "And when you say these things, you paint a bad picture of Evin."

"The world has heard about what goes on here, like the death of Zahra Kazemi," I said. My mother, who must have understood only the journalist's name, punctuated my words with "Yes! It's true!"

"It's not like that here," the agent countered. "Anyway," he said, turning to my father with a sly smile, "I should inform you that we found fifteen classified documents in your daughter's home."

Fifteen? This was the first time I had heard a number put on these allegedly classified materials. I whispered to my mother that she should tell my father not to believe the agent. She replied that she felt uneasy about the young man.

Javan glowered at me. "If you keep talking to your mother like that, you won't have in-person meetings from now on," he warned. "Don't translate anymore."

When Javan finished with his instructions, he informed us the visit was over.

I embraced my father and said in his ear that he should continue to speak to the media. "Don't worry," he told me. "We know. We've learned what to do."

I also told my mother quietly in my broken Japanese, "Tell the media that from Thursday, *tâbemâsen*, I won't eat." I hoped by then I would have seen my new lawyer. "Trust me. I know what I'm doing."

I could tell from the look in her eyes that she was concerned, but with a subtle nod of her head, she indicated she knew I was determined to take this step and she wouldn't try to stop me.

I ended up starting my hunger strike that evening. I had decided not to wait any longer to protest my verdict, despite learning that both President Ahmadinejad and Judiciary Chief Shahroudi had made encouraging statements about my case.

IRIB reported that Shahroudi had ordered a "careful, quick, and fair" appeal of my sentence. And Ahmadinejad had requested that Iran's judiciary ensure justice and a fair investigation into my case and that of the Iranian Canadian Hossein Derakhshan, who had become known in Iran as the Blogfather after helping to popularize blogging in the country. His whereabouts had been unconfirmed since his arrest in November 2008.

I hoped the officials' statements would make a difference, but I couldn't be certain. Regardless of whether Ahmadinejad had known of my arrest all along, perhaps he now viewed my detention as an obstacle to improving relations with the United States. He might have wanted to be seen as supporting rapprochement as a way to increase his popularity among a large number of Iranians less than two months before he was to stand for reelection.

But even if Ahmadinejad and Shahroudi had meant what they said, I had no way of knowing how much power even they held over the hard-liners who seemed bent on keeping me in jail.

I concluded that the officials could pursue their agenda, and I would pursue mine.

When I informed Haj Khanom of my decision to go on a hunger strike, she handed me a piece of paper and told me I had to formally notify the director of the detention center.

I did as she said. Haj Khanom retrieved the paper from me but forgot the pen, which I tucked under my blankets.

A few minutes later, she was back at our cell. The director wanted to see me.

Haj Khanom led me to a room on the first floor, where a man's voice instructed me to remove my blindfold. I recognized the director from the last time I had seen him, when he had come to my cell over the New Year's holidays to check on my diabetic cellmate.

He stepped out from behind his big desk and offered me some fruit, which I declined. Then he informed me that if I went on a hunger strike, he would have to relocate me from my cell to another section, where I would have to spend my days with *nâjur,* or uncongenial women. I assumed he meant the regular prison, where my first cellmate Roya had suggested I room with the murderers. *That could be one of those challenges I could turn into an opportunity,* I thought, recalling Mahvash's outlook on life. *Maybe I could learn something new from those women, too.*

"Please do whatever you think is right," I told him.

The bearded man looked a bit mystified, then warned, "If you don't eat, we can't allow you to make calls to your parents."

"That's OK. My aim is not to make a phone call. I am on a hunger strike to protest the unjust sentence I have been given."

He eyed me curiously. "But you have gone on hunger strikes before, and you saw they didn't help you at all."

"Those were not really hunger strikes," I said. "This time is different. This time, I am going to continue until the end."

CHAPTER TWENTY-ONE

Over the next few days, I reduced my diet to only sugared water and, once or twice, a spoonful of honey. As earlier, my first three days without food proved the most difficult, but defiance numbed me to the pangs of hunger.

Gradually, the fleshy areas around my shoulders and ribs began to disappear. My thighs shriveled to the size they were in my teens, and my stomach became flatter than I had ever seen it. My cheeks, however, remained fairly round.

As the fat dissolved from my body, I grew colder. I slept bundled in my prison sweatsuit, *roopoosh*, and chador; my socks; and extra clothes that Mahvash and Fariba lent me. To keep my head warm, I wore my *maqna'e* day and night.

On Thursday, April 23, the fourth day of my strike, one of the guards told me I had to go to the dispensary. There, a doctor checked my blood pressure, pulse, and sugar level. He said these were all fine, but when I stepped on the scale, he observed that since my last visit just five or six days earlier, my weight had fallen from 114 pounds to 104. Since I had reached my height of five feet, five inches back in high school, I had never weighed so little.

By now, I had only enough energy to sit up for a few minutes each day. Lying down, though, had become uncomfortable because I couldn't figure out where to place my hands. Resting them on my belly hurt, putting them on my chest impeded my breathing, and laying them beside me added pressure to my tailbone, which was more exposed than ever to the hard floor.

I was too feeble to walk during *havâ-khori*, but one day Mahvash and Fariba helped me go outside, where I sat and watched them as they circled the concrete yard, kicking a deflated plastic ball another prisoner must have left behind. As they passed it back and forth, I couldn't help thinking that just three months earlier, I was sprinting across a soccer field at a European school in Tehran, where I could take off my head-scarf and play with men, both Iranians and foreigners. Although Iran had recently created a women's national soccer team, many of them had marveled at my audacity the first time I had shown up to take part in what they considered a male sport. When they realized I could keep up (I had been playing soccer since I was five), they welcomed me to their weekly scrimmages. If only they could see me now. Just watching the ball roll across the pavement wore me out.

Despite my discomfort, I was encouraged to know that I wasn't waiting idly in my cell, relying solely on supporters outside Evin to push for my release. I, too, was doing what I could.

I predicted that if I could sustain my hunger strike, the Iranian authorities would either have to hook me up to an intravenous drip every few days—which could turn into a public relations nightmare for them—or set me free. I didn't know how many days a person could survive on what little I was consuming, but I highly doubted my captors would let me die. If they did, however, after all I had seen in this place, I had come to believe that death under these circumstances would not be meaningless. At least it might bring attention to the injustices of this system. I had gone from fearing death to being ready to die for a cause, a profound change brought on by my captors themselves.

During this time, my two cellmates insisted on washing my clothes for me, saying I had to conserve my energy. Occasionally, I would catch Mahvash gazing in my direction with moist eyes, and once, after I prayed aloud for us in English, I noticed a tear gliding down Fariba's cheek. I assured them I would be all right, but they didn't seem convinced.

Otherwise, my cellmates were as serene as ever, even when Heidarifard, Haddad's assistant, informed them one day that they faced a new charge: spreading corruption on earth. We laughed at the absurdity of it, though it was deadly serious. My cellmates told me this charge, like two others they faced, could result in the death penalty. In fact, several Baha'is in the early years of the revolution had been convicted of spreading corruption on earth and executed.

"Don't you ever get mad at these people for treating you this way?" I asked the two women.

They shook their heads. "Of course we miss our families and our freedom," Mahvash said, "but we believe in love and compassion for humanity, even for those who wrong us."

I told them that I realized one should, as the saying went, hate the sin, not the sinner, but it took enormous effort not to feel hatred toward Javan, Haddad, Heidarifard, Judge Moqiseh . . . for what they had done to me and surely done to countless others, and I couldn't grasp how I was supposed to love mankind when I despised these people.

"How do you not *hate* your captors?" I wanted to know. "Especially you, Fariba." She had told me her father had been tortured in prison years earlier and died shortly after his release.

"We forgive them," Fariba replied. "We don't want to become like them."

"But what about justice?" I asked. "Aren't these people treating you unjustly? Don't you ever wonder if *they* will be brought to justice?"

She smiled and answered softly, "We hope God will help us show them a better way."

As the week passed, I grew impatient to hear when I would meet my new attorney, but no news came. Fariba and Mahvash continued their daily routine, while I spent most of my time resting. Reading had begun to tire my arms, which had become too weak to prop up books, even the light paperbacks my parents had brought me. So all day, I watched TV. The three of us closely followed the news headlines, alert for any reports that might hint at our own fates.

IRIB was broadcasting more and more coverage of Iran's upcoming presidential election. Mir-Hossein Mousavi, Iran's prime minister in the 1980s, was considered the main reformist front-runner who would challenge incumbent Ahmadinejad. Mousavi enjoyed the support of former president Mohammad Khatami, who had withdrawn his own candidacy in March.

I recalled how Ahmadinejad's win in 2005 had shocked many observers. When the former Tehran mayor registered his candidacy that year at the Interior Ministry, he was considered such a long shot that many journalists took a tea break rather than shoot footage of him. Only a handful showed up at his preelection news conferences. After he won, we found ourselves scrambling for a chance to interview him.

Many Iranians later told me they hadn't bothered to vote. "They're all the same," was a common explanation for this apathy.

Yet Ahmadinejad appeared to have gained substantial support in rural and lower-class areas, including southern Tehran. Basij members I interviewed said they voted for him because they admired his simplicity, honesty, and self-proclaimed battle against corruption. A few also admitted that their commanders had strongly suggested they vote for him.

If Ahmadinejad won again this year, the Basij, Revolutionary Guards, and hard-liners who backed them would likely gain even more power during his second term than they had during his first. The Guards, which was thought to have around 125,000 active members, was the Islamic Republic's most powerful military institution, held command over the Basij, and had oversight of the country's nuclear program. The corps had also spread its reach into politics and the economy, having formed many companies in fields such as construction and oil and gas exploration.

An Ahmadinejad victory would allow these forces to further limit domestic freedoms under the guise of protecting national security. That would not bode well for political prisoners like us. In the meantime, however, my cellmates and I hoped Ahmadinejad's government would release some prisoners as a goodwill gesture in the run-up to the June election.

I n late April, we were joined by a new cellmate. At first, she asked us many questions about ourselves, making me wonder whether she was an informant planted by our captors, as former cellmates had told me sometimes happened in prison. But as I got to know Mahshid Najafi, I realized she simply craved conversation following a month and a half of solitary confinement.

Mahshid, an attractive woman in her forties with long, thick hair, was the spokeswoman for Iran's El-Yasin Community, which she described as a coalition of individuals, NGOs, and publications aiming to raise awareness about "interpreting the words of God" and "different methods of thinking." Mahshid called it a spiritual-cultural organization, but her captors claimed it was an anti-Islamic cult organized around its thirty-six-year-old leader, Peyman Fattahi.

Fattahi promoted spiritual freedom and criticized the use of violence in the name of religion, Mahshid told me. She said he had become so popular that sometimes large auditoriums had overflowed with Iranians eager to hear him speak and that he had helped boost El-Yasin's mostly Iranian membership to around two hundred thousand since the group was founded in 1996. Many of these followers were young people looking for a deeper understanding of spirituality and religion, including Islam.

I had found a similar trend in Iranian society while doing research for my book. Although numerous Iranians supported the brand of Islam propagated by the regime, many others were distancing themselves from it. Many had tired of what they considered the political manipulation of the pulpit and were making religion a more personal experience or looking to other forms of faith. Some Iranians were turning their backs on the clergy; others, on religion altogether.

One Iranian I had met who had become disenchanted with the state's ideological Islam was a young father named Farzad.* He considered himself religious, but he preferred to worship within his own home rather than at state-sponsored Friday prayers or in the mosque, settings that he saw as a show of support for the regime.

"In the name of Islam," Farzad had said to me, "the regime bans satellite television and uses force to make youngsters wear its own idea of Islamic clothing. In the name of Islam, the authorities have told many lies. They promised economic welfare, but instead, they have brought corruption, inflation, and more poverty and prostitution. This is not true Islam."

A few of my former cellmates held similar beliefs. One had declared to her interrogators that their fundamentalist Islam was nothing like the moderate Islam she espoused. Another was an atheist.

Given hard-liners' rigid views of religion, I wasn't surprised to hear Mahshid say that over the years, the authorities had curtailed El-Yasin's activities. They had shut down the community's NGOs and publications and detained some of the group's supporters. The teaching of El-Yasin's ideas had also recently been banned.

Mahshid told me the group's leader, Fattahi, was now detained in Evin. He had been held in solitary confinement for the previous few months, and El-Yasin members feared he was undergoing severe torture, as they said he had during his previous detention in 2007.[*]

Mahshid directed a publishing company that had printed a book by Fattahi and many works about spirituality. It, too, had been forced to close. She was now accused of propaganda against the state, a charge she said stemmed mainly from interviews she had done with foreign media, including Voice of America.

Since Mahshid and her son were arrested without a warrant on March 2, they had not had any contact with each other or with their families. Her interrogator pressured her to make false statements about herself and

---

[*]   According to Paris Keynezhad, spokeswoman for El-Yasin Human Rights and International Affairs, during Fattahi's first imprisonment, he was subjected to electric shocks and toxic injections that led to internal bleeding. He said his interrogators, who accused him of heresy and atheism, insisted he had a confidential bulletin and pressured him to admit to "misusing people" and having illicit relations—all charges he denied.

Fattahi, but she refused, even though she could have been freed in return for making a false confession, as had at least two other El-Yasin members. Once released, they had recanted their lies in videos they circulated on YouTube and were now in hiding out of fear of the Intelligence Ministry.

"I will never lie as they want me to," Mahshid vowed. "I will not sell my dignity at any price."

Mahshid had an exceptionally positive attitude toward her incarceration. She believed it was possible to find something to be happy about each day, even in prison, whether it was catching a rare glimpse of the moon through our mesh-covered window or eating a particular meal, even if only rice soaked in oil and topped with one thin slice of zucchini. She savored every bite, often taking an entire hour to finish her food. Mahshid applied similar concentration to brushing her teeth five minutes every morning and five minutes every evening. She joked that when she was free, she had never had the time to clean her teeth this meticulously. "We can make paradise for ourselves," she liked to say, "even in hell."

Keep your feet up!" a male guard was hollering in the corridor behind us late one night. "Wash them with cold water! Sulking won't help!"

The four of us stirred awake. It sounded as though the guard was yelling at an inmate who had just had his feet flogged. We couldn't hear the prisoner respond. He either could not or would not talk.

For hours after that, we lay awake, not speaking but knowing that each of us was suffering in our own way with the unknown man on the other side of our wall.

Skinny handed me a mixed bouquet of flowers.
It was early evening on Sunday, April 26, and she and a male guard had driven me to another building on the prison grounds, one I had never been to before. Then, without any explanation, she had given me the bouquet and told me to walk inside.

The last time I got flowers was exactly one year earlier, for my birthday, when more than thirty friends had crammed into my apartment, and we ate, sang, and danced late into the night.

I wobbled into a small room, where I was startled to find my parents. I was about to smile and hug them when I noticed a video camera pointed in my direction. I couldn't see any red lights indicating that it was rolling, but I was leery. I refused to allow the authorities to record video of me happily embracing my parents with flowers in my hands. They could use it as propaganda to claim they had been kind to me on my birthday.

I thrust the bouquet at my mother and tried to look grave as she and my father hugged me and we sat down on a couch. I had just turned thirty-two, and my parents had waited hours to get permission to see me on a nonvisitation day. Javan stood in one corner, off camera, coolly observing us.

It was the seventh day of my hunger strike, and my father informed me that staff members of the Paris-based media-rights group Reporters Without Borders were planning to start fasting to show solidarity with me.

I found it hard to believe what my father was telling me. Total strangers were going to deprive themselves of food because of me?

"Please tell them to keep eating!" I begged him. "They need energy to work and live. In prison, I can lie on my back all day, hardly burning any calories."

"They will continue until you stop your strike," he said. "They will do it so you don't have to."

"But I have no plans to quit," I said resolutely.

My parents sank into the couch. They must have been terribly worried about my health, although they didn't admit it.

When our time was up, my parents gave me a bunch of fresh-cut red roses that they had brought. I sniffed their sweet fragrance until I reached the entrance to Section 209, where the male guard confiscated them.

T his is a movement toward world unity," Mahvash said with shining eyes, when I told my cellmates that night about the people who planned to go on a hunger strike on my behalf.

I smiled. I had learned that Baha'is believed the world was destined to one day achieve peace and unity.

"With the attention that your case has received," Fariba said, "you have been given an opportunity to highlight the issue of human rights in Iran."

"Roxana," Mahvash added, her face turning serious, "when you go back to America, please tell others that our country is not only about the nuclear issue. It is also about people like us."

M y father began to speak, but my mother interrupted him. It was Monday, a regular visitation day and the day after my birthday, and I was sitting at a round table with my parents, with Braces wedged between my mother and me. Braces had ordered me to speak only in Farsi and stressed that my father, not I, must translate for my mother. Other than a male agent who sat nearby, no one else was in the hall.

"This time, let me speak first," my mother said.

My father nodded, and she went ahead. "Roxana, we are very anxious about your health. We want you to eat."

I looked at my mother, then at my father. Both appeared pale, with lines etched deeper into their faces than I could remember. They had bags under their eyes, and their clothes sagged a little, a sign that they had lost weight in recent weeks.

"I understand your concerns," I told my father in Farsi, who translated for my mother. "But this time, I am determined to continue my hunger strike."

I paused. My next words would alarm my parents, but I wanted to say them in front of the agent and Braces so they could include them in their reports to their bosses.

"I am even ready for death," I declared.

My mother waited for my father to translate, then burst into tears. She set her forehead on the plastic table and sobbed loudly, her shoulders heaving as she gasped for air.

I sat stiffly, torn over what to do. I had never seen my mother cry. She had always been so level-headed and in control of her emotions. I had never even glimpsed a tear on her lashes. Each sob ripped into my heart, but I could not back down from my hunger strike now.

"I don't want you to die, Roxana!" my mother wailed, her head still on the table.

I began to caress her hair, trying to calm her as I blinked back tears. I wished I could tell her that even though I was prepared to die, the authorities probably wouldn't let me. But I didn't want my captors to know I thought this, so all I could say was, *Negarân nabâsh, negarân nabâsh*, or "Don't worry, don't worry," as I ran my fingers through her hair, frustrated at having to use a language she could barely understand.

My father took her hand as Braces looked on, stone-faced.

Eventually my mother raised her head and dried her tears. "I'm sorry," she sniffled. "This is the first time I've cried since your arrest. Your father has been very strong. He cried only once, and that was back home."

Her words stung me. I knew that my imprisonment had been rough on my parents, but until now, they had hardly revealed their suffering. This ordeal was destroying them. A daughter should never cause her parents so much pain, I chastised myself. At the same time, I needed them to support my hunger strike.

"Please, Mom," I entreated. "Please understand. I have to continue my strike."

She managed a melancholy smile and clasped my hands in hers.

CHAPTER TWENTY-TWO

S kinny inspected my hair, pants, and socks when she fetched me from my cell, as the guards normally did whenever prisoners went in and out of Section 209. But this time, she even peeked inside my underwear.

"Sorry," she said.

"It's OK," I replied. "I know you're just doing your job."

Fortunately, she didn't pull up my sleeve to see my left arm.

I had woken up early that Tuesday morning to review what I wanted to say to my new lawyer, Soltani, whom my father had told me I was to meet at the deputy prosecutor's office that day. I knew this would probably be my only chance to talk to Soltani before my appellate trial, so I had to be prepared. With the pen Haj Khanom had forgotten the week before, I squiggled a few notes on my arm. I did this under my blanket, in case one of the guards spotted me through the peephole. Then I rolled down the sleeve of my prison shirt. When I put on my pants, I had to fold the waistband over three times to prevent them from falling off.

T wo guards drove a male prisoner and me to the Revolutionary Court. When we got out of the car, I noticed that my fellow inmate was limping. I wondered whether he was the man on the other side of our cell whose feet had been flogged. We shuffled forward at about the same pace, I weakened by the ninth day of my hunger strike and he, visibly in pain.

One of the guards took me to the second floor. There, I was overjoyed to see Bahman, along with my father, Khorramshahi, and a man I assumed was Soltani, sitting in the hallway and chatting with one another.

Bahman was the first to notice me. He stopped speaking, his eyes lit up, and for a second he appeared about to leap out of his seat toward me. Then the rest of the men looked up. Soltani gave me a warm, reassuring smile. I liked him already. I was about to say something to Bahman when my father stood and hugged me. I quickly whispered, "Tell Mom not to worry. I don't think they'll let me die."

The guard stepped forward, rebuked me for speaking, and led me to the office of Haddad's secretary, where I was to wait until the deputy prosecutor arrived. I slumped in a chair by the door, exhausted.

The room was stuffy, and though I had been feeling cold throughout my hunger strike, I began to sweat. My stomach was growling, having been awakened from its slumber by the intrusion of one date I had eaten that morning to gain energy for my important meeting. I was growing dizzy, and my mouth felt parched. A water cooler stood near my chair, but I was too proud to ask the guard for a drink. I longed to lie down.

After several minutes, Bahman threw the door open and flew into the room. He strode up to the guard, held out his identity card, then said beseechingly, "Please let me speak to this woman to convince her she must start eating." The guard jumped up, grabbed Bahman by the arm, and pulled him out of the room.

I watched, stupefied.

After what seemed like an hour, Haddad strolled by without acknowledging me and entered his office. A few moments later, his secretary told me to go in.

Haddad glanced up and, without speaking, motioned at me to sit down. "How are you?" he asked disinterestedly.

"OK," I said.

"I hear you're on a hunger strike."

"Yes."

His eyes narrowed as he surveyed me. "You don't look like it. I've seen the faces of people on hunger strikes, and yours does not show that you haven't been eating."

I could have ripped off my chador to give him a better look at my scrawny body or told him to ask the prison doctor about my weight loss, but I knew there was no use arguing with a man like this.

"Hunger strikes have no effect on our decisions," Haddad continued, then picked up his phone and ordered his secretary to tell my father and Khorramshahi to enter. When they did, Haddad said to me, "I hear you want a different lawyer."

He had spoken these words pointedly, as if he wanted to imply that I was ungrateful for Khorramshahi.

"I don't want a *different* lawyer," I clarified. "I want a *second* lawyer."

"Why?"

"Because I believe one plus one can equal three, not two."

Haddad's jaw hardened. "So whom else do you want?"

I was certain he knew the answer already, but I told him anyway. "Mr. Soltani."

One side of his upper lip shot up, turning his mouth into a snarl. "That's not possible," Haddad said sharply. "You can have any attorney but him."

"Why?" I asked, taken aback.

"Because he once filed a complaint against me."

I had no idea what Haddad was talking about. "But that has nothing to do with me," I protested, "and Mr. Ahmadinejad said my legal rights should be observed."

Haddad scoffed. "Your rights *are* being observed. You can have any lawyer except for Soltani."

I wasn't going to give up this easily. "But *you* have a problem with him, I don't," I asserted.

"*I* don't have a problem with him," Haddad spat back. "*He* has a problem with me."

"But I thought my file has gone to the appellate level," I persisted. "Why are you the one to decide who can be my attorney?"

Haddad paused a moment, his face twisting in distaste. Then he said, "If you take Soltani as your attorney, I will prevent him from ever meeting you, and if the appellate court rules in your favor, I will *e'terâz*, I will object."

I looked at him, flabbergasted. After what Haddad had done to me in the past, I didn't doubt the seriousness of this threat. I was beginning to once again feel powerless. Soltani was sitting just a few steps away, yet he was beyond my reach.

My father bent toward me and whispered in my ear, "Roxana, we have to do as he says. Choose someone else."

I bristled at the unfairness of it all. Then again, why should I have expected fairness now when I hadn't received it in the past?

I rubbed my temples. "Fine," I said resentfully. "Then I will take Mr. Dadkhah and Mrs. Ebadi."

Since my father had brought up Dadkhah's name before my first trial, I had learned from my cellmates that he was Soltani and Ebadi's colleague at the Center for Human Rights Defenders. The authorities had shut down the center's office in December 2008, but its lawyers were still taking on new cases. And even though Ebadi was overseas, maybe she would return to represent me.

"Human-rights lawyers are very outspoken," Haddad said. "They will not help your case." Then he added, enunciating each word, "They—will—only—*hurt*—you."

I pressed some more. He repeated his warning. My father again whispered to me to choose someone else.

"What about Mr. Nikbakht?" Khorramshahi proposed, bringing up the same name he had suggested the last time we had spoken.

I replied that I knew nothing about him. Khorramshahi said Nikbakht had already been helping him prepare for my next trial.

"Mr. Nikbakht is very good," Haddad interjected. "He is highly respected by the courts."

There must have been a reason that Haddad found Nikbakht acceptable while Soltani, Ebadi, Dadkhah, and all human-rights attorneys, for that matter, were not. But Khorramshahi then named a couple of famous reformists whom Nikbakht had defended a few years earlier. If he had represented those men, I thought, he must be all right.

"If I take Nikbakht, will I be allowed to meet with him before my trial?" I asked Haddad.

"Of course," he replied.

I sat back and exhaled slowly. These new and unforeseen threats were jumbling my mind, which was already sluggish after days without nourishment. The only thing I could think of was to tell my father to speak to both Nikbakht and Dadkhah and do what he thought was best.

Haddad instructed me to leave the room a few minutes after my father and Khorramshahi. Bahman was waiting alone in the hallway. My guard had already warned me not to talk to anyone on the way out. I complied, but Bahman approached me, his eyes clouded with worry and desperation.

"Please, please, stop your hunger strike," he implored. "It's killing me to see you suffering like this. Please."

The guard turned to admonish him, giving me a chance to mouth, "It's OK. I'm strong."

Bahman kept pleading with me as I entered the elevator. I sought his eyes and held them until the door closed.

Mahshid was sitting by herself in our cell when I returned. Mahvash and Fariba had been transferred to another cell, she told me. They were sorry the guards hadn't given them a chance to say good-bye to me. I was sorry, too.

I eased myself onto my blankets and lay there for hours, drained of energy and filled with disappointment.

My mood only worsened that evening, when, on IRIB, an English-language headline scrolled across the bottom of the screen, stating, "Iranian judicial official denies U.S. reporter is on hunger strike."

Fury pumped through my veins, and if I had had the strength, I would have banged on the walls. This judicial official must have been none other than Haddad. How dare he try to make me look like a liar and negate the only form of protest I had. I felt totally helpless, trapped in this stinking cell without a way to tell the public the truth. I could only hope that my father would deny Haddad's lie.

Haddad had lied about me before, I had discovered a few weeks earlier, when reading my cellmates' *Keyhan* newspaper. It said he claimed I had accepted the accusations of espionage activities and that the court had no evidence I had any nationality other than my Iranian one. Even though I was sure many people would doubt his statements, his lies still infuriated me.

"I am going to stop drinking sugared water, too," I swore aloud to Mahshid.

"Don't do that," she counseled, trying to settle me down. "You don't know when your trial will be, and you'll need enough energy to make it until then."

She had a point. But I was defiant. I would cut out all sugar and continue with only water.

A few times a day, I felt nauseous. Mahshid would stand up and hit the black button, which in itself had become a struggle for me, and I would wait until a guard ambled down the corridor to open our door. Then I would lift myself to my feet, blinded momentarily by colorful dots flashing before my eyes, and stagger down the hallway to the bathroom. There, I would squat with my head over the toilet and dry heave. On one occasion, I looked up to see Skinny in the doorway, staring at me.

"Sorry," I apologized. "Was I making too much noise?"

She nodded.

"I want to vomit," I mumbled, "but I can't."

"*Ma'lume,*" she replied, "that's obvious. Your stomach is empty. You can eat some honey, you know, or drink a little tea. We won't tell anyone."

"No," I croaked, and stumbled back to my cell.

On Friday, the twelfth day of my hunger strike, Glasses notified me that the doctor wanted to see me. I told her I didn't want to see him. She left and came back a few minutes later, saying I had no choice. So I went through the labor of getting dressed and teetered behind her to the dispensary. The doctor informed me my weight had fallen to about ninety-nine pounds, a loss of roughly fifteen pounds since my strike began, and he said my blood pressure had sunk to a dangerous level. He wanted to hook me up to an IV, but I declined. He also advised me to stop my hunger strike.

The next day, I was taken back to the dispensary, where this time I let the doctor attach me to the IV. He seemed offended when I asked for a clean needle, but given the prevalence of drug addiction and risk of HIV infection among the prison population, I felt the request was necessary. He injected my left arm, then left me with Cheeks, as I watched a yellowish liquid drip from a clear plastic bag down a tube and into my body.

After what seemed like an hour, the doctor returned. I was sure if he had taken any longer, my bladder would have burst.

That night, my body began to regain some energy. The doctor had warned me I would soon be forced to go through the same process again if my strike continued. "Your strike is useless," he had said. "We'll keep you alive, just as we have others like you, through any means."

I wished Javan and I hadn't arrived before my parents. It was Monday, May 4, and he was sitting on a chair across from me in the visitation room, with nothing but a thick wall of silence between us.

I couldn't stand to look at my *bâzju*, and I longed for my mother and father to relieve me of the torment of being alone with him. But then I realized this was an opportune moment to ask him a question that had been on my mind for weeks.

"Why did you allow my confession to be perpetuated when you told me yourself you knew it was false from the beginning?" I asked.

Without hesitating, he replied, "Because lying to the authorities is itself a crime."

"What a stupid answer," I muttered. I was about to point out that he and his colleagues were the ones who had coerced me into lying in the first place when my mother entered the room, with Tasbihi and my father behind her. She was crying again.

"Please start eating," she wept, as she sat down beside me, "or I will go on a hunger strike from today!"

I held her hand and asked her to be brave so that I could stay strong. Eventually she quieted down, and my father gave me an update.

He and Khorramshahi had spoken to Nikbakht, who had agreed to represent me on the condition that he would not do any media interviews.

My father also told me he had written a letter to the supreme leader and had it hand-delivered to him through a "well-placed friend." In front of the two agents, I couldn't ask who this friend was or what was in the letter.

Then my father said he had refuted Haddad's statement that I had not been on a hunger strike and added that Haddad told him there were hidden cameras in the women's cells, proving I had been eating my cellmates' meals.

I laughed. So did Javan. "We don't have hidden cameras in the cells," he said. "Whoever said that is a liar." Apparently he hadn't heard my father attribute the statement to Haddad, or he wouldn't have contradicted the deputy prosecutor.

"Why are you on a hunger strike anyway?" Javan asked, his eyes glimmering with derision. "It's contradictory to do so when you are waiting for an appeal. A strike implies you don't have hope; an appeal implies you do."

I replied in English, paraphrasing a lesson I had learned from Plutarch, "Because I believe that one must always hope for the best but expect the worst."

Javan pretended to look confused. "Sorry," he said in Farsi, "I don't understand English."

"How is it that you don't understand the language now, but you were correcting my English statements in interrogation?" I asked him, still speaking in English.

He smiled innocently.

"And tell me again," I added, switching to Farsi, "why you are letting my confession carry on when you knew it was false from the start."

"I don't know what you're talking about," he claimed, refusing to repeat his earlier reply in front of my parents. "Anyway, you can't have hope and expect the worst at the same time," he sneered, still in Farsi.

My parents interrupted to ask Tasbihi if one of the guards could bring me lunch. I insisted I didn't want any, but the food came, and my father held a spoonful of yogurt up to my lips until I relented and ate a few bites. As my mother looked on, she began to smile widely and massage my back.

"This doesn't mean I've decided to eat," I emphasized.

The time soon came for me to return to my cell. Before Tasbihi took me away, Javan said if I decided to discontinue my hunger strike, I could call my parents that night to tell them the news.

That afternoon, I agonized over what to do. I believed that my mother had been completely serious when she said she would go on a hunger strike. I couldn't bear the thought of her enduring even more pain because of me. Moreover, my father had reminded me that many people abroad were offering to continue their strikes if I were to stop mine. But I had already made it through two weeks of fasting, and I was afraid if I quit now, no one would take me seriously if I had to start again after the appellate trial.

I talked all this over with my cellmate. She urged me to stop so that I wouldn't collapse before my trial.

I decided to break my fast with dinner that night. Afterward, I was allowed to call my father and tell him my decision. I heard my mother clapping excitedly in the background. My father, too, sounded relieved. I would need my strength for my trial, he said, which he had just learned would take place in eight days, on May 12.

H addad laced his hands together on his desk, tilted his head to one side, and asked, "What exactly is your relationship with Bahman Ghobadi?"

This question caught me off-guard.

"We were . . . contemplating marriage," I said, repeating the answer I had given during interrogation.

"Mm-hmm," Haddad said, nodding slowly. "Mr. Ghobadi has been coming here every day for the past several days, trying to see you. Do you want to see him?"

"Yes," I answered, although I couldn't understand why Haddad was suddenly being nice to me. It was Wednesday morning, May 6, and he had summoned me to his office for what I thought was to be the meeting he had promised I could have with my new lawyer, Nikbakht. But no one had been there except Haddad, sitting behind his desk. I had sat down several feet away in the row of plastic-covered chairs against the wall.

Haddad told his assistant to allow Bahman to enter. A few seconds later, Bahman swept in, tears streaming down his cheeks.

My heart ached. I longed to embrace him, take his hand, or merely touch his arm. But I doubted Haddad, who was looking on with raised eyebrows, would allow that. So I just smiled sympathetically.

"Sit over there," Haddad directed Bahman, pointing at a chair a few seats down from me.

Bahman obeyed and, amid his tears, thanked Haddad for this opportunity to talk to me. Haddad nodded and allowed him to begin.

"I'm so sorry I hung up on you when you called about Zahedan," he said, as he dried his face on his sleeve. "I will never, ever forgive myself."

"It's OK, *azizam*," I tried to assure him. "I understand."

He dug a slip of paper out of his shirt pocket. "I wrote down some notes to help me remember what I wanted to tell you," he continued.

I watched him speechlessly, astonished that after more than three months, the authorities were finally permitting Bahman and me to meet with each other.

"For days," Bahman said, looking up from his notes, "I've been visiting various officials, asking for their help to release you, and one of them convinced Haddad to let me see you today."

My face flushed. Considering Bahman's own problems with the regime, I knew he would have never ordinarily approached these people for anything.

Bahman kept talking, hardly stopping to catch his breath. He felt he had also been imprisoned because he could never rest while I was behind bars. To feel closer to me, he would pace back and forth outside Evin for half an hour every night.

Tears were again rolling down his face. I had never seen him cry like this. I yearned to speak to him privately. I had so much to tell him, and I was sure he was censoring himself because Haddad was listening.

I turned toward Haddad. "May we sit a bit closer?" I asked. He nodded.

Bahman moved to the seat next to mine. I lifted my hand to his face and silently wiped away his tears. He seemed surprised by my calm demeanor. It was true that although I had been greatly moved by seeing him, no tears had fallen from my eyes. I had not forgotten the pledge I had made to myself just before Nowruz not to cry until my release.

"It seems he loves you more than you love him," Haddad remarked, with a little cackle.

Without responding, I took Bahman's hands in mine and hid them from Haddad in the folds of my chador.

"Roxana," Bahman said, dropping his voice to a whisper, "I don't want you to worry, but you should know that intelligence agents came after me a while ago, beat me up, and detained me in a private house in northern Tehran for four days."

I squeezed his hands.

He explained that the agents claimed I had been sleeping around behind his back and advised him to forget about me—statements reminiscent of what my *bâzju* had told me about Bahman. The agents also wanted him to say I was a spy, an allegation he had denied, and they warned he should not speak out in support of me. Bahman had remained quiet, hoping I would soon be freed. After my eight-year sentence, however, he had gone to the media and written an open letter calling for my release.

I pressed his hands tighter. I was about to speak when Haddad said, "Miss Saberi, why don't you just tell the truth in court?"

Anger overcame me as I spun around to face him. "I have been telling the truth," I said adamantly. "If you mean I'm supposed to say I'm a spy, I won't do that because I am not a spy."

"No, no!" Haddad said. "I didn't mean that. But you can say you had a classified document—the one on Iraq—that you didn't know was classified, and apologize for it."

I eyed him, confounded by these words. Haddad seemed to be saying he knew I wasn't a spy and was telling me what I should say in court.

"He's giving you a hint," Bahman whispered to me. "He's looking for a way out."

I turned to him and whispered back, "But I don't think I had any classified documents, and these people won't even let Khorramshahi see them."

"Roxana," Bahman said gravely but quietly, "I know what this regime is like. If you fight it, you can't win. These people are dangerous and have no pity for people like you. If you don't do what they say, they will keep you in prison for years, and who knows what will happen to you then. If they want, they could hurt or even kill you."

He smiled as he spoke, to prevent Haddad from discerning what he was saying.

"I think you should just do what he says," Bahman continued, so softly I could scarcely hear him. "The whole world knows this regime tells lies. Your parents are worried about you. Get out of jail and out of the country while you can, then tell your side of the story."

Perhaps the best thing to do, I thought, would be to ask my new lawyer, Nikbakht, what he thought about Haddad's suggestion. Earlier that day, Haddad had told me to sign a form appointing Nikbakht as my second attorney. I had agreed, but I still had doubts about him.

"Your time is up," Haddad informed us.

"Excuse me," I said. "I would like a third lawyer, Mr. Dadkhah."

Haddad frowned, then repeated his previous warning that human-rights lawyers would make things *sholugh*, or confused, and harm my case. He reiterated that I should be satisfied with Nikbakht.

I looked at Bahman.

"It's better you do what he tells you, Roxana," he repeated. "When he says Mr. Dadkhah will be detrimental to you, he means it."

I decided to take Bahman's word for it. Besides, with my trial in less than a week, I doubted I could find anyone else by then who would meet with Haddad's approval.

Another English-language headline rolled across the bottom of the TV screen that Saturday, informing me of my future: "Appeals court to hear case of jailed U.S. reporter on Sunday."

I was alarmed. My trial was supposed to be two days later than that. I had not even been allowed to talk to Nikbakht. I would ask for a postponement, but just in case my request was denied as before, I decided to prepare my defense on my own.

The guards had confiscated my pen, so I ran through the major points in my head, forming acronyms to remember them. This was all I felt I could do to get ready for a trial whose verdict, like my last one, may have already been determined.

Some time after midnight, I lay down, but sleep didn't come. I gazed at the ceiling for hours. Finally, as the call to morning prayers arose from the prison loudspeakers, I fell into a dreamless sleep.

CHAPTER TWENTY-THREE

Roxana!" one of the journalists gasped. I wasn't sure why she was so startled. Then I realized I must have been quite a sight: still frail from my hunger strike, flip-flopping along in plastic bathroom slippers, and wearing a chador that failed to hide a forehead full of what were by now bloated, burning pimples.

I had been driven that day to an austere courthouse in southern Tehran. There, on the second floor, I had been surprised to see, in addition to my father, two Iranian journalist friends and a close family friend. They all hastened to their feet when they saw me coming.

"Dad," I called out, as my guard hustled me past the group, "I'm not ready for the trial. I haven't met with Mr. Nikbakht yet."

The guard led me down a hallway and into a room on the left. It was a small courtroom with a few rows of chairs facing a slightly raised platform topped with three desks. Two middle-aged men with neatly trimmed beards were sitting behind two of the desks. I supposed they were judges.

The man on the right, the taller of the two, gestured at me to sit down. As I did, Heidarifard came in, carrying numerous files, just as I had last seen him. He sat at the third desk, to the judges' right. Then Baby Face, the representative from the Intelligence Ministry who had taken part in my first trial, entered and sat down in one of the rows behind me.

I watched this procession from the edge of my seat, distraught that all the pieces were being put in place for another trial I was not prepared for.

Soon Khorramshahi walked in, accompanied by a gray-haired, gray-mustached man with glasses. Khorramshahi took a seat on my right, while the other man sat on my left. He introduced himself to me as Mr. Nikbakht.

"Your Honor," I asked the tall judge. "Could we please delay the trial? I have not yet had the chance to speak to my new lawyer."

"No," he said abruptly, "but you can talk to him during the few minutes the prosecution needs to prepare itself."

Protesting, it seemed, would be useless. I turned to Nikbakht and asked if he had been allowed to see my file. He said he had not, so he had prepared his defense based on some notes Khorramshahi had shown him. Then Nikbakht pulled some papers from his briefcase and quickly read for me his main argument. The trial court, he would contend, had not had grounds to sentence me for "collaborating with a hostile state," in this case the United States, because Washington and Tehran could not be defined as being hostile toward each other.

I half listened to this technical argument, then shared with Nikbakht what Haddad had told me a few days earlier in his office: that I should apologize for having a classified document that I didn't know was classified, even though, I emphasized to Nikbakht, I didn't think it was really classified.

Nikbakht nodded and whispered, "Yes, do that."

Before we could continue, the tall judge spoke up. "What's your relation to Bahman Ghobadi?" he asked me.

I didn't know what this had to do with my trial, but I gave him the answer I had always given, that "we were contemplating marriage."

Then the judge announced that the trial was starting. This time, I requested and was given a pen and paper to take notes.

Heidarifard began by reading off the prosecution's accusations against me. I tried to follow as best I could.

"Miss Saberi was using her book and journalism work as a cover to spy on Iran for Mr. D, who paid her to do so and who has ties to the CIA," Heidarifard declared. This was the first time I was hearing "journalism work" thrown in as part of my supposed cover. "She was well qualified to be a spy," Heidarifard went on, "because she was acquainted with both Iran and America, she is a woman, and she had access to individuals in various political and diplomatic centers of Iran."

Then he added, repeating what had by now become a familiar refrain, that I was exactly the type of person the CIA needed in Iran: someone on the ground who could interview people and gather analysis.

Heidarifard adjusted his reading glasses with one hand and continued. He said I had ties to the Aspen Institute, which he claimed, as he had in my previous trial, was striving to overthrow the Islamic regime in a soft revolution.

"Miss Saberi also conducted many interviews and gathered information, including classified documents," he said in an accusatory voice. "Her goal through these activities was to collect news about U.S.-Iran relations to give to organizations in the United States."

Finally, Heidarifard quoted Mr. V, whom Baby Face had brought up at my first trial, as admitting to having given me many classified documents, allegedly at my request, because he was smitten by my "feminine attractiveness" and I had supposedly promised to marry him.

The tall judge squinted at me. "Miss Saberi, how many men did you promise to marry?"

"But those statements are not true," I protested. "First of all, to the best of my knowledge, I never received any classified documents from either Mr. V or anyone else. Secondly, I didn't promise to marry him, and we were just *dust-e âdi*, ordinary friends."

"You were what?" the judge asked, as if he had never heard this term before.

"Ordinary friends," I repeated.

"Your Honor," Heidarifard interjected, "Mr. V said the two went to a restaurant together."

"Is it illegal to have lunch with a friend?" I asked.

"It is in our country," the judge said sternly, "if the man and woman are *nâ-mahram*." He was referring to men and women unrelated to one another through either marriage or close family ties.

I was sure the judge knew very well that if the authorities really enforced that, Iran's restaurants would go out of business. I also wondered how he would respond if I asked him why four men were allowed to interrogate me in a small room with no other woman present. And what would he say if I told him I had recently heard that a woman prisoner at Evin had been freed only after agreeing to have sex with her interrogator?

"Sir," Heidarifard interrupted, "Miss Saberi also used her femininity to get close to certain Iranian officials . . ."

I recoiled in my seat at this false allegation.

". . . in order to get her brother exempted from military service in Iran."

Unbelievable. Jasper had never even thought about coming to Iran, and even if he had wanted to, I had been told that the government allowed Iranians abroad to visit for a few months a year without being drafted. Besides, my captors knew he was in the U.S. Army. The suggestion was absurd.

"I object, Your Honor," I said sharply. "I find these accusations insulting." Referring to a verse I had read in the Koran, I added, "And according to the Koran, you need four witnesses to prove illicit relations."

Heidarifard lowered his papers and locked his small, round eyes on me for a few seconds. Then he looked back at the judge and announced that he was resting his case. Now it was time for my defense.

I turned to Khorramshahi, then to Nikbakht, wondering which one would go first, but they motioned at me to begin. I again wished I had studied Iranian law.

I took a deep breath and closed my eyes. *God*, I prayed, *please cherish me, guide me, and take care of me. I trust in you that if I tell the truth, you will protect me.*

I opened my eyes and started to read aloud the notes I had just written. The Mr. D story was false, I said, then explained how I had been pressured to make it up. "Moreover," I continued, "the Intelligence Ministry knows very well that I didn't see Mr. D on the dates stated in my false confession because, as my interrogators informed me, they accompanied me on my trips abroad."

"Your Honors," Baby Face cut in from behind me, "we didn't travel *everywhere* with her."

The tall judge dipped his chin at him, encouraging him to continue.

"But we know she sent Mr. D information electronically," the agent said. "She made a CD for him and also sent him information through e-mail."

"Excuse me," I said, turning slightly toward Baby Face, "but I never made a CD for Mr. D. And if I had actually e-mailed any information to him, show me proof of those e-mails, which you must have because you monitored my communications very closely."

Baby Face lowered his eyes.

I continued my defense. I touched on the Aspen Institute, restating what I had said during my first trial, and I described my book and the types of news reports I had prepared, none of which amounted to a cover for anything.

As for the documents Heidarifard had referred to, I said, as far as I knew, none of the articles I had was classified and all were public information.

No sooner had these words left my mouth than Heidarifard thrust his fist into the air, gripping the article on the U.S. war in Iraq, and announced, "Miss Saberi said she copied this report and got it at the Center for Strategic Research."

"There was nothing on that report to indicate it was classified," I said, as calmly as I could. "And from what I recall, it is old—dated from before the war even started—and does not contain anything that hasn't been publicly stated a thousand times by Iranian officials."

"But did you copy it?" the tall judge asked.

"Yes."

"And who told you that you could copy it?"

My mind began to spin. I didn't want to say that employees at the center let me copy materials because even though I didn't think this report was classified, if it really was, I didn't want to get anyone there in trouble. Not only was the center filled with moderates, but hard-liners had also accused one of its directors of espionage in 2007, though he was later given a suspended sentence for a lesser charge and resumed his work there.

"No one told me," I said. "I copied it myself . . . out of curiosity."

The judge nodded grimly. Then he turned to my lawyers and told them they could continue with my defense.

Khorramshahi rose to his feet and gave a five-minute argument, similar to what Nikbakht had earlier read to me about the United States not being a hostile state. Then Nikbakht stood up and repeated the argument, although he spoke with much more confidence and stretched out his speech for what seemed like thirty to forty-five minutes. I couldn't follow his references to this or that article and this or that precedent. I began to listen closely when he started speaking about the so-called classified documents.

"None of the materials she had is classified," Nikbakht said emphatically.

"None is classified," the tall judge said, "except the one on Iraq—according to the trial court."

I couldn't help rolling my eyes.

Nikbakht countered: "The report on Iraq does not have a classified stamp on it. It has no signs of being classified. Also, it is an outdated article, and it contains nothing sensitive or secret. In any case, Miss Saberi apologizes for copying it and had no bad intentions."

Actually, I had not apologized.

Nikbakht peered down at me with raised eyebrows. He must have been waiting for me to say what we had discussed before the trial.

I raised my eyebrows back at him.

He gave me a quick but firm nod.

I sighed deeply. Nikbakht appeared to know what he was doing. It seemed I should repeat at least a version of what he and Haddad had advised.

"If it really was classified," I said slowly, "I didn't know it, and I apologize. In any case, I didn't use it, I didn't plan to use it, and I didn't give it to anyone."

There. I had to some extent said what everyone seemed to have wanted me to say, even though I still didn't think I had any classified materials. I looked at Heidarifard. I thought I detected a smile of self-satisfaction.

It was Baby Face's turn to speak. Most of his allegations of suspicious activities were similar to those I had heard on earlier occasions, such as my interview with the Hezbollah official in Lebanon and my short chat with the Japanese ambassador to Tehran. I defended myself as well as I could and argued that these actions were harmless.

The agent also repeated his claim that I had been under no pressure when interrogated and that I was questioned in a "completely friendly atmosphere." This time, I reminded him that I had been held in solitary confinement, barred from having a lawyer, blindfolded, repeatedly interrogated by four men, and cut off from the outside world. Baby Face replied only that such treatment was "natural in security cases."

The tall judge then asked several questions about my book and wanted to know why I had interviewed "so many people."

Time passed quickly, and when the trial was finished, I discovered that it had lasted around four hours. Like my first trial, it was badly flawed. Neither my lawyers nor I had been able to examine the supposed witness, Mr. V, or what the prosecution called evidence (although my attorneys had not even asked for permission to do so), but at least the two judges had not cut off my statements as Judge Moqiseh had.

I couldn't tell by looking at my lawyers what they thought of the trial. They told me all we could do was wait for the verdict, which might be announced in a week or two.

As I was leaving the courtroom, the shorter judge, who had sat mutely most of the time, held up his palm to stop me. "Your next book," he said, with a quiet, sinister laugh, "should be about Guantánamo Bay."

The guard led me back down the deserted hallway, my father and friends nowhere to be seen.

W*hatever the result of my appeal will be*, I told myself that night in my cell, *I must do my best to accept it with strength, courage, and patience.*

I expected my sentence to be reduced, but I didn't know by how many years. I vowed that if I was given a short sentence, I would try to make the most of my experience with the women in the regular prison. If I was given a long sentence, I would resume my hunger strike.

CHAPTER TWENTY-FOUR

My ears perked up at the sound of someone snapping. It was Mahshid. She entered our cell the next morning, clicking her fingers above her head and performing a little Iranian dance. Still on her feet and panting, she told me she had just had her first family visit with her husband, brother, sister, and son, who had been freed some days earlier.

"And," Mahshid added, with sparkling eyes, "my sister has read online that you will soon be freed."

I yanked her down to the floor. I couldn't believe what I was hearing. Mahshid's sister must have misread the article. Maybe it had actually quoted Khorramshahi saying he *hoped* I would be freed. And how could the court have reached a decision so fast? Mahshid replied that her sister had spoken with certainty.

Noon passed, and I had no news of my parents' routine Monday morning visit. Then, around one o'clock, Skinny told me to put on my chador and blindfold. By now, I had become so used to walking with my eyes covered that I nimbly followed her outside to a Peykan. But instead of being driven toward the visitation building as I was expecting, I was handcuffed and taken off Evin compound, toward the appellate court where I had been the day before.

My driver today was my guard from the previous day. He was driving like a maniac, swerving in and out of traffic and ignoring stoplights as if they were merely decoration. When a diligent police officer stopped our car, the guard roared at him to mind his own business. I groped for a seat belt, but as in the backseats of many Iranian cars, either there wasn't one or it was buried so far into the dirty cushioning that I opted to let the driver play with my fate.

As we tore around a corner, the driver yelled back at me, "Were you the winner of a beauty pageant?"

This was the first time since my arrest that anyone had raised this subject. "Yes," I said, a bit hesitantly, "but it was a scholarship competition and not just a beauty pageant."

He and his colleague asked me a few questions about it. They seemed intrigued, so I found myself explaining to two Iranian prison guards how a young woman went about competing for Miss America.

This time when I entered the courtroom, only the tall judge was there, and he allowed the two guards to sit in the back. Khorramshahi and Nikbakht soon arrived, and the judge began to read out the verdict in a loud, monotone voice.

What little I could understand sounded awful. Nikbakht was looking on stoically, while Khorramshahi's face was tense. The judge droned on. I wished he would just tell me how much longer I would have to remain in prison.

At last, he reached what appeared to be the last page. The vocabulary was so complex that I couldn't follow it well, although the tone of the text and the judge's voice seemed to have become a little more positive. I heard him say something about "Islamic forgiveness," a suspended sentence, and not being allowed to work as a journalist in Iran for five years.

I turned to Khorramshahi. A slight smile had formed on his lips.

"Does that mean I'm free?" I whispered, as the judge continued to read.

Khorramshahi's smile broke into a grin.

"Thank God!" I said softly, my hands rising toward the ceiling. I wanted to kneel on the ground and cry out these words, but I restrained myself.

The judge finished reading and looked up at me. "Just be good to Islam and Iran," he said. Then he informed my lawyers that they could tell my parents to pick me up at the prison in two hours.

Nikbakht thanked the judge profusely, as I just sat there, unable to move or speak. *Would I really be freed?* I wouldn't believe it until I was out of jail and with my parents. Khorramshahi called them with the news as the two guards led me back to the car—this time, without handcuffs.

"We can't believe you'll be released," the driver told me, as we set out toward Evin.

"Yeah," his colleague added, "we didn't think eight years would be reduced to a suspended sentence."

I hadn't, either.

The driver was driving like a madman again. Now that I was to be a free woman, I asked him to slow down.

The two guards wanted to know if I liked Iranian food and if I had eaten the chicken kabob the previous evening. I said yes. One said white meat was healthier than red meat. The other agreed. Their bantering continued until we reached a narrow street near the prison, where the driver stopped in front of a bakery. The guard in the passenger seat hopped out, bought a large stack of steamy white bread, and offered me some. The guards had never been so friendly. I had heard that captors often warmed up to prisoners who were about to be freed, so that when they were released, they would be less likely to badmouth prison officials. I declined the offer. I was too excited to eat, anyway.

"Were you at court today?" Skinny asked me when I arrived at the women's ward. I could tell by the inquisitive look on her face that she wanted to be the first to find out about the latest development in my case, which I had discovered the guards had been following as closely as *The Prophet Joseph*.

"Yes," I replied, without elaborating.

Skinny filled the silence immediately. "Well, what happened?" she asked impatiently.

"It's a wonderful day," I said.

"What do you mean?"

"I mean, I'm going to be freed," I replied, a smile stretching across my face.

"Really?" She looked at me in a peculiar way.

Skinny didn't say anything else as she ushered me into my cell. Mahshid was standing in the middle of the room in her chador, saying her afternoon prayers. She raised her eyes.

All I had to do was smile.

"I told you!" she cried.

"I still can't believe it," I said.

She hugged me, and we jumped up and down with joy. But suddenly, I froze.

"What's wrong?" Mahshid asked.

"I'm glad I'm being released," I said, "but what about you?"

"Don't worry about me," she replied, stroking my arm. "I have learned to accept what is happening to me. I realize I am serving a purpose by being here, perhaps even more than if I would be outside."

She was smiling broadly. She seemed to really mean what she said.

Our cell door opened. "Gather your belongings," Skinny ordered me in the same tone as always, "except for your blankets."

I had heard her and her fellow guards say this to so many other prisoners, and now she was saying it to me.

When I was ready, Skinny pulled me out of the cell, without giving me a chance to hug Mahshid one last time. She led me down the corridor, past a few chadors hanging on the wall next to cell doors with their barred windows sealed shut. I wondered when the prisoners who wore those garments would be freed.

I had often heard the rustling of trash bags that signaled other inmates going home. And now Skinny was handing me the bag that held my own clothes. I put them on—they were at least three sizes too big, but how I had missed them!

She told me I still had to wear my blindfold as she took me to the office of the detention center's director. The man who had warned me not to go on a hunger strike wanted to emphasize that I wasn't being released because of it. I nodded. I just wanted to get out of Evin.

Skinny left me in another room with a male guard who returned my tote bag, laptop, flash drive, and some of my books and notebooks. He said my *bâjzu* wasn't at Evin that day, and my passports and cash, as well as the rest of my belongings, were in his hands. The guard told me to check back in a day or two. Peeking under my blindfold, I signed some papers and was fingerprinted.

"Now don't go around telling people we tortured you here," he said, as he dropped me off at a van outside 209 and told me I was free to uncover my eyes. In one swift movement, I ripped off the cloth and gave it to him.

Another guard drove me toward a prison gate I had not seen before. "We're taking you to another exit," he explained, "so that the journalists at the main gate won't see you."

The van's windows must have been tinted, because as we pulled up to my parents, I could see them waiting for me, but they couldn't see me waving at them. When our vehicle came to a halt, my mother stuck her head in the passenger-side window and spotted me in the rear seat. She was beaming. The guard let me out, and I hugged her tightly, soaking up the scent of her freshly shampooed hair. Then my father stepped forward and enveloped me in his arms. My mother was so happy, she tried to shake the hand of my guard, who, flustered at the possibility of a *nâ-mahram* woman touching him, offered her his wrist.

My parents led me to a friend's car, which he had been permitted to drive onto the prison grounds. I climbed into the back with my mother, and we pulled out of the gate.

As we entered an alley behind Evin Prison, I looked over my shoulder at the tall walls and barbed wire. When we rounded a corner, they faded from my sight.

Finally, I wept.

EPILOGUE

My tears were of both joy and sorrow: joy at my freedom but sorrow for the prisoners of conscience I was leaving behind, who were being punished simply because of their peaceful pursuit of basic human rights or for their beliefs.

Why was I freed while many others were not? Was it because as a foreign citizen, I was fortunate enough to receive international support, while others' plights were less known outside Iran or perhaps even unknown beyond their families?

On May 11, the day of my release, I stayed at a friend's home while my parents returned to my apartment, where a neighbor had reported that several journalists were camped out. I wasn't ready to face them, and I knew that the authorities would be closely monitoring my every word. News of my freedom was all over the satellite TV networks, and both local and foreign journalists wanted to interview me.

Many Iranians, I learned the next day, had been following my story. A driver at my neighborhood taxi agency refused to accept my money, and I was shocked when he told me a local bazaar had been selling "Roxana scarves," like the blue one I had worn in a photograph circulated in the media. The manager of an office where I had some business called his wife and child to come from home to get their picture taken with me. And when I returned to my apartment complex through the back door that day, my neighbors, even the ones who had been too frightened to visit my parents while I was in jail, said they had prayed for me. Close friends called, brought flowers, or stopped by to visit. Nearly everyone who saw me apologized for the way I had been treated, which they said was contrary to the hospitality that Iranians like to show their guests.

I was greatly moved that the regime's propaganda against me did not appear to have influenced them, and I told them honestly that my affection for the Iranian people had not at all diminished.

Other than these brief encounters, as well as a message of thanks that I shared with journalists on my second day of freedom, I tried to maintain a low profile, not wanting to give the authorities any excuses to hold on to my two passports. My father went to Evin twice to try to retrieve them, but he was told that my *bâzju* was unavailable. Meanwhile, Iran's Intelligence Minister announced to the media that in his eyes, I was still a spy, making me feel an even more urgent need to leave the country.

When I saw Bahman, we spoke for hours, trying to catch up on all that had happened during my incarceration. We talked softly in case his apartment was bugged and hurriedly, as if we feared being pulled apart again at any moment. He agreed that I should leave Iran as soon as possible, and he contacted a high-level official who made a few phone calls about my passports. Bahman, too, was preparing to move overseas. The movie he had secretly filmed, *No One Knows About Persian Cats*, was about to screen in France. It was openly critical of Iran's sociocultural restrictions, and he predicted that the Iranian authorities would give him an even tougher time after that.

On May 13, Bahman departed for the Cannes Film Festival, and I bade him farewell, knowing we would meet again soon outside Iran. The next night, with both of my passports in hand, I left for the airport with my parents and a family friend, having kissed my neighbor's Koran and passed under it three times for protection on our voyage.

I was ecstatic when I made it through passport control at Imam Khomeini International Airport. But just as my parents entered behind me, a plainclothesman with a walkie-talkie began shouting my name.

"Miss Saberi," he said breathlessly, "you are not allowed to leave the country!"

My mother collapsed onto the floor, and the man ordered us to move to a lounge to avoid creating a scene in the middle of the airport. After he woke up his superiors at their homes, he realized what we had been telling him—that the court had not barred me from leaving Iran—was true.

Finally, when our Austrian Airlines flight lifted off the runway, I released a deep sigh of relief, even though I couldn't help wondering whether an Iranian agent was watching me from another row of seats. A few hours later, we arrived in Vienna, where we rested for about a week at a friend's home before returning to America.

I now relished the freedoms I had taken for granted before my imprisonment. I went for a slow jog in the streets, ate chips, and flossed my teeth. I slept with the lights off and my head on a pillow. I spoke to my parents, made phone calls, and wrote e-mails whenever I liked and without fear of being monitored.

One of the first people I contacted was Mr. D. When I explained the terrible falsehoods I had been pressured to state about him, he was truly understanding. "If that tale helped save your life," he told me, "then I am glad."

*

Since those early days, I have been gaining new perspectives on my experiences by speaking to former prisoners, human-rights advocates, lawyers, analysts, and others who followed my case.

I discovered that what happened to me was remarkably similar to what many people in Iranian prisons endure. Human-rights activists call the mix of intimidation and manipulation that I experienced "white torture," which does not leave a physical mark but devastates one's mind and conscience. Numerous prisoners have suffered harsher treatment; some have reacted much as I did, others have not.

Many people detained in Iran are held without due process of law, their whereabouts are kept secret, they are placed in solitary confinement, and they have little or no contact with their families or attorneys. They often suffer severe psychological—and in some cases, physical—torture aimed at forcing them to make confessions and to write or speak about their friends and colleagues. Some, like Iranian-Canadian journalist Maziar Bahari, who was detained for 118 days in 2009, have been pressured, as I was, to become agents of the regime. Families are often told to avoid talking to the media.

The world heard much more about the use of such methods in the aftermath of Iran's disputed June 12, 2009, presidential election, when thousands of people were detained and dozens killed during the most significant civil unrest since the Islamic Revolution. A presidential candidate reported prisoner allegations of rape and sexual abuse, and the authorities acknowledged that at least three people died in custody, although human-rights groups say the death toll was likely higher. A number of journalists, reformist politicians, student activists, and dissidents prosecuted in mass show trials were portrayed in the Iranian media as confessing to crimes against the Islamic Republic. More than one hundred people received jail terms of up to fifteen years, and several defendants accused of taking part in protests following Ahmadinejad's reelection were sentenced to death. Crackdowns by Iran's increasingly repressive security forces largely subdued demonstrations that broke out after the election in support of the opposition Green Movement.

Just as I was, many prisoners have been warned that if they did not confess and repent, they wouldn't be released, and their loved ones could be harmed. Some former detainees have reported being forced to sign confessions they were not even allowed to read, while others, like me, were guided by their captors about what to say, or they negotiated with their interrogators over the content of their statements and whom they would implicate. As author and historian Ervand Abrahamian explained to me, interrogators often give prisoners a list of topics they should mention but let them write their own confession in an attempt to make the wording fit the victim, sound believable, and therefore, serve as a tool for swaying public opinion. As a result of these tactics, captors such as mine like to claim they never force anyone to make a false confession and that prisoners confess voluntarily.

Omid Memarian, a former Iranian journalist who was detained and coerced into making a false confession in 2004, told me that interrogators rarely believe the confessions they force out of prisoners, just as my *bâzju* eventually admitted knowing from the start that mine was not true. "If they believed those confessions," said Memarian, who retracted his after he was released, "they wouldn't release anybody. The fact is that they have freed several supposed spies and people who have allegedly acted against national security. They are incapable of finding real spies, if there are any, and by arresting innocent people, they want to intimidate others.

"Even when you learn that they do not believe your confession," he added, "you still know they can keep you in prison on the false accusations for years. Their threats are very real. They make you feel you have no control over your life. You even smell your own fear."

Not all prisoners, however, are pressured to confess. It is often those who represent something, such as a group, an ideology, or a foreign country, whose confessions have propagandistic, symbolic, or other value for their captors. For example, high-profile activists, political figures, and people such as Silva Harotonian and me who have had contacts with Americans are more likely to be coerced to confess than are lesser-known prisoners, such as most of my other cellmates.

Some prisoners have been released relatively quickly after making confessions. Apparently it was enough for their captors to be armed with these statements, which could be used to further their own aims.

But making a confession does not always guarantee freedom. Iranian-American scholar Kian Tajbakhsh, who was released soon after his so-called confession was broadcast in 2007, was arrested again in 2009 and according to Iranian media, confessed that American institutions like the nonprofit he once worked for were involved in attempting a soft revolution against the regime. He was later sentenced to fifteen years in prison on various trumped-up charges, including espionage, before an appellate court reduced his sentence to five years. Since March 2010, he has been on temporary release from prison but unable to leave Iran.

Amnesty International has reported that numerous prisoners in Iran have even been executed with confessions extracted under duress used as the sole evidence against them.

Some prisoners have retracted their confessions before their release, though this can jeopardize their chances at freedom. In my case, I unknowingly recanted shortly after Deputy Prosecutor Haddad had publicly announced I would be released within a few days, evidently prompting the authorities to reverse this decision. Many other prisoners have waited to recant until they were freed, and still others have remained quiet. Recanting, particularly for those who stay in Iran, can be dangerous not only for themselves but also for their families.

Whether or not prisoners recant, their confessions are widely doubted by ordinary people in today's Iran. As author Abrahamian says, many see such confessions as a sign of being human rather than as a sign of weakness, and they are likely to ridicule the interrogator while pitying the prisoner.

I have also understood more about another form of white torture—the practice of pressuring detainees to write about people they know, often forcing them to write lies. Iranians even have a name for this: *taknevisi*, which refers to writing about relatives, acquaintances, friends, and colleagues one by one on separate sheets of paper. This is required especially of prisoners who are considered social hubs or who have had contacts with many people. It is common for them to have to write about reformist politicians and other well-known figures, many of whom are potential targets for future arrests. One reason interrogators collect even seemingly insignificant information is to scare future prisoners into talking by making them think their captors know more than they actually do—a method I later realized my interrogators used with me. Interrogators also often lie to captives by claiming that their friends made statements against them.

I have also learned that some prisoners have been falsely accused, as I was, of having classified documents. Shortly after my release, I was surprised to hear that my attorneys had begun to announce to the media that I had copied a classified document, contradicting what they themselves had said at my trial. I do not know why they made this and other untrue statements about me. Perhaps they were intimidated by the Iranian authorities into colluding with them to try to discredit me. Other attorneys have told me that some Iranian lawyers face such severe pressure from the authorities that they sometimes sacrifice their ethics and responsibilities to their clients. Lawyers who defy this pressure can end up in prison themselves. This was the case with human-rights advocates Abdolfattah Soltani and Mohammad Dadkhah, who were both detained for several weeks after the June 2009 election and still await their trials.

It was not until more than a month and a half after my release that I became absolutely certain the article I had was not a classified document. By then, I had talked to various Iranian legal experts, including Nobel Peace laureate Shirin Ebadi, whom Haddad had warned me not to retain as my lawyer. They all told me there is no way an official document in Iran can be marked classified with a *mim*, handwritten or otherwise. To be considered classified, an article like the one I had must have the word CLASSIFIED either printed on it at the time of publication or stamped on it. As Ebadi told me, "It was all a trick."

Maybe, in the end, the Iranian authorities promoted this falsehood as my main "crime" because amid the international outcry, they were hoping to save face by presenting a pretext for my imprisonment other than a confession whose validity I had denied while still in custody. Or, they may have wanted all along to frame me to implicate the Center for Strategic Research, which is linked to moderates and pragmatic conservatives who have been open to dialogue with the West and has come under increasing pressure by hard-liners since Ahmadinejad became president in 2005.

Many people have asked me if I understand the reasons behind my arrest. I cannot be sure. Iran's regime comprises many different players and factions, and its inner workings are far from transparent.

As both my *bâzju* and the deputy prosecutor suggested to me, they knew I was not a spy. So my captors must have had other motives for my incarceration, such as possible political reasons, wanting to justify their investment in monitoring me, and making demands such as having me spy for them.

They also seemed extremely bothered by the fact that I could move freely around Iran to interview people in their own language and without a government minder for a book the authorities could not censor. They may have thought it would be much easier to put a stop to the information my book was meant to provide than to control the Iranians who were willing to be interviewed by me—and there were many more than sixty, as I counted after my release. From the illiterate to the scholar and from the reformist to the conservative, they wanted to share their views with me. They were proud of their country and sought to help me create a more comprehensive picture of it for outsiders.

I also cannot be certain why I was released. I believe that international pressure had a lot to do with it, publicity of my two-week hunger strike appeared to further annoy my captors, and the regime must have concluded that keeping me in prison would be more costly than releasing me. The decision to free me, I have heard, was likely made even before my appellate trial.

When I was released, there was speculation that Tehran and Washington may have reached some kind of behind-the-scenes deal, but I have been told by officials close to my case that this was not so. And when, in July 2009, America handed over five Iranian officials it had detained in northern Iraq, the State Department denied that this was linked to my release.

*

At the time of this writing, I am aware of at least two of my former cellmates who are still in prison. After their trial starting in January 2010, Mahvash Sabet and Fariba Kamalabadi, along with their five male Baha'i colleagues, were told they received twenty-year sentences, reduced to ten years, though they have not been notified of these rulings in writing. Since my release, I have learned that all seven refused to make false confessions.

Silva Harotonian was transferred to the regular prison when her sentence was upheld on appeal. After an international publicity campaign calling for her release, she was allowed to leave Iran in March 2010. Mahshid Najafi, my last cellmate, was released in July 2009, but her file remains open, and she awaits a court hearing.

In September 2010, Iranian-Canadian blogger Hossein Derakhshan, whom authorities confirmed was in Evin Prison, was sentenced to nineteen and a half years in prison. Omid Reza Mirsayafi, another blogger and a journalist, died under suspicious circumstances inside Evin while I was there, on March 18, 2009. Numerous other journalists have been arrested since the 2009 election, making Iran the world's largest prison for journalists, according to Reporters Without Borders.

Iranian-American student Esha Momeni was allowed to return to the United States in August 2009, but two of three American hikers, who Iranian authorities claimed illegally crossed into Iran from Iraq in July 2009, remain detained in Evin and are accused of spying, a charge their families and friends say is ridiculous. And in 2010, according to Amnesty International, at least twenty-three Iranian prisoners convicted of politically motivated offenses were executed.

*

Someday, I would like to return to Iran. I hope that day will be what one Iranian friend called "a time when everywhere [in Iran] will be safe and prosperous, and we will have no political prisoners."

"You must return," he said, "because Iran is your father's country and because your name is Iranian, and you are Iranian."

I remain proud of my Iranian roots, and it pains me to see the suffering of Iranians who endure repression and brutality when peacefully standing up for fundamental human rights such as freedom of expression, association, and assembly. Yet I am also inspired by their nobility, courage, and hope for a brighter future.

Iran is a sophisticated nation with a rich culture and civilization spanning thousands of years and a history of democratic movements. Its people deserve much more than the injustices they have been facing. I experienced the impact that international support can have, and it is my hope that similar attention can be given to others who are wrongly treated and that human-rights abuses will not be overlooked in the international community's political dealings with the Islamic Republic.

I do believe that certain Iranian authorities are genuinely trying to address some of their country's human-rights violations and shortcomings. However, they face fierce opposition from extremists who seem blinded by their own pursuit of power and their failure to recognize that the key to long-term security lies not in control and intimidation but in tolerance, an exchange of ideas, and winning the hearts and minds of disaffected groups and independent thinkers. This security also depends on addressing the roots of problems instead of suppressing the people who speak or write about them. While suppression might silence people in the short run, it breeds discontent and distrust toward the regime in the long run. It can also push advocates of moderate change underground, where they might turn from evolutionaries into revolutionaries.

*

A year and a half after my release, I still look over my shoulder sometimes to see if someone is following me. I can't help it, just as I can't help having occasional nightmares about my time in Evin. Like many former prisoners, I have emotional scars such as these to deal with, but the universal lessons I gained from my experiences and my cellmates—including those about compassion, courage, integrity, and the power of faith—have been helping me heal. As I have traveled across the country and abroad and heard from many readers, I have also realized that we all have our own prisons in life, and while staying true to our principles and beliefs is at times the hardest path to follow, it is, as I have seen, the surest path to real freedom.

My recovery has been further aided by supportive friends and a loving family. My parents' lives have returned to normal, while Jasper got married and plans to go back to graduate school. My ordeal brought us all closer, and we value our time together much more than before.

After many months, Bahman and I decided to go our separate ways. He lives in Iraqi Kurdistan, where he is working on his next film. After leaving Iran, he openly criticized the government's repressive measures, and if he returns, he could be imprisoned or at the very least barred from departing the country.

As for me, I have spent much of my time joining others in speaking out against human rights abuses in the Islamic Republic, although my message is not limited to Iran, for injustice to one is injustice to all, and each of us can make a difference in addressing it, whenever and wherever it occurs. I also plan to resume writing my next book on Iran—the one that I was working on at the time of my arrest.

While I wish I had never been imprisoned, I realize my captivity has created interest in what I have to say about Iran. It has also given me a newfound determination to speak out. That's because although I had witnessed injustice before I was arrested, I never really understood it— until I *lived* it and felt the pain of others who endure and stand up to it.

I have spoken openly and freely, hoping to give a voice to the many Saras, Faribas, and Mahshids who are struggling to achieve their most basic rights. From them, I have learned that in the dark, there is light, and that though there will always be those who suffer, eventually the truth will prevail.

January, 2011
United States of America

ACKNOWLEDGMENTS

I am deeply indebted to the people who supported me during my six years in Iran and my one hundred days in prison. If I could, I would thank them all here by name. I hope wherever they are in the world, they will accept my heartfelt gratitude.

I would not have moved to Iran if Simon Marks had not taken a chance on me by sending me to Tehran to become the first Iran correspondent for his agency, Feature Story News. Thank you, Simon, for having confidence in me, for paying me to do something I loved, and when I was imprisoned, for helping to coordinate efforts for my release with several news organizations. Special thanks to ABC, BBC, Fox News, NPR, PBS, and the *Wall Street Journal*, which along with Simon issued a joint statement to Iranian authorities on my behalf.

There were many fellow journalists from America to Asia and from Europe to New Zealand who kept my story alive. Several wrote reports and editorials that sought to humanize my case. Numerous journalists also went beyond their professional duties to seek my release and offer my parents comfort, help, and guidance. I will not attempt to list them here because I know I cannot name them all.

Calls for my release were made by dozens of journalism groups, including Asian American Journalists Association, Association of Independents in Radio, Committee to Protect Journalists, National Press Photographers Association, Overseas Press Club, Radio Television Digital News Foundation, Society of Professional Journalists, and UNITY: Journalists of Color. Reporters Without Borders devoted considerable time, energy, and resources to my case and drew public attention to it in creative ways. After learning of what these and other journalism groups did for me, I appreciate even more their work in support of journalists around the world.

Human-rights activists and groups, such as Amnesty International, Human Rights Watch, and the International Campaign for Human Rights in Iran, also played an invaluable role by raising awareness, advocating on my behalf, and keeping the media spotlight on my detention and prosecution.

I also thank the team of volunteers who set up the freeroxana.net Web site, which kept a blog on my situation and allowed individuals to sign up for a hunger strike in solidarity with me, just after the one by Reporters Without Borders began. The Web site, along with www.roxanasaberi.com, showed what new media combined with big hearts and enthusiasm can do.

A blanket thanks to the many people around the world who urged my release on social networking Web sites such as Facebook and Twitter. Thank you to all those who signed petitions and wrote letters, fasted, took part in rallies and vigils, prayed for me, and once I was freed, sent me congratulatory e-mails, cards, and flowers. I was deeply moved that friends, strangers, and people who had met me only briefly years earlier showed such compassion. Without it, it is quite likely I would still be in prison.

I am also immensely thankful for the efforts of many faculty, staff, students, alumni, and former classmates from my alma maters in Fargo Public Schools, Concordia College, Northwestern University's Medill School of Journalism, and the University of Cambridge. The North Dakota and Minnesota communities, Fargo-Moorhead residents, and the Fargo VA Medical Center, where my mother works, were enormously understanding and generous. While my parents were in Iran, their neighbors watched over their home, planted flowers in their yard, and started a yellow-ribbon campaign. The Miss North Dakota and Miss America organizations, the Aspen Institute, and Rotary International, which all knew me before my imprisonment, were also among the many groups that called upon the Iranian authorities to release me.

I was very fortunate to have had the support of President Barack Obama, Secretary of State Hillary Clinton, and the State Department, as well as North Dakota Governor John Hoeven, U.S. senators Kent Conrad and Byron Dorgan and Representative Earl Pomeroy of North Dakota, and Senator Amy Klobuchar of Minnesota. Among others, the North Dakota congressional delegation wrote a letter to the supreme leader requesting my release. North Dakota's state legislature passed a resolution supporting Congress in its efforts to obtain my freedom.

The Swiss Embassy in Iran played a vital role as the representative of U.S. interests there. Swiss Ambassador Livia Leu Agosti had a number of high-level contacts with different Iranian authorities, pushing for a fair trial and quick release. She and her colleagues closely followed the developments in my case and regularly communicated with the State Department and my parents. Swiss President Hans-Rudolf Merz also raised the issue with President Ahmadinejad on April 19 at a meeting in Geneva.

The Japanese government and embassy in Tehran were tremendously helpful as well, and then–Foreign Minister Hirofumi Nakasone expressed concern about my case in a meeting with his Iranian counterpart in early May in Tehran.

I also thank the European Union, which issued statements on my behalf despite the fact that, as my interrogator pointed out, I am not European. I was told that my case was also discussed at several meetings of E.U. ambassadors in Tehran. I am grateful for this, as I am for the efforts of Michael Postl, the then–Austrian ambassador to Tehran, a friend who lifted my parents' spirits and used his extensive contacts in Iran to push for my release.

Nechervan Barzani, the then–prime minister of the Kurdistan Regional Government in Iraq, also requested that Tehran free me. Politicians and officials in other countries, including Britain, did the same, while on several occasions, U.N. Secretary-General Ban Ki-moon discussed my imprisonment with the Iranian government.

The Iranian diaspora was extremely active in publicizing my case and calling for my freedom. I especially appreciate the efforts of Farsi-speaking journalists, whose news reports and analyses reached the Iranian people and the regime.

I am also grateful to Iranian attorneys Shirin Ebadi and Abdolfattah Soltani, who publicly and courageously announced my innocence despite risks to themselves, and who have maintained that I should not have been arrested in the first place. Soltani, I have learned, tried several times to see me in prison so that I could sign the papers needed for him to represent me, but the authorities did not let him. I have no doubt that if he had been allowed to defend me, he would have done so with skill and principle.

My parents would have had a much tougher time during their stay in Iran if it were not for my friends and acquaintances there who kept them company. I would like to thank in particular Aresu Eqbali, Payam Mohebi, and my neighbor Nahid for never fearing to be friends with my parents and with me.

Months after my release, I found on the Internet an open letter to Iran's judiciary chief, written by Sadegh Zibakalam, a political science professor at the University of Tehran. I was touched and amazed by his boldness to declare my innocence at a time when the regime's propaganda machine was trying to paint me as one of the worst kinds of criminals. "Roxana Saberi's only crime," he wrote, "is excessive love of Iran, a sentiment that finally ran her into trouble."

During the past several months, I have greatly benefited from the sound advice of my attorney, Robert Barnett, and his colleagues Deneen Howell and Margaret Keeley. Publicists Denise Godoy and Reenie Kuhlman of GoodPR and Gretchen Crary of Harper-Collins have guided me through the unfamiliar terrain of being the interviewee instead of the interviewer.

Guillermo Arriaga, Alice Boelter, Hadi Ghaemi, Afshin Molavi,

Karim Sadjadpour, Andrea Sanke, Stephanie Sy, Shane Tedjarati, Mindy Trossman, and Alastair Wanklyn read this entire manuscript and offered their insight and opinions. I am also thankful to others who did the same but prefer to remain unidentified.

Victoria Rowan helped me polish these pages, while Hossein Abkenar made suggestions to bring scenes to life. Omid Memarian helped me with research, double-checked facts, and provided his unique perspective on Iran's political system and judiciary. The BBC kindly allowed me to use its news monitoring service to search its archives.

My editors, Margo Melnicove and Serena Jones, clarified my thoughts and encouraged me when I doubted my writing. Serena helped keep my writing succinct and has a talent for asking questions that need answering. Margo's passion for the project was tireless, and she edited countless drafts with an eye for detail and an ear for authenticity that are second to none. Tim Duggan, vice president and executive editor at HarperCollins, kept me on track and used his expertise to help me see the larger picture. Shannon Ceci, the senior production editor, was understanding and thorough as we put the finishing touches on this manuscript. Although in many ways, writing this book has been therapeutic, it has also been emotionally challenging, and I thank you all for guiding me through its most difficult days.

Bahman Ghobadi has always wanted the best for me and stood by me during very trying times. He also brought his screenwriting expertise and creativity to this book and shared his insight into Iranian culture and society. Thank you, Bahman, from the bottom of my heart.

To my parents, who, more than anyone else, helped rescue me from prison, thank you for loving me unconditionally and for always believing in me. You and Jasper have been pillars of patience, strength, and selflessness. I love you all.

I feel blessed to have met my former cellmates, who are some of the most admirable people I have ever come to know. Thank you for helping me face my fears, for showing me that a person can have hope even in the bleakest moments, and for teaching me so much about what really matters in life.

I will eternally appreciate the countless Iranians who welcomed me as one of their own and taught me lessons not only about Iran but also about humanity. Thank you for your hospitality, warmth, and willingness to better acquaint me with my father's homeland, and for your well wishes and calls for my release when I was in prison. I know that many of you prefer to remain anonymous, and I hope if you are reading these words, you know who you are.

What is most beautiful to me is that so many of those who supported me did so not for any personal benefit but out of love. *Nemi-dânam bâ che zabâni az shomâ tashâkkor konam*. I do not know with what words to thank you.

January, 2010

GLOSSARY

Az to harakat, az khodâ barakat. God helps those who help themselves; Do your best, and God will do the rest; Take one step, and God will shower you with blessings.

azizam. My dear.

bâzju. Interrogator; investigator.

Basij. A militia devised as a volunteer force, which backed up the Iranian army in the Iran-Iraq War. Alongside the Revolutionary Guards, who have formal command over the Basij, its roles have included defending the country against foreign threats, enforcing ideological and Islamic values, and maintaining domestic law and order, which has involved suppressing civil unrest.

Châdor; chador. A shapeless, head-to-toe outer garment or cloak worn as one form of *hejâb*; hejab.

dust-et dâram. A term of affection that can mean "I like you" or "I love you," depending on the context.

Hâj Âghâ; *Hajj.* The pilgrimage to Mecca, obligatory for any Muslim able to make the journey. *Hâji* or *Hâj* is used before the name of a man or woman who has made the pilgrimage. The term *Hâj Âghâ* is often used more generally to show respect to a man.

havâ-khori. To breathe air; to take recreation in the open air.

hejâb. Literally, "veil" or "curtain." Any dress that is said to follow Islamic principles. By law, women in the Islamic Republic are required to observe *hejâb* by concealing the shapes of their bodies and covering their hair in public places and in front of *nâ-mahram* men who are not closely related to them.

Imâm; Imam. Religious leader; the title of one of the twelve descendants of the Prophet Mohammad, who, according to Shiites, succeeded him as the leader of Muslims.

javân. Young; young person; youth.

Khâk bar saram. Literally, "Dirt on my head." It can also be defined as "Shame on me" or "Woe is me."

mahramâneh. Classified; confidential; secret.

maqna'e. A hoodlike cloth used to cover a woman's hair and neck.

monâfeqin. Hypocrites; Iran's Islamic regime uses this term to refer to the opposition group known as the Mujahedin-e Khalq.

nâ-mahram. Men and women unrelated to one another through either marriage or close family ties.

nazr. A vow solemnized to God. A person might make a nazr when he or she is in a difficult situation and begs God for assistance to solve the situation, promising to do a good deed in return. Very often associated with giving money for a good cause.

Nowruz. The Iranian New Year.

pârti bâzi. Literally, "playing" of one's connections, as a way to get things done; favoritism; nepotism; partisanship.

Qurân. Muslims' holy book, the Koran.

riâl; rial. Currency of Iran; equal to one-tenth of a *tomân*.

roopoosh. Uniform; gown; a kind of jacket of varying lengths that is worn over the clothes in Iran as a form of *hejâb*.

shâh; shah. King; sovereign; the title of Iran's monarchical rulers before the 1979 Islamic Revolution.

Shi'ite; Shiite, Shia. A follower of the branch of Islam that recognizes the Prophet's son-in-law, Ali, and his descendants as the rightful successors of Mohammad.

sigheh. Temporary marriage; a Shiite practice that allows couples to marry for a period of their choice, from a few minutes to ninety-nine years, by reciting a verse from the Koran. *Sigheh* is frowned upon by many Iranians who see it as a front for prostitution or as a way for men and women to legitimize extramarital relationships, but it has also become a practical method of dealing with the Islamic regime's crackdown on couples who are dating.

ta'ârof. A complex system of formalized courtesy common in Iran and elsewhere in the Middle East and in much of Asia, though known by different names there.

tasbih. Prayer beads; rosary.

tomân; toman. Unit of currency equal to 10 *riâls*. At the time of my imprisonment, 1,000 tomans was equivalent to just under $1.

velâyat-e faqih. Rule of the Islamic jurisprudent; refers to the Islamic Republic's supreme leader, a cleric who is to have ultimate authority in the absence of the Shiites' Twelfth Imam, who was said to have disappeared in the ninth century.

NOTES ON SOURCES

In *Between Two Worlds*, most of my work involved personal observation, experience, and interactions with others during my one hundred days in Evin Prison and my six years in Iran. However, I also benefited greatly from written materials and interviews, and I have listed below those that were most useful for this book. I have not cited widely reported news available from several sources or interviews with people who preferred to remain unidentified.

CHAPTER 2

Amnesty International, "Iran: Preserve the Khavaran Grave Site for Investigation into Mass Killings," www.amnesty.org/en/library/asset/MDE13/006/2009/en/4c4f2ba8-e7b0-11dd-a526-05dc1810b803/mde130062009eng.html, Jan. 20, 2009.

Haleh Esfandiari, *My Prison, My Home: One Woman's Story of Captivity in Iran* (New York: HarperCollins, 2009), 178. Esfandiari writes that the Intelligence Ministry spliced two of her sentences in her videotaped interview to make her appear to admit to something she had not done.

CHAPTER 4

International Federation for Human Rights, "Iran/Death Penalty: A State Terror Policy," Apr. 2009.

CHAPTER 5

Plutarch, *Plutarch: Selected Lives and Essays*, trans. Louise Ropes Loomis (Roslyn, NY: Walter J. Black, 1951), 69.

Mahatma Gandhi, *The Essential Gandhi: An Anthology of His Writings on His Life, Work, and Ideas*, ed. Louis Fischer (New York: Vintage, 1962), 185.

CHAPTER 6

Michael Slackman, "Americans Often Misunderstand Iranians, Whose Style of Conversation Often Hides Their Feelings," *New York Times*, Aug. 6, 2006.

CHAPTER 8

Anthony Cordesman, "Iran's Revolutionary Guards, the Al Quds Force, and Other
    Intelligence and Paramilitary Forces," Center for Strategic and International
    Studies, working draft, Aug. 16, 2007.
"Covert Terror: Iran's Parallel Intelligence Apparatus," Iran Human Rights
    Documentation Center, http://www.iranhrdc.org/httpdocs/English/pdfs/Reports/
    Covert%20Terror-Iran%27s-Parallel-Intelligence-Apparatus.pdf, Apr. 2009.

CHAPTER 10

National Anthem of the Islamic Republic of Iran, translated by Reza Saberi

> The Eastern sun appeared on the horizon,
> The light of the eyes of believers in Truth.
> Bahman is the glory of our faith.
> Your message, O Imam, of independence and freedom is imprinted on
>   our souls.
> Martyrs, your cries ring in the ears of time.
> May the Islamic Republic of Iran last forever.

CHAPTER 11

Jim Muir, "Iran 'Brothel' Plan Rejected," BBC News, http://news.bbc.co.uk/2/hi/
    middle_east/2156975.stm, July 28, 2002.
May 2007 data collected by the State Prisons Organization and Security and
    Corrective Measures. According to Iran's Anti-Narcotics Headquarters, the
    country has more than 2 million drug addicts. "Nearly Half of Iran's Drug
    Addicts Are Under 29 Years Old," BBC Farsi, Aug. 17, 2009. Some observers
    claim the actual statistic is much higher.
Abdullah Yusuf Ali, *The Meaning of The Holy Qur'an*, Amana Publications,
    Beltsville, Maryland, 10th ed., 1999.

CHAPTER 12

Mâ Hastim's official Web site, http://www.mahastim.org.
"Guide to Iranian Media and Broadcasts to Iran," BBC Monitoring, Mar. 27, 2007.
"Five Million Internet Sites in the Country Have Been Filtered," Mehr News
    Agency, www.mehrnews.com/fa/newsdetail.aspx?NewsID=784979, Nov. 18,
    2008.
Iran's 1385 (2006) Census, Statistical Centre of Iran, http://www.sci.org.ir/portal/
    faces/public/sci_en/sci_en.selecteddata/sci_en.yearbookdata.

CHAPTER 13

"Iran's Fight Against HIV," Press TV, www.presstv.ir/detail.aspx?id=78486, Dec. 14, 2008.

"High Risk Sexual Behavior: The Current Cause of the Spread of AIDS in Iran," BBC Persian, www.bbc.co.uk/persian/iran/2008/11/081129_mg_aids_incidence.shtml, Nov. 29, 2008.

CHAPTER 14

"The Population of Young Iranian University Students Has Increased by Six Times in the Past Thirty Years," IRNA, Apr. 28, 2009.

Behzad Yaghmaian, *Social Change in Iran* (Albany: State University of New York Press, 2002), 75.

Ali Afshari, "The Challenges of the Student Movement in the Post-Reform Era," Gozaar, www.gozaar.org/template1.php?id=936&language=english, Jan. 20, 2008.

Akbar Ganji, *The Road to Democracy in Iran* (Cambridge: MIT Press, 2008), xiii.

CHAPTER 16

"Gender Details for the College Entrance Exam Were Announced," Mehr News Agency, www.mehrnews.com/fa/newsdetail.aspx?NewsID=644513, Feb. 24, 2008.

Miles Menander Dawson, *The Conduct of Life: The Basic Thoughts of Confucius* (New York: Garden City Publishing, 1941), 57.

Matthew 6:31, quoted here from the Good News Translation, American Bible Society, 1976.

CHAPTER 17

Baha'i International Community, www.bahai.org/dir/worldwide/persecution.

"A Look at the Religious Minorities and Ethnic and Language Groups in Iran," Public Relations Office, Iranian Embassy in Athens, www.iranembassy.gr/per/policy_minoritiesinIran.htm.

Hafez, *Divan of Hafez*, Sonnet 250, trans. Reza Saberi (Lanham, MD: University Press of America, 2002), 302.

Will Durant, *The Story of Civilization*, vol. 5, *The Renaissance* (New York: Simon & Schuster, 1953), 160.

Viktor Frankl, *Man's Search for Meaning*, 3d ed. (New York: Simon & Schuster, 1984), 75.

CHAPTER 19

Ali Mostashari and Ali Khodamhosseini, "An Overview of Socioeconomic
    Characteristics of the Iranian-American Community Based on the 2000
    Census," Iranian Studies Group, MIT, Feb. 2004.
William Samii, "Iran's Brain Drain: Causes and Trends," Radio Free Europe,
    www.rferl.org/content/article/1342765.html, Jan. 7, 2002.

CHAPTER 21

El-Yasin's official Web site, www.ostad-iliya.org.

EPILOGUE

Amnesty International, "Freedom of Expression," www.amnesty.org/en/freedom-
    of-expression. Iran denies having not only political prisoners, but also *prisoners
    of conscience,* a term Amnesty International uses for people who have never
    used or advocated violence and who are detained or imprisoned because of
    their "political, religious or other conscientiously held beliefs, ethnic origin,
    sex, color, language, national or social origin, economic status, birth, sexual
    orientation or other status . . ." Not all political prisoners, whom Amnesty
    describes as people accused of politically motivated crimes, are considered
    prisoners of conscience.
Maziar Bahari, "118 Days, 12 Hours, 54 Minutes," *Newsweek,* www.newsweek
    .com/id/223862, Nov. 21, 2009.
Laura Secor, "The Iran Show," *New Yorker,* www.newyorker.com/talk/
    comment/2009/08/31/090831taco_talk_secor, Aug. 31, 2009.
Michael Slackman, "Top Reformers Admitted Plot, Iran Declares," *New York
    Times,* www.nytimes.com/2009/07/04/world/middleeast/04confess.html, July 3,
    2009.
Free Kian 2009, www.freekian09.org.
Free the Hikers, http://freethehikers.org.
Amnesty International, "Iran: Election Contested, Repression Compounded,"
    http://www.amnestyusa.org/pdf/mde131232009en.pdf, December 2009.
State Department Daily Press Briefing, www.state.gov/r/pa/prs/dpb/2009/
    july/125892.htm, July 9, 2009.

SELECTED BIBLIOGRAPHY
AND SUGGESTIONS FOR
FURTHER READING

BOOKS

Abdo, Geneive, and Jonathan Lyons. *Answering Only to God: Faith and Freedom in Twenty-first-Century Iran.* New York: Henry Holt, 2003.

Abrahamian, Ervand. *Tortured Confessions: Prisons and Public Recantations in Modern Iran.* Berkeley: University of California Press, 1999.

Afshari, Reza. *Human Rights in Iran: The Abuse of Cultural Relativism.* Philadelphia: University of Pennsylvania Press, 2001.

Brumberg, Daniel. *Reinventing Khomeini: The Struggle for Reform in Iran.* University of Chicago Press, 2001.

Buchta, Wilfried. *Who Rules Iran? The Structure of Power in the Islamic Republic.* Washington, DC: Washington Institute for Near East Policy, 2000.

Ebadi, Shirin, and Azadeh Moaveni. *Iran Awakening: A Memoir of Revolution and Hope.* New York: Random House, 2006.

Entekhabifard, Camelia. *Camelia, Save Yourself by Telling the Truth: A Memoir of Iran.* New York: Seven Stories Press, 2007.

Erlich, Reese. *The Iran Agenda: The Real Story of U.S. Policy and the Middle East Crisis.* Sausalito, CA: PoliPointPress, 2007.

Ganji, Akbar. *The Road to Democracy in Iran.* Cambridge: MIT Press, 2008.

Ghahramani, Zarah, and Robert Hillman. *My Life as a Traitor: An Iranian Memoir.* New York: Farrar, Straus & Giroux, 2008.

Kar, Mehrangiz. *Crossing the Red Line: The Struggle for Human Rights in Iran.* Costa Mesa, CA: Blind Owl Press, 2007.

Keddie, Nikki R. *Modern Iran: Roots and Results of Revolution.* New Haven, CT: Yale University Press, 2003.

Majd, Hooman. *The Ayatollah Begs to Differ: The Paradox of Modern Iran.* New York: Anchor Books, 2009.

Miller, Frederic P., Agnes F. Vandome, and John McBrewster, eds. *Human Rights in the Islamic Republic of Iran.* Beau Bassin, Mauritius: Alphascript Publishing, 2009.

Molavi, Afshin. *Persian Pilgrimages: Journeys across Iran.* New York: Norton, 2002.

Moslem, Mehdi. *Factional Politics in Post-Khomeini Iran*. Syracuse, NY: Syracuse University Press, 2002.

Nemat, Marina. *Prisoner of Tehran: One Woman's Story of Survival Inside an Iranian Prison*. New York: Free Press, 2007.

Price, Massoume. *Iran's Diverse Peoples: A Reference Sourcebook*. Santa Barbara, CA: ABC-CLIO, 2005.

Sciolino, Elaine. *Persian Mirrors: The Elusive Face of Iran*. New York: Simon & Schuster, 2000.

Semati, Mehdi, ed. *Media, Culture and Society in Iran: Living with Globalization and the Islamic State*. New York: Routledge, 2008.

Slavin, Barbara. *Bitter Friends, Bosom Enemies: Iran, the U.S., and the Twisted Path to Confrontation*. New York: St. Martin's Press, 2007.

Varzi, Roxana. *Warring Souls: Youth, Media, and Martyrdom in Post-Revolution Iran*. Durham, NC, and London: Duke University Press, 2006.

ARTICLES AND WEB SITES

Human Rights Watch. "Like the Dead in Their Coffins: Torture, Detention, and the Crushing of Dissent in Iran," www.hrw.org/en/reports/2004/06/06/dead-their-coffins, June 6, 2004.

Human Rights Watch. "You Can Detain Anyone for Anything: Iran's Broadening Clampdown on Independent Activism," www.hrw.org/en/reports/2008/01/06/you-can-detain-anyone-anything-0, Jan. 6, 2008.

International Campaign for Human Rights in Iran lists links to further information on human rights in Iran at www.iranhumanrights.org/links.

Iran Human Rights Documentation Center. "Forced Confessions: Targeting Iran's Cyber-Journalists," www.iranhrdc.org/httpdocs/English/pdfs/Reports/Forced%20Confessions%20-%20Targeting%20Iran%27s%20Cyber-Journalists.pdf, Sept. 2009.

Reporters Without Borders. www.rsf.org.

INTERVIEWS AND CORRESPONDENCE

Abrahamian, Ervand, author and professor, e-mail correspondence with the author, Nov. 2009.

Ala'i, Diane, Baha'i International Community representative to the United Nations in Geneva, various interviews with the author, 2009.

Alexander, Paige, vice president of International Research & Exchanges Board, various interviews with the author, 2009.

Auerbach, Elise, Iran specialist for Amnesty International USA, various interviews with the author, 2009.

Batebi, Ahmad, journalist and former Evin prisoner, in-person interview with the author, Jan. 21, 2009.

Ebadi, Shirin, attorney and 2003 Nobel Peace Prize winner, telephone interview with the author, July 30, 2009. Ebadi, the lawyer for Zahra Kazemi's family, said the Iranian-Canadian journalist died from a blow to her head but that details of the doctor's report about her death were incorrect. Ebadi also confirmed that the reporting I was doing without a press pass was not illegal according to Iranian law.

Esfandiari, Haleh, former Evin prisoner and the director of the Middle East Program at the Woodrow Wilson International Center for Scholars, e-mail correspondence with the author, 2009.

Ghaemi, Hadi, International Campaign for Human Rights in Iran, various interviews with the author, June–Nov. 2009.

Javanfekr, Ali Akbar, President Ahmadinejad's advisor for press affairs, e-mail interview with the author, Tehran, Oct. 11, 2008.

Kamalabadi, Iraj, brother of Fariba Kamalabadi, in-person interview with the author, Sept. 23, 2009.

Keynezhad, Paris, spokeswoman for El-Yasin Human Rights and International Affairs, telephone interview with the author, Oct. 20, 2009.

Lahidji, Abdol-Karim, president of Iranian League for the Defense of Human Rights, e-mail correspondence with the author, 2009.

Memarian, Omid, journalist and former Evin prisoner, various interviews with the author, Aug.–Nov. 2009.

Mirebrahimi, Roozbeh, journalist and former Evin prisoner, telephone interview with the author, Nov. 18, 2009.

Moeni, Reza, Reporters Without Borders, e-mail correspondence with the author, Oct.–Nov. 2009.

Mohammadi, Majid, author and professor, e-mail correspondence with the author, Oct. 2009.

Molavi, Afshin, senior research fellow at the New America Foundation, telephone interview with the author, Dec. 14, 2009.

Montazeri, Ahmad, son of Grand Ayatollah Hossein-Ali Montazeri, in-person interview with the author, Qom, Dec. 24, 2008.

Moradkhan, Klara, Silva Harotonian's cousin, various interviews with the author, 2009.

Sadjadpour, Karim, associate at the Carnegie Endowment for International Peace, various interviews with the author, 2009.

Setayesh, Hamidreza, UNAIDS country officer for Iran, in-person interview with the author, Tehran, Sept. 9, 2007, and e-mail correspondence, Oct. 2009, when he was UNAIDS Middle East and North Africa regional program advisor.

Soltani, Bahram, IRIB communications director, in-person interview with the author, Tehran, Jan. 13, 2008.